C000065286

A lot of books have been written about modern   ell
you an ideology, but fall short in explaining how   is
book fixes this gap. It brings together the plet   rn
product manager, from creating a Vision to leading an Agile development team. Highly
recommended for any product manager looking to increase the impact of the digital
products they are creating!

Pieter Hens, *Product Coach and Professor of Product Management*
at the University of Leuven

This book delivers an excellent and practical guide to digital product management
skills, culture and mindset. It is particularly useful for those new to, or interested in,
the product management discipline as well as current practitioners wishing to develop
their skills. It provides engaging insight into core product management capabilities and
ways of working which are invaluable to any digitally-centred team, business unit or
organisation.

Roy Kee Son, *Product Management Consultant, Orange Pie Consulting*

This book provides a very good introduction into the emerging field, both for product
managers transitioning from physical to digital product roles and for people moving
laterally into product management from other careers. I particularly enjoyed the relevant
choices and emphasis on practices which embody what makes product management
both special and critical. The authors help pull the readers past a superficial cataloguing
of activities and into an understanding of what makes for good product management.
You'll be glad you read it, as I am.

Scott Sehlhorst, *President, Tyner Blain;*
Product Management and Strategy Consulting

This book is perfect for a business analyst who is looking to transition into a product
focused role or wants a better understanding of the stakeholders they interact with.
It covers the complete life cycle, not only how product decisions are made, but how
these ideas are developed into actionable products that deliver value to the customer.
The chapter on software development is essential reading for those who are looking to
transition into the digital space.

Martin Pendlebury, *Senior Business Analyst;*
Senior Leadership Team, Young Business Analysts (YBA)

I wish this had been available when I first started a digital product management role as
a postgraduate. This book effectively captures the essence of product management – a
perpetual juggling act between the needs of the customer and the business – and equips
readers with the tools to balance strategic vision with the realities of software delivery.
I would recommend it to any business analyst or software professional interested in
exploring this exciting role.

Alexandra Koyfman, *Analyst, PDMS;*
Senior Leadership Team, Young Business Analysts (YBA)

This is an excellent introduction to product management and gives an in-depth view into how this discipline has evolved to cater for digital products. The inclusion and focus on how to deliver value to your customers is particularly valuable, giving thorough, understandable advice, backed up by data to underpin the reader's understanding. I would highly recommend this to any colleagues wanting a go-to manual for digital product management.

Joanne Fahy Gilbertson, *Senior Business Analyst, University of Manchester;*
Senior Leadership Team, Young Business Analysts (YBA)

Having recently expanded my remit at work to include digital product management, I've been delighted to read through this offering from BCS. It has given me a great grounding in the discipline, and I look forward to returning to it as my journey with digital product management continues.

Dr Craig W. Docherty, *Business Analyst, BJSS (Scotland);*
Young Business Analysts (YBA)

Anyone interested in product management would find this book a useful addition to their library. It contains a core set of tools that you can use to succeed in a product management role. The book starts by explaining the differences between traditional product management and digital product management – a distinction which organisations have to embrace as the world becomes more digitised. The book goes on to explain how to deal with the challenge of having unstructured problems. The book was particularly unique in its explanation of how different members of digital product teams can contribute to specific areas, leading to success of the product. I found the book very insightful, and will be keeping a copy nearby for reference.

Kay Hardy, *Senior Service Designer;*
Cofounder, Young Business Analysts (YBA)

This book offers a deep and practical insight into how to effectively manage the entire end to end product lifecycle. It offers advice that is relevant to any business trying to form and deliver customer led products. It is full of effective tools that can be referred back to at any time to keep any product manager on their toes. A must read for those starting out in product management and established product managers alike or for anyone seeking new and optimal ways to deliver valuable customer led products.

Samantha Bland, *Senior Product Manager*

DIGITAL PRODUCT MANAGEMENT

BCS, THE CHARTERED INSTITUTE FOR IT

BCS, The Chartered Institute for IT, is committed to making IT good for society. We use the power of our network to bring about positive, tangible change. We champion the global IT profession and the interests of individuals, engaged in that profession, for the benefit of all.

Exchanging IT expertise and knowledge
The Institute fosters links between experts from industry, academia and business to promote new thinking, education and knowledge sharing.

Supporting practitioners
Through continuing professional development and a series of respected IT qualifications, the Institute seeks to promote professional practice tuned to the demands of business. It provides practical support and information services to its members and volunteer communities around the world.

Setting standards and frameworks
The Institute collaborates with government, industry and relevant bodies to establish good working practices, codes of conduct, skills frameworks and common standards. It also offers a range of consultancy services to employers to help them adopt best practice.

Become a member
Over 70,000 people including students, teachers, professionals and practitioners enjoy the benefits of BCS membership. These include access to an international community, invitations to a roster of local and national events, career development tools and a quarterly thought-leadership magazine. Visit www.bcs.org/membership to find out more.

Further information
BCS, The Chartered Institute for IT,
3 Newbridge Square,
Swindon, SN1 1BY, United Kingdom.
T +44 (0) 1793 417 417
(Monday to Friday, 09:00 to 17:00 UK time)
www.bcs.org/contact
http://shop.bcs.org/
Printed by Henry Ling Limited at the Dorset Press, Dorchester, Dorset DT1 1HD

DIGITAL PRODUCT MANAGEMENT

Kevin J. Brennan, Sallie Godwin and Filip Hendrickx

© BCS Learning and Development Ltd 2022

The right of Kevin J. Brennan, Sallie Godwin and Filip Hendrickx to be identified as authors of this work has been asserted by them in accordance with sections 77 and 78 of the Copyright, Designs and Patents Act 1988.

All rights reserved. Apart from any fair dealing for the purposes of research or private study, or criticism or review, as permitted by the Copyright Designs and Patents Act 1988, no part of this publication may be reproduced, stored or transmitted in any form or by any means, except with the prior permission in writing of the publisher, or in the case of reprographic reproduction, in accordance with the terms of the licences issued by the Copyright Licensing Agency. Enquiries for permission to reproduce material outside those terms should be directed to the publisher.

All trade marks, registered names etc. acknowledged in this publication are the property of their respective owners. BCS and the BCS logo are the registered trade marks of the British Computer Society charity number 292786 (BCS).

Published by BCS Learning and Development Ltd, a wholly owned subsidiary of BCS, The Chartered Institute for IT, 3 Newbridge Square, Swindon, SN1 1BY, UK.
www.bcs.org

Paperback ISBN: 978-1-78017-5324
PDF ISBN: 978-1-78017-5331
ePUB ISBN: 978-1-78017-5348

British Cataloguing in Publication Data.
A CIP catalogue record for this book is available at the British Library.

Disclaimer:
The views expressed in this book are of the authors and do not necessarily reflect the views of the Institute or BCS Learning and Development Ltd except where explicitly stated as such. Although every care has been taken by the authors and BCS Learning and Development Ltd in the preparation of the publication, no warranty is given by the authors or BCS Learning and Development Ltd as publisher as to the accuracy or completeness of the information contained within it and neither the authors nor BCS Learning and Development Ltd shall be responsible or liable for any loss or damage whatsoever arising by virtue of such information or any instructions or advice contained within this publication or by any of the aforementioned.

Website links up to date at the time of publication.

Publisher's acknowledgements
Reviewers: Samantha Bland, Craig Docherty, Joanne Fahy Gilbertson, Kay Hardy, Naj Hassan, Pieter Hens, Alexandra Koyfman, Kent McDonald, Martin Pendlebury, Steve Rogalsky, Scott Sehlhorst, Roy Kee Son and Paul Wilkinson
Publisher: Ian Borthwick
Commissioning editor: Rebecca Youé
Production manager: Florence Leroy
Project manager: Sunrise Setting Ltd
Copy-editor: Denise Bannerman
Proofreader: Barbara Eastman
Indexer: Matthew Gale
Cover design: Alex Wright
Cover image: istock/zorazhuang
Typeset by Lapiz Digital Services, Chennai, India

To my mother, Jo, who taught herself how to program mainframes back in the 1960s.
Love you, Mum, and thanks for everything.

Kevin

To my husband and first proofreader, Oli, who now knows a lot more about product
management than he expected to! With love and thanks.

Sallie

To the BA community. Thanks all of you for being so knowledgeable and supportive.

Filip

CONTENTS

LIST OF FIGURES AND TABLES

AUTHORS

Kevin J. Brennan is a globally recognised expert in product management, business architecture, organisational effectiveness and enterprise design. He currently works as an independent consultant and as a professor at George Brown College in Toronto, Canada. He is best known for his work as EVP, Product Management and Development at IIBA Global where, among other accomplishments, he led the creation and development of the guide to the *Business Analysis Body of Knowledge* (*BABOK® Guide*) and IIBA's other professional development programmes; helped to found the annual Building Business Capability Conference; and led the development of IIBA's first strategic plan. Kevin is a past member of the IIBA Global Board of Directors and served as the first senior staff officer of the Canadian Federation of Library Associations (CFLA-FCAB). He has a Master's degree in Corporate Innovation and Entrepreneurship from Penn State University.

Sallie Godwin is a product manager with over 10 years experience working in product teams, where she has been called a business analyst, product manager, a product owner and even a product analyst. Along the way she has learned how to join up strategy with delivery, sort out the absolute 'must haves' from the 'should dos' and redrawn her roadmap more times than she cares to remember. Previously she has worked in financial services, media organisations, central government and at the British Library. She has an MA in English Literature from Sidney Sussex College, Cambridge.

Filip Hendrickx is convinced that established organisations can, and should, become corporate startups. To help them achieve this, he follows a structured yet pragmatic approach, by bridging business analysis, product management, design thinking, Lean startup and innovation techniques. His background of over 10 years in business consulting and his previous 10 years in software engineering and research enable Filip to connect strategy and portfolio management with project execution and product development. As co-founder of the BA & Beyond Conference and IIBA Brussels Chapter president, Filip helps to support the business analysis profession and grow the BA community in and around Belgium. Filip is co-author of *Brainy Glue*, a business novel on business analysis, innovation and change, and *Cycles*, a book, method and toolkit enabling faster innovation.

FOREWORD

AUTHORS

'What does your dad do?'

I had been working in software for 20 years, and still my kids had trouble answering this question. 'He helps people with computers'. 'He does agile! But I don't know what that means'. 'Something about getting people to work together in teams?' And while my adult family members tried to have conversations with me about my work with questions like 'How is the agile going?' it was clear they couldn't answer the 'what does he do' question well either. Their best answers ranged from 'IT guy' to 'project management'. While I love project managers, the good ones know as well as I do that I fall short of that qualification despite some practice in that skill set.

You see, I had spent the last 15 years as a consultant while working for two different firms. For most of my engagements, I was hired to fill a gap. Sometimes that meant coding, sometimes acting as team lead or architect and yes, sometimes 'agile coach'. But the mixed bag of roles and companies didn't help my family answer that simple question; they didn't know what I 'did'.

The experience I gained in those years, however, was invaluable. After some difficult early lessons, our team began to excel at executing on any given problem. I had a front row seat watching how companies operate and how their leaders led. It was fun. But one issue stuck out. We never really owned which problem to solve. And looking back five years, was it even the right problem to have solved in the first place? I started to feel the pull of wanting to be more involved in those long term questions and the long term effects they would have.

The parallel storyline is that I began to engage in the agile and lean communities. I started attending, speaking, and then running user groups and conferences with some friends of mine. I met and became friends with some of the influential thinkers in our space. People like Kevin Brennan. And eventually, I began contributing to the wider community of thought in software development. While my early contributions were focused on execution, I started shifting to vision, strategy and discovery. I was discovering product management but didn't even realise it had a name at that point. I did realise, however, that working at a consulting firm would limit my ability to practice and learn that broader skill set.

So I made a career decision to look for, and join, a company that practiced product management. I was thrilled to join D2L and haven't looked back. I began as a technical product manager and immediately started trying out those vision, strategy and discovery skills about which I had been speaking. In no time I was exploring new questions like, 'what does a great customer facing roadmap look like?' I still remember the excitement I had when I was involved in my first data driven decision that guided both what we were going to work on, and how we should tackle it. In addition, I learned about the customer experience and how product decisions impacted that entire experience. I was able to use the influencing skills I gained while consulting to engage the team in problem solving. I could focus on outcomes and not output. I was a product manager at last.

It is because of the hard-won and meandering lessons from the last 25 years of my career that I'm able to recommend this book with certainty. Whether you are looking to shift to product management or are just starting out in your career, if becoming a product manager is what you desire, this book is for you and may help you get there more efficiently than I did. This book doesn't spend a lot of time on execution; there are plenty of other excellent books on that topic. It does, however, take a careful and thorough look into vision, strategy, discovery, roadmaps, data driven decisions, and the customer experience. I have tried, and lived through, many of the techniques and problems described here. Read this book, and go find a company that allows you to practice these skills.

I'm happy to say that my kids approve of my new profession because they can finally tell their friends what I do. 'You know that software you use every day at school? That's what my dad does. He focuses on making learning easier and more engaging through software. The things you like in there, that's his team. The things you might not like yet, they are working on making those better too'. Long term impact. Now they know what I do.

Steve Rogalsky
Vice President, Product Management, D2L
July 2022

ACKNOWLEDGEMENTS

Kevin J. Brennan

This book has taken a longer road to publication than we ever envisioned. When I first agreed to write it, I had just recovered from cancer and organ transplant surgery, and we were heading into a global pandemic (and me without a working immune system!). The last few years made it harder to write this book than anything I've written before. I'd like to thank my wife Leslie and our children, Áine and Ciarán, for their love and support during this time and every other.

I also must thank the BCS team for their patience and determination to see this project through, including Ian Borthwick, Becky Youé and Florence Leroy, as well as my co-authors Filip and Sallie for joining in and making this a better book than the one I would have written alone. Our reviewers Samantha Bland, Craig Docherty, Joanne Fahy Gilbertson, Kay Hardy, Naj Hassan, Pieter Hens, Alexandra Koyfman, Kent McDonald, Martin Pendlebury, Steve Rogalsky, Scott Sehlhorst, Roy Kee Son and Paul Wilkinson all added immeasurably to the quality of this book through their insights and recommendations.

Julian Sammy, who passed away from his own battle with cancer while this book was in development, pushed me to think deeply about product management and business analysis over the years, and I'm sorry he never got to see some of the ideas he had and others he sparked in print.

And of course, I'd also like to thank all the product teams I've worked with over the years. I would never have written this without you.

Finally, thank you to the anonymous donor whose liver saved my life and to their family. Without you, I wouldn't be here at all.

ABBREVIATIONS

AARRR	Acquisition, Activation, Retention, Revenue, Referral
AI	artificial intelligence
B2B	business to business
B2C	business to consumer
BDD	behaviour-driven development
CEO	chief executive officer
CTO	chief technology officer
CX Pyramid	Customer Experience Pyramid
HiPPO	highest paid person's opinion
JTBD	job-to-be-done
MMP	minimum marketable product
MoSCoW	must have, should have, could have, won't have
MVP	minimum viable product
PM	product manager
QA	quality assurance
R&D	research and development
RICE	Reach, Impact, Certainty or Confidence, Effort
SaaS	software-as-a-service
Sammy VCM	Sammy Value Concept Model
SME	subject matter expert
TDD	test-driven development
UI	user interface
UX	user experience
WEIRD	white male, educated, industrialised, rich, democratic

PREFACE

Kevin J. Brennan

My first brush with product management came in 2001. It was at a company building a electricity billing system, a product we brought to market readiness only to see the market disappear on us when the government re-regulated energy. I would gradually re-enter the product management world during my time in the executive leadership team at IIBA. This experience gave me a solid view of product development from the executive level and forced me to learn to think about products as part of a portfolio and business strategy. I would take on both product management and business architecture consulting roles in the years after that, and each of those engagements taught me something new.

In 2019, I looked at what had been the business analysis space, and what I saw was a rapid change in the way companies were developing and launching new products and internal systems. Many companies were shifting to a 'product' approach to development, but business analysts weren't being made aware of the tools they needed to adapt. Everything that was out there either focused on the 'product owner' role, teaching Agile 101, or was written by people who learned the job in startups. Neither fit the needs of many new product managers, the people for whom agile methods aren't enough but who also don't have the freedom of action found in 'product-led' companies.

Much of my frustration with the talk about product ownership stemmed from knowing that people were confusing it with product management and including just enough product management in their descriptions of the Scrum role to make sure you realised that you had a bunch of new responsibilities without giving you the tools to meet them. For all the talk about strategy and responsibility for business outcomes, most product ownership training I've seen focuses on the product owner's relationship with the development team.

Business analysts have a great deal in common with product managers. Both roles are interdisciplinary, helping teams with diverse skill sets and viewpoints communicate with one another. Both facilitate difficult conversations and use a range of analytical techniques to develop vital insights. Both have to manage through influence much of the time instead of formal authority. The primary difference is that business analysts focus on the internal workings of a company, and project managers focus on the work performed by a team.

That simple distinction hides a world of differences. Business analysts work in very complex environments, but ones in which it is frequently possible to get definitive answers. When those answers aren't obtainable, the problem is usually a conflict between stakeholders and their interests, or the result of external forces. The end goal is usually defined, even if that goal changes over time. None of this is meant to suggest that business analysis is easy or simple, but rather that business analysts are generally faced with structured problems (or at least ones amenable to structuring).

Product managers, on the other hand, are usually dealing with open-ended questions to which there is no definitive right answer. A product manager will be faced with many choices and options, and the end goal will be based on business outcomes – no matter how good the product is, it will be seen to have failed if it doesn't generate those. The challenge is usually in finding usable information to give you an insight that's better than your gut feelings. Product managers deal with unstructured problems.

Many project managers are being faced with the same transition and are dealing with similar challenges. A project has a beginning, middle and end – it is done with a defined scope, cost and budget, and one cannot change without affecting the other two. The project will change along the way, of course, but there is always an end goal in sight and once that goal is completed the project team moves on to other engagements. In contrast, digital products don't end, they die because they are no longer producing enough value to justify continued development. There are goals and objectives, but they will be business targets and not deliverables. A traditional project is literally built from a set of defined deliverables in the work breakdown structure. A product manager must never make the mistake of focusing on deliverables rather than the outcome.

If you find those thoughts exciting, then product management may be the career for you. In this book, we've tried to focus on the parts of the job that will be new to you. We assume that you know how to facilitate discussions and lead brainstorming exercises, how software development works, and at least the basics of project management and requirements development. What we've tried to give you in this book is a core set of tools that you can use to succeed in a new product management role and a sense of what to expect. The approach in this book isn't the only way to be an effective product manager. It's a place to start.

1 WHAT IS DIGITAL PRODUCT MANAGEMENT?

Kevin J. Brennan

INTRODUCTION

The demand for product managers is growing rapidly. If you're an experienced IT professional, you may have wondered if you should consider moving into this space. In this chapter, we will discuss the reasons for the rise of product management, and how they connect to digital transformation. We will discuss the key members of digital product teams and how the product manager works with them to add value. Finally, we will touch on one of the biggest shifts an IT professional may face in moving to product management: the need to broaden your horizons and think on every level, from the long-term strategy to the day-to-day work of the product team.

DIGITAL TRANSFORMATION AND DIGITAL PRODUCTS

'Software is eating the world.'

Marc Andreessen (the co-founder of Netscape®) wrote those words in 2011.[1] In an op-ed published in *The Wall Street Journal*, he made the case that companies were going through a profound transformation, one that we've seen accelerate in the years since. He argued that the ability to build and deliver products and services through software – in other words **digital products** – would be the critical capability that enabled companies to survive in the 21st-century economy. Many traditional products, such as cameras, movies and television, had already been completely disrupted and transformed by digital technologies. TV channels and networks are in the process of disappearing and being replaced by online streaming services that operate on a global scale.

Even industries that relied on a physical value chain and distribution network were being changed irrevocably by software. Uber® disrupted taxi companies all over the world, and today that disruption is spreading to other industries. In the city where I live, many restaurants are now doing more business through online delivery services than they do in their physical location, and 'ghost kitchens', which only prepare meals for delivery customers, are becoming commonplace. In the past, this kind of business used to be limited to those franchises big enough to employ full-time drivers, but the existence of a digital middleman allows them access to a fleet of drivers whenever an order comes in.

---

1 Marc Andressen (2011) 'Why software is eating the world'. *The Wall Street Journal*. Available from www.wsj.com/articles/SB10001424053111903480904576512250915629460

It's now becoming common for entire industries to face whole-scale disruption through the entry of software-driven competition. For a number of years, the standard wisdom was that this process was inevitably fatal for incumbents. Disruption theory, developed by Clay Christensen and first described in *The Innovator's Dilemma*,[2] provided a compelling argument explaining why. According to Christensen, disruption typically occurred because companies found ways to enter market segments that existing providers would consider to be low value and which would damage their profit margins to try and serve.

For instance, Uber got started by offering services strictly in the luxury car market, tapping into a pool of cars that otherwise spent a significant amount of time sitting unused. This high-end market posed little threat to traditional providers, because it let them generate additional money from drivers and vehicles they already had in place. However, disruption theory also predicts that disruptors will eventually move into other adjacent markets in search of growth, and that's where the trouble starts for incumbents. They may start with creating demand among over-served[3] market segments, but they don't stop there. The capabilities and business model that work in their niche, usually low-end, market often allow them to offer a better value proposition to a broad range of customers as their product capabilities are improved over time. So, naturally, they do. The disruptor moves into other markets that their new capabilities can serve, and does so more efficiently at a lower cost. By the time this happens, the incumbent is typically years behind in developing their needed capabilities, and hobbled by business models that can't easily adapt.

This happened with Uber when they decided to pursue the opportunity to move out of the luxury market and compete with regular taxis. They were able to do so because they had built an existing customer base and infrastructure, and a product that offered a superior user experience to traditional taxi companies. However, rather than partner with those companies to offer a front-end to their services, Uber instead enabled new drivers to compete with them without going through the traditional licensing process, increasing the availability of service and in many cases offering lower costs. Despite intense resistance, which escalated to actual violence in some places, Uber was successful.[4] While some companies tried to offer a similar ride-hailing service working with existing taxi firms, these generally failed to be competitive with Uber's offering.

INTRODUCING DIGITAL PRODUCTS

In recent years, though, the predictions of disruption theory haven't borne out as often as they did in the past. Why? Well, in a sense, disruption theory disrupted itself. Firms became aware of this dynamic and decided that if they were going to be disrupted anyway, they might as well accept the hit to their bottom line that it brought early in the process and be prepared to disrupt themselves. The new business model might

---

2   Clay Christensen (1997) *The Innovator's Dilemma.* Harvard Business Review Press.

3   An 'over-served' market is one that doesn't demand all the features and capabilities built into the product. People in this segment will happily switch to a product that offers only the features they need at a lower price.

4   At gaining market share, anyway. Profitability has remained an issue. At the time of writing, Uber had been profitable for the first time in 2021 but was expected to lose money in the coming year. A frequent challenge for tech startups is the need to move from prioritising growth at all costs to developing a sustainable business model.

not be as lucrative as their existing one, but they were certainly more lucrative than bankruptcy! Those firms that were willing to make this transition benefited from the market advantages that came with incumbency, including brand recognition, industry expertise, and of course money, resources and skilled people.

However, they couldn't respond to disruptive competitors with traditional products and services. If they were going to disrupt themselves, they needed to do so using the same practices and methods as the venture, capital-backed startup firms. One of the key practices in question is a modern approach to digital product management.

Traditional product management

In the past, product management meant the management of **physical** products. The discipline originated with Proctor & Gamble in the 1930s, where it was applied to consumer packaged goods. These products needed to be prototyped, engineered, and have a manufacturing process developed to produce them before they were transported and distributed to consumers. There are many products that still follow this model: medicines, cars, phones, consumer electronics, cleaning products and many more.

It's worthwhile for us to take a little time to discuss the physical new product development and product management life cycle before we dig into digital product management. You may find product management guides that are targeted at this kind of product development, and knowing how it works will help you to determine what does and does not apply to your situation.

These products require a significant upfront investment in their creation and development. It is expected that they will earn back that investment over a period of time. The development and manufacturing process can be very lengthy, as a supply chain has to be developed, materials and packaging need to be created and approved, regulatory approval must be secured, and on and on. In this world, products take years, even decades, to develop and may also earn revenue for years after release.

Because of this reality, traditional products have a well-known life cycle model, pictured in Figure 1.1.

Figure 1.1 The product life cycle

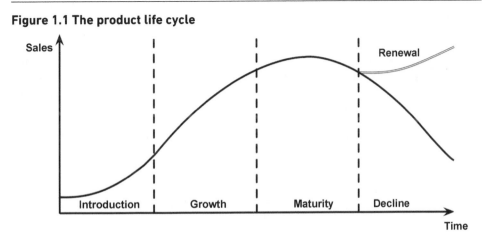

New product development traditionally begins with the creation of a **product concept** or **vision**. This captures the idea behind the product and why the company believes it will be successful in the market. Because new products require a considerable investment of time and resources, this phase focuses on validating whether or not that investment is justified. This involves significant effort in market research, investment in feasibility studies, prototyping, and other research and development (R&D) to make sure that the market for the product is real, and it's possible to manufacture and distribute the product at a viable price. Effects of scale, expected product lifespan and similar factors will end up being considered in that equation.

This phase usually ends with the proposed product reaching a **stage-gate**, where the information is reviewed and approval is given to move the product into development. The creation of a new product is treated as a project, with a project team assembled to turn the concept into something that will ship. The product is developed through a single waterfall[5] effort or through a series of iterations until it reaches a state of quality and functionality that makes it ready to launch. While the effort put into the development of the product concept will mitigate some risks, it's normal for problems to be discovered and resolved during this stage, and not unusual for this part of the product development process to result in significant delays or cost overruns that may affect the long-term viability of the product.

The nature of that development process varies a lot by industry and usually requires very specific expertise in that space. For instance, auto manufacturing will require engagement with product engineers, regulatory agencies and experts in supply chain management. The development of this industry expertise is generally a key capability of companies, one that can be hard or even impossible to match for potential new entrants.

The product **launch** is often where the product team finally gets to see whether or not the product is truly viable. It also represents a major transition in the life cycle of a traditional product, as the product moves from the responsibility of the development team, and management becomes the responsibility of sales and marketing. The transition takes place as the company gears up for the product launch. The sales and marketing team will work to line up orders for the new product and make sure that the market is paying attention to the launch. The product launch represents the best opportunity to convince existing customers to upgrade and get non-customers to switch. If done right, the product launch will start a period of growth as customers purchase the product and use it, and market awareness grows. If done badly, the launch may lead to the product rapidly disappearing into obscurity. Do you remember New Coke®?

Following the product launch, the product will move into its **growth** phase, as the company seeks to generate a return on its investment. During this phase, the goal will be to acquire new customers, upsell existing ones and possibly move the product into new market areas. While some of the product team may continue to be needed to develop new features or solve maintenance issues, the number of people working on it usually drops significantly while marketing efforts ramp up. The goal of most companies is to keep growth continuing for as long as possible.

---

5 'Waterfall' projects are expected to pass through a series of phases, beginning with business case development, followed by analysis, design, development and testing.

However, as a product or market matures, it will become harder to reach new customers – a phase known as product **maturity**. Companies eventually have to shift to getting more attention and use of the product from existing customers (and possibly working to cross-sell those customers on related products), or protecting their product's market share from new competitors. In maturity, a product is often treated as a cash cow. The focus of the remaining product team shifts to lowering the costs of manufacturing, distributing and servicing the product, with the goal of maximising profit margins. Despite this, prices may still fall as competition heats up because features that were once new and unique become easier to match.

Eventually, the market for the product will head into **decline**, either due to structural changes, such as changes in taste or new technologies, or because competitors develop superior alternatives. At this point, most of the potential profit has already been captured and the firm must choose whether to let the product ride out the decline, terminate it or invest in enhancements needed to renew it for the future. Spending on the product and on product marketing will be minimised as revenue streams dry up. Eventually, the product becomes a pure commodity, with prices not far above what it costs to manufacture, or is shut down. Either way, there's very little product management to be done.

For a real-world example, look at the history of video tapes. The concept of recording movies on optical discs has been around for decades and was first brought to market as the LaserDisc in 1978. For a long time, though, most customers found the format too expensive, and not many movies were released in that format. It's also fair to say that the general video quality of televisions themselves wasn't good enough to drive a lot of demand. Over the next 15 years or so, they remained a niche product with a limited market. That changed when the major computer manufacturers pressured companies to adopt a unified format.

Once DVDs entered the market, they rapidly displaced video tapes as the main format for video sales. A chart is reproduced in Figure 1.2.[6]

As you can see, the trend in sales looks a great deal like the product life cycle. DVDs grew, rapidly hit maturity, and then dropped into rapid decline. The culprit, of course, was streaming video. DVD had its growth phase from 1998 to around 2004 or 2005, a period of maturity from 2005 to 2010 and since then has been in decline. By 2019, the total volume of physical video media (largely DVDs and Blu-Ray) had fallen to 48 million units, only slightly above their 2001 level.[7]

Digital product management

Modern digital products don't follow this traditional life cycle, and so they require a different approach to product management. It's not only because they're software applications; in fact, until the last decade or so most software products followed variations on the traditional product life cycle. Microsoft Windows® and Office ®, for instance, followed this exact life cycle for years and through multiple versions.

---

6 'DVD and Blu-ray sales statistics'. Available from www.avforums.com/threads/dvd-and-blu-ray-sales-statistics.2004986/

7 'Physical video retail unit sales in the United Kingdom (UK) from 1999 to 2019'. Statista.com. Available from www.statista.com/statistics/238863/retail-video-sales-in-the-uk-by-volume/. This number includes different types of media, such as Blu-ray.

Figure 1.2 DVD sales in the UK, 1996–2014

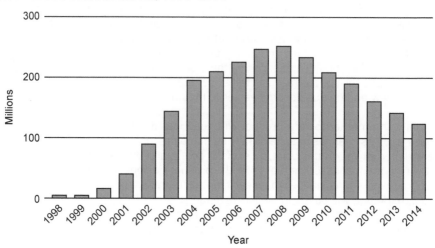

I remember when the release of a new software application or version was a major event, with people even lining up at stores to buy them!

Digital products aren't different because the **products** are digital; the most important change was that the **distribution** of those products became digital as well. The development of the internet, the Apple App Store and Google Play as the central points for distributing most software (as mobile devices now outnumber computers) was the key event that changed the way products were built and developed. Before then, digital products had to be shipped to customers on physical media through traditional channels. While it was still possible to patch and update those products, it could be a lot of work to do so and you couldn't assume that those changes would get out to your customer base in any reasonable amount of time. Customers had to specifically go online to use any connected features of your application.

Once distribution moved online, though, that was no longer true, especially as bandwidth increased. With almost non-existent distribution costs, and cloud computing radically changing the economics of scaling up, the incremental cost to serve a new customer dropped close to zero.[8] Products could send data back and forth on demand. They could be updated as often as needed. Agile methodologies and DevOps increased the speed at which companies could develop and implement new features. Products didn't need to be 'complete' to ship – they just needed to be good enough to get customers to use them. Products didn't need to be developed by a project team – the product team could keep on developing them as long as the demand for new features existed.

These changes break the traditional life cycle model, because the product itself is no longer fixed. You have to simultaneously explore new product directions, build new product features, grow the product in the market and defend against competitors who will be trying to copy your innovations (and who will be able to do so far more quickly

---

8 Ben Thompson developed this insight as part of his work on Aggregation Theory. For more information, see the Stratechery website. Available from https://stratechery.com/aggregation-theory/

than they can with physical products). A new version of a product can be deployed in weeks, months at worst – but much more importantly, it can be updated and improved continually as long as the product is worth improving. This capacity for rapid and even constant change means that product managers have to think very differently about how to handle a digital product. Rather than the product life cycle happening at a leisurely pace and following a well-defined order, a digital product will undergo continual change and evolution until it is no longer worth investing in.

Today's digital products may be offered on a subscription basis, as a purchase in an online App Store, or combination of both. They may be embedded in hardware or firmware that allow for ongoing upgrades. They often aren't a standalone application, and are supported by or integrate with business processes. In many respects, a digital product is more like a service than it is a traditional physical product. Quite often, the distinction is minimal – a digital product may be a channel through which a service is delivered.

You may have noticed that this history, and the difference between the approaches, is very similar to the difference between traditional project management and agile approaches. That's because they are largely the same story. The shift we've just discussed is a large part of why agile methods came to be dominant in software development.

Many products today are developed through a hybrid of these methods. An obvious one is cell phones. Phone hardware is developed through a traditional, multi-year process. Prototypes of new components are tested extensively and integrated into potential designs, which are evaluated as the technology matures to determine when they can be incorporated into manufacturing at a reasonable cost and profit margin. The software that runs on those phones, in contrast, is continually evolving and will regularly be installed on older hardware.

DIGITAL PRODUCTS ARE A TEAM SPORT

This change in the product life cycle also led to a profound change in the nature of how products are managed. In the traditional life cycle, there were different groups in the organisation that 'owned' the product at different points in its development. The different phases and stage-gates often included formal handoffs to different teams. I don't want to overstate the case here – product management has always required people to collaborate. However, with digital products, the handoffs and transitions in responsibility are greatly reduced.

A digital product requires three key skill sets in addition to product management. These skills may be represented within the product team itself, or in different departments across the company, or both. The first are developers or engineers – the people who will code, test and deploy the digital application that will be used by customers. Second are experts in customer or user experience who focus on how the product and associated services will be used by the customer, and who create the user interface, services and other interactions with the customers. The third are sales and marketing experts, who will actually get customers to use the product. In many cases, a product manager will have a background in one or more of these areas. Most likely, developers and user/customer experience professionals will be part of the product team, and the sales and marketing group will be separate. This grouping of product management, development and customer experience is often referred to as the 'product triad'.

Developers are the people who will actually build the digital product. While most people on these teams are software developers, this may include other IT professionals. If you're coming from a development background, you may have worked as a business analyst, Scrum master, project manager or even as a product owner. Most development teams for digital products use agile methods, but there are some exceptions. Sometimes these exceptions are driven by corporate culture, but they can also be driven by real constraints in interacting systems or processes that the product team needs to accommodate. For instance, there may be legacy systems or hardware components that are part of the product development cycle, or regulatory requirements that the product or the development process must follow.

The user or customer experience team includes people who specialise in understanding how customers interact with your products. This work involves a great deal of research, prototyping and experimentation. The product experience is more than what's commonly understood as part of the term 'user experience'. It covers every interaction that the customer has with your product and your company. That means, with a digital app, the product experience may start before your customer even visits your website or downloads your app from the App Store or Google Play. The experience includes the process of signing up for your service, every time that the customer interacts with it, and every interaction that the customer has or has to have because your app can't provide a service – in short, the complete customer journey.

Many digital products also have a service component. Those services may be delivered by customer support or customer success departments, by the sales team, by retail employees or by other groups. Those experiences may actually matter more in terms of customer acquisition or retention than the ones driven by the performance of the product itself. You will need to understand how these services affect the overall customer journey, which is covered in greater detail in Chapter 5.

However, it's not enough to simply build and design a product. The ultimate test of any product is its effectiveness in the market. Different products will strike a different balance in the need for sales and marketing. In the digital world, sales teams tend to be more important for business-to-business (B2B) products, while marketing teams are more influential for business-to-consumer (B2C) products. It generally won't be hard to figure out which is important in any given company, though.

Sales are most important when revenue is generated from a smaller number of customers who can place a large order. In these cases, each buyer is influential, and the product team may need to consider whether to incorporate specific features and functions demanded by customers to close a deal. For many products, the buyer and the user are different people and the buying decision may not be related to the factors that drive user satisfaction.

In contrast, marketing is more important when selling a product to large numbers of buyers who make individual purchase decisions. The benefits and value of the product will be communicated in a uniform way to a mass audience (although there may be marketing targeted at specific niches). The marketing team will need to distil the product value proposition down to a compelling narrative that can be used to get the attention of possible customers.

While executives are not formally part of the product team, a product manager (PM) must also keep in mind their needs and expectations. They will be defining the overall strategy of the company – which markets it will play in, which customers it will focus on and how it will win in those markets. Your product strategy must be aligned with these higher-level strategies, and these stakeholders will often seek to influence or even direct product decisions, in ways that may or may not align with your product strategy.

THE ROLE OF THE PRODUCT MANAGER

The need for constant cross-functional collaboration across the organisation has led to the growth and widespread adoption of product management as a formal role. Product managers work across the organisation to ensure that the right products are actually built. Product managers must have a strong relationship with every part of the product team, with other stakeholders in your company, and with suppliers and vendors. Most of all, product managers are accountable to the company for the market success of the product. Product management is, in short, a leadership role, even if much of that leadership comes from influence rather than authority. If you've worked as a business analyst or project manager, you've already developed many of the needed skills and contacts across your company.

Because you're accountable for your product's success, you'll have to work across the organisation to get things done. You're going to run into problems that are a first for you and possibly a first for your company. On the positive side, you're also going to be in a position to demonstrate your direct contribution to your company's bottom line – something that can give you a lot more influence, if not authority. Success as a product manager is something that gives you the opportunity to move up the ranks to senior leadership positions.

You can be assured that your internal stakeholders will have strong opinions about how your product should be developed, what the roadmap should be, what key features you need to add and when they need to be delivered to make sure your company wins. You'll have to navigate internal politics to make sure that your team gets the resources and attention they need – and, sometimes, to make sure that they don't get attention that they **don't** need.

Like any good manager, a big part of your job will be to clear obstacles to make sure that your team is able to deliver a successful product. This includes helping members of your team and others better understand the product strategy and improve their product management skills. A product team will be stronger if everyone is thinking about what your customers need and how you can meet those needs. Your team members will bring their own perspectives and unique insights to these problems and the result will be a better product. See Chapter 8 for more advice.

However, most of this book will actually focus on the things you need to do so that your team **can** create that product. A product team is a complex balance of people with different skills, approaches and outlooks. When it works well, that mix can create a product that becomes an important part of helping your customers to achieve their goals. When it doesn't, the result can be an unworkable mess. Your job is to get that team collaborating on solving the right problems. These are the ones that simultaneously solve problems for your customers, for which they're willing to pay,[9] which are aligned with your business strategy and which your company is poised to solve more effectively than your competitors. In short, the job is about getting your team to focus on solving the right problems, and solving those problems in a way that no competitor can easily match.

PRODUCT MANAGER VERSUS PRODUCT OWNER

This might be a good place to explain the difference between a product manager and a product owner. The confusion between the two stems from different uses of the word 'product'. A product can be a good or service offered in a market, or the work output of a team. In Scrum, a product owner is the person who defines the work output of a development team. Product managers, on the other hand, are more broadly concerned with how to develop something that succeeds in the market – the development work is an important part of that, but only a part. As a product manager, you may also act as the product owner for the development team, or that responsibility might be delegated to someone else.

HORIZONS OF DIGITAL PRODUCT MANAGEMENT

To do that, you need to be constantly thinking at multiple levels. Unlike a typical software project, you can't focus on the project goal or the next release while leaving other considerations for the future. Those things are important, and you need to be thinking about them too! Product managers need to think about the direction of their product over three distinct time horizons: strategic, tactical and operational (Figure 1.3).

Figure 1.3 Digital product management horizons

---

9   In government and non-profits, 'willing to pay' may not be relevant, but they still need to prefer your product to other options available to them (including doing nothing).

The strategic horizon

Decisions and changes at this horizon usually play out over the course of a number of years. At this horizon, you'll be thinking about the long-term direction of the product, as expressed in the product vision.

To be able to define a product vision, you must know:

- who will use the product and under what circumstances;
- what they hope to accomplish using your product;
- what makes it special and different from alternative products that could do the same thing;
- and how that product will create and capture value.

The answers to these questions will be articulated as the **product strategy**. One of the most important parts of your job is to be able to articulate the answers to these questions to everyone who needs to know them. The product vision tells everyone **what problem are we solving?** Beyond that, it tells us that the problem we're working on is a problem **worth** solving, and who we are solving it for.

Another major thing that a product strategy must articulate is where the product fits in the market. Your goal, as a product manager, is to make sure that the product has some kind of competitive advantage – that is, it better meets the needs and desires of a specific group of customers than any alternative, and it does so in a way that other companies can't easily copy.

That seems like a lot to ask for, in a world where software can rapidly be developed and deployed and key features reverse-engineered. Nevertheless, it is possible – usually through finding a way to serve customers that cannot be matched given the strategic choices that your competitors have made. This competitive advantage is usually rooted in the overall strategy of your company and in the unique capabilities that it has developed. Product managers should identify those and find ways to leverage them to make their products more compelling to their customer base.

The tactical horizon

Decisions at the tactical level will play out over no more than a year to 18 months, depending on the pace of competition in your market.[10] At this level, you'll be concerning yourself with developing product roadmaps, anticipating competitive actions, and scanning for shifts in the market and in customer preference. The tactical horizon is where you take actions that will have a major impact on customer metrics such as acquisition, retention or revenue. Here, you need to be able to articulate to the team:

- How is the performance of the product in the market being judged?

---

10 Discussed further in Chapter 3.

- What changes need to be made to it to keep up with competitive pressures?

- What are the most important improvements to focus on?

- How do we create a compelling customer experience?

The plan for responding to these issues will be captured in the product roadmap and in a set of product metrics.

The product roadmap is used to communicate to all of the important stakeholders what the plans are for the longer-term development of the product. That information will be used to sell the product to customers,[11] plan for longer-term resourcing needs, coordinate work between departments and allow for scheduling. The roadmap serves as a communication tool, first and foremost, rather than a project plan. The further out something is on the roadmap, the less certain it is that the feature in question will be developed.

Digital product development is predicated on continuous improvement of the product and, like all continuous improvement efforts, it needs to be guided by clear metrics and goals. Those metrics tell the team if a change is resulting in improvement or not. The metrics that a team uses to judge success are critical – they will shape team behaviour and, if badly chosen or incentivised, can lead to teams building stuff that improves the chosen metrics but causes other counterproductive behaviours.

The operational horizon

Here, the product manager must focus on the specific capabilities offered in the product. You will collaborate with the product team to design, develop and deploy enhancements. This horizon focuses on enhancing the speed at which improvements can be deployed into the market. This space is still evolving, with a few companies instituting dedicated product ops roles. However, there are three critical elements that matter to the operational horizon.

First is the speed and effectiveness of the digital development team. How quickly can they build and deploy new features? Are they managing and limiting their technical debt (see Chapter 7), which, if allowed to grow out of control, will eventually make it extremely difficult to add new features? Do they have the tools and environments they need? Can they respond quickly to a change in the market and refocus their efforts accordingly?

The second element of product operations is the need for continual value stream management. While some digital products are entirely online, many others exist as a front-end to a set of business processes or in some way have a service element to them. The digital product is only part of the customer experience. The human work that needs to be done to complete the value delivery to the customer is no less important, and if those processes are unable to change at the same pace as the digital elements of the product, they'll end up as a constraint on the ability to change along with the market.

---

11 Most product managers intensely dislike this use as it causes customers to view that roadmap as a commitment to them, making needed changes difficult. However, if your product is sold to enterprises, it will be hard to avoid.

That means that agile software development needs to be paired with continuous process improvement methods, such as Lean, Theory of Constraints, and Six Sigma. The appropriate use of those methods will allow operational teams to implement changes and improvements to the business side, keep staff up to date with features, and eliminate and control operational costs to keep the product profitable. Historically, product managers haven't had to pay close attention to this aspect of the business but if we want to deliver a unified and desirable customer experience, it can't be neglected.

Managing the value stream means looking at each business process or sub-process to assess how it contributes to customer or business outcomes and, analogously, to development value streams, removing the things that get in the way of delivering that value or which make it harder to change the process at the pace that's needed. It involves understanding where delays or wasted effort reoccur and redesigning the underlying process to eliminate those problems.

Finally, the last element of product operations is implementing the systems to collect data and feedback to help us learn more about the customer and how they are using our products. All the emphasis on speed of change and delivery mean little if you don't actually have the information you need to tell if those changes are working. Many of the metrics that guide product success are lagging indicators. A solid product strategy may take months or years before you get the outcomes you're looking for, but you don't want to take that long to make decisions about new features, so ...

As a digital product manager, you need the systems in place that will allow you to connect with your customers and provide you with insights into how your app is being used and what you can do to make it better. That real-time, or nearly so, insight into customer behaviour is what enables you to increase the pace at which you improve your product without spending a lot of time and wasted effort.

PRODUCT MANAGEMENT IS ABOUT MANAGING

The reason that it's important for product managers to be able to think at multiple levels is that product management isn't just about the product. Your team is filled with experts in their own areas, and those people don't need you to tell them how to do their jobs. What they **do** need is somebody who is looking across all of the different groups that contribute to product success and who focuses on enabling them to create the needed outcomes. This is known as 'servant leadership'.

Product managers usually have a limited influence over who is on the team. You might get to pick some of the players, but certainly not all. You don't get to decide on the strategic direction of the company. You may not even get to decide on the strategy for your product, although you had better understand what it is. Instead, as a product manager, you have to **influence** and **persuade**. You have to instill your vision in the product team so that they can execute on it better than you could. You need to be the person your team needs in order to succeed, because you will be held accountable for the outcomes they produce. You generally won't have many people reporting directly to you, and may not even have full control of your budget. You may have offshored team members or vendors responsible for delivering on critical product capabilities, and contracts in place that restrict what changes you can ask for and when. Your job is to get results anyway.

It would be very easy to read all of this discussion of the role of the PM, see all of the discussion about vision and leadership, and come to the conclusion that the job of the product manager is to drive the rest of the team to deliver their singular sense of the product into the market. There are certainly no end of stories about Silicon Valley *wunderkinds* who are hagiographically described in the business press and in their biographies as the sole inventors of a new industry.

However, even if it is sometimes possible for a single visionary to take full responsibility for a product, that doesn't make it a good idea. Even if we assume that you are a product visionary and genius, with incredible insight into your market and customers, this approach still places everything on **you**, and the performance of your product will be limited to **your** abilities.

The best product managers realise that success is a team effort. They do what they need to do to keep their teams focused on building a product that will solve a customer problem and meet customer needs, but tap into the insights of everybody on the team. Your team knows what's possible and desirable based on their differing experiences and knowledge, and can find opportunities that never occurred to you. You need to make sure that you're not getting in the way of that, and also make sure that others in your organisation aren't either.

Product management is a cross-functional role and because of that you'll need to adapt your style to fit the realities of the organisation you work in. It's quite likely that you'll have limited freedom to shape the direction of the product itself, as your plans need to fit with the overall strategy of the organisation and possibly the rest of the product portfolio. Product teams may be closely collaborative or deeply siloed. You may have to work with difficult people because they're the ones that are available to you. Successful product management and PM styles will differ from place to place. It's generally true that the best digital product teams follow a certain template, but how close you can come to that ideal may be out of your hands.

Ultimately, the job of the digital product manager is to enable the product team to focus on the problems of the customer – and find creative and innovative solutions for them – and not on internal issues or conflicts. A product team that spends most of its time looking inward is a team that's going to deliver products that customers don't need. They can't do great work if they're constantly firefighting and dealing with conflicting imperatives and demands, because then they're being pulled away from the customer problem. If your team isn't working on ways to increase customer value, you aren't being effective as a product manager.

In the end, you are accountable for the success of the product but you can't do that without your team. Furthermore, you should be taking advantage of their insights and skills. If you insist on dictating exactly how your product works, it can only be as good as your insight. If you engage your team, it can be as good as the best insights all of you have.

Digital products are complicated. Success in delivering and improving them requires many different parts of a company to work together. Developers need to understand what features the application needs to have and what's most important to change at any given time. Designers need to know who the customers are and how and when they'll use the product. Sales need to know what the plans are for future development and how the product compares to alternative offerings from competitors. Marketing needs to know what the value proposition is and what the product has to offer to customers. Operational units need to have the systems and processes in place to offer supporting services.

Product management is the glue that holds all of these functional groups together. The job of the product manager is to develop and communicate the product vision to the different members of the team and make sure that they are all pulling in the same direction. That sounds simple, but it's not. A product vision needs to be rooted in a very clear understanding of the value proposition of the product and how it gets used by the customer to achieve their goals. It needs to clearly define what progress means from the perspective of the customer and how that progress is enabled by the product. It needs to guide the addition of new features to the product as well as the design of the product. And it needs to turn the product into an operational reality.

As a product manager, your job is to lead the evolution of the product over time to meet the conflicting demands of management, partners and customers. There's no one right way to do that, because every organisation is a little bit different in culture, decision-making authority and capabilities. A product manager is much like a conductor of an orchestra or a coach. All of the players know their jobs and can do them better than you can. Your job is to make sure that they all play together as a team, and that they can work towards a harmonious and coordinated result. If you do that job correctly, they will come together and build a product that will lead the market. In short, the role of a product manager is to do the things that will enable the product team to succeed.

CASE STUDY: UNPARKR

To provide a concrete example of how this could play out, we will follow the progress of a new digital product developed by HumberTel, a company that offers web-conferencing and teleconferencing capabilities to its enterprise customers. While this product and the company are fictional, the case study will explore many of the challenges that you may encounter during the development and ongoing management of a typical digital product. HumberTel is trying to differentiate its conferencing offerings from those of many other service providers, and its executive team believes that it has a good opportunity to move into an adjacent market by creating a web and mobile application that helps customers to have more effective remote meetings.

The new application has been named **Unparkr**. While HumberTel intends to bundle Unparkr with its existing services, it will also be made available to other external customers for an appropriate fee to allow HumberTel to generate revenue outside its existing service geographies, and build a new marketing channel that will allow the company to expand its customer base. This means that Unparkr will need to be independent of HumberTel's existing services, although it may offer incentives for the app to be purchased as an add-on. Unparkr is also expected to be revenue-positive in its own right after a couple of years to build up a presence in the market.

The product team will need to find answers to many problems over all three horizons for Unparkr to succeed, such as the following.

Strategic problems

- Who will drive demand for this product? Will it be sold to enterprises, aiming for adoption across the organisation? Or will it aim at individual team members and seek bottom-up adoption?

- Will Unparkr be integrated with other office productivity suites, and if so which ones?

- What competition will Unparkr face?

  - Are there other companies offering a similar tool?

  - Will major productivity suites begin offering similar functionality bundled for free?

- How quickly must they act to secure a place in the market?

Tactical problems

- What features does it need to focus on first to gain traction?

- What are the key features that will let it validate the product concept?

- What is the minimum set of features it will need for a market launch to begin generating revenue?

- How will it drive awareness in its customer base and bring people onboard?

- What platforms should it target? Mobile, web or desktop?

- Are there any ethical problems that could arise from misuse of the application?

Operational problems

- Does HumberTel have people with the right experience available to build this sort of product?

- Are development environments set up properly to support agile development and DevOps?

- Are key stakeholders willing to support the effort?

- How can it bring a new team together, one which may be matrixed across the organisation, and ensure that it is able to focus on this product?

- What data does it need to make the product better, and can it collect this?

- Are there ethical or business concerns about that data collection? Will customers consider that information confidential?

KEY TAKEAWAYS

- Digital products are becoming critical to the success of the vast majority of businesses, as every customer has a computer in his or her pocket.

- Successful digital product management isn't the sole responsibility of any one person. An effective product manager will need to work closely with developers and user experience professionals.

- Product managers must be integrators who reach across their organisation and out to customers, and who align the product team and key stakeholders to a shared vision.

- Product managers must develop long-term strategies, do medium-term planning and operational work, and support the day-to-day work of the product team.

- Product managers won't be given a clear scope and objectives for a product. You will have to work that out for yourself, and make sure that other stakeholders agree with your view.

2 PRODUCT VISION: ENABLING CUSTOMER VALUE

Kevin J. Brennan

Product managers and their teams need to do a great many things to create and improve a successful product. However, if I were asked to pick one of those things as more important than any of the others, it would be **the ability to solve a problem for your customers**. If you haven't built something that meets a real customer need, all the slick user experience (UX) design and marketing in the world won't make it successful. On the other hand, if you find a truly meaningful need, your product can still have a bad user experience and limited functionality and be a hit.

In this chapter, we're going to discuss approaches and techniques that help you to see the world through the eyes of your customers, to understand the problems and challenges they face and to envision solutions for them. While much of the discussion here will examine the work needed to develop a new product, it's equally relevant when managing an existing product. You can't assume that the customer base you have today will stick with you no matter what, and there are many examples out there of products that failed after their initial success because their creators came to focus on the wrong things and lost sight of the actual customer problem.

We'll begin by looking at some of the methods you can use to build an understanding of your customer's needs. That understanding will guide you in determining what is important to include in your product, and what should be left out or even removed. To do that, you need to understand what value really is and how that perception changes in the mind of the customer.

We will look at how you capture that problem in the form of a statement about the job-to-be-done, or JTBD. JTBD is an analysis technique that asks 'what is the customer hiring the product to do' – the idea being that there is always a larger problem that your product helps the customer to solve. From there we'll expand on some other useful tools, including empathy maps, expanding the JTBD into the beginnings of a story map, and Kano analysis.

So, let's start with the most basic question: why is this product being developed?

Companies may have many different reasons for building a digital product. They may be concerned about customer retention, looking to develop a new revenue stream or even simply trying to match what a competitor is doing. Perhaps someone in your company has pitched an idea that has caught the imagination of an executive, or your leadership team is afraid that your industry will be upended or disrupted. These can all be valid reasons to create a new product but, ironically, focusing on them is almost certain to deliver what will be, at best, a mediocre, 'me too' application.

If you want a product to actually matter, you need to think like your customers. Every product should start as a solution to a customer's problem. A product starts when you see something that's harder than it ought to be, or an opportunity to make somebody's life a little bit easier or more convenient in some way. It might make it easier for people to communicate with your company, to do business with you when it's convenient for them, or let people do things that were impractical or difficult to do without it.

Problems can vary significantly in size and complexity, and a product doesn't have to solve a big problem to be successful – it has to be better enough than the current solution that people use it instead. Remember, there is a cost to the customer to switch, even if it's just the formation of new habits. People will stick with what they know unless the change is worth the perceived effort.

The basis of a sound product strategy is to find the correct problems for your customers and potential customers – ones that you can solve and which are a basis for a viable business. The customer problem has to be one that the customer is willing to pay to solve. Even if your app isn't directly revenue-generating, it still has to give customers a reason to spend their money with your company rather than a competitor, or give them a reason not to switch. It also needs to be a fit with the rest of your business.

If you're developing an app for the government or a non-profit, this framing may be difficult for you to apply at first, because your customers don't 'pay' as such (or only pay nominal fees). But even if no money is involved, you are still trying to get your clients or citizens to spend their time using the app rather than whatever alternatives might exist (which may include doing nothing at all). It still needs to be easier for customers to do their 'job' with the app than without.

The 'good' news when you're developing a digital product is that it's almost certain that your customers have problems with their existing solutions – quite possibly problems that your company caused! To solve them, you'll have to explore what they are trying to accomplish in their interactions with you, where there's an opportunity to step in and offer a better solution, and what would motivate them to seek out and use that solution.

EXPLORING CUSTOMER NEEDS

If you want to know what your customers need, there's no substitute for 'getting out of the building' and interacting with them. **None.** You need to make a point of going out to see customers in the environment where your product is used on a regular basis. Many experts recommend you do this at least once a week. If that's not possible for you, do what you can – any amount of in-person interaction will help, but I would suggest a minimum of once per month. This doesn't literally have to be out of the office – you can get real contact with customers through support requests or other forms of interaction – but the key here is unscripted and unmediated contact. This is true for your team as well. The better that UX designers, developers, product owners and other team members understand the context of your customers, the better they will be able to identify solutions to their problems.

There are many different ways of gathering insights into your customers and the context in which they may use your product, and you should use as many of them as you practically can. Each vector of information gathering will provide you with unique insights and will have its own set of blind spots. No product manager has failed from knowing their customers too well.

There are several methods you can use to get to understand potential customers, including the following:

- **Interviews.** Interviews allow you to have an in-depth conversation with individual customers about their habits, needs and desires. The free-form nature of an interview allows you to adjust the script as you learn more and when unexpected or surprising information is discovered, but the one-on-one nature of the discussion means that you cannot easily determine whether any particular interview reflects the general opinion of your customers. Interviews are also relatively easy to arrange and conduct, but their informal nature and distance from the actual situation in which your customers perform their tasks can lead to things being missed. However, they are generally significantly easier to organise, and interviewing as few as 5–7 customers will likely give you substantial insight into your target market.

- **Focus groups.** In a focus group, several customers or representatives of a targeted group will participate in a facilitated discussion with a prepared script. The facilitator should not be the product manager or a member of the product team, as it is important that they do not subconsciously bias the focus group by words or actions (a problem that can occur in interviews as well). This script should be consistent across groups to allow analysis and comparison, but the facilitator retains the option to expand on topics as required. Like all group meetings, however, a focus group is vulnerable to groupthink and domination by forceful individuals.

- **Testing.** Another option for gathering data is user testing – that is, allowing potential customers to interact with prototypes or a working application under controlled conditions so that their behaviour can be tracked and analysed. Even a non-working prototype, with interactions simulated by the product team, can reveal customer reactions and opinions that would never be spotted in conversation, such as when customers become frustrated with a particular task. You can also test competing products to see the practical differences in the way apps work. Testing under realistic circumstances, and using insights gathered from that activity, will often generate insights into your customers that would be impossible to collect through interviews.

- **Observation.** You and the team should regularly go and observe customers in the actual context where your product will be used. This does not consist of collecting data from the app (see Chapter 6 for more on that) but rather on watching how they shop, deal with problems and perform related activities in reality. This can take many forms, from spending time in a retail location to taking calls in the customer service department. The advantage of this approach is that it is likely to reveal pain points or usage patterns that would otherwise have been missed.

However, the product team will typically need to perform additional research to identify workable solutions.

- **Surveys.** A survey is useful when you have well-defined questions you want to ask your customers and you need to ensure that the answers reflect the breadth of your customer base. A well-designed survey campaign will have the advantage of being statistically valid. Although a survey can be relatively cheap to run, you need to be careful in the drafting of the questions to not bias the results. Furthermore, some significant effort may be needed to verify that the survey results properly reflect the demographics of your customers. It may be helpful to engage specialised market research companies in the drafting and distribution of the survey. However, a survey is only as good as the questions you ask, and it's unlikely to suggest innovative ideas.

A WORD OF WARNING

The challenge you face in exploring customer needs is that customers may not themselves be able to articulate these problems, and you shouldn't assume that they will be able to figure out the best solution. If you're coming into product management with a project/business analysis background, don't make the mistake of relying on them to tell you. Customers aren't like business subject matter experts (SMEs) who can tell them what their business processes are, what business rules need to be enforced, what decisions need to be made and so on. There's no scope and nobody can tell you what needs to be done.

Please don't misunderstand what I'm saying. As a product manager, you absolutely should make the time to sit with customers and listen to their opinions and ideas. If you do, they'll tell you about all sorts of things that they'd like to have, things that would make them happy and many new features that they would like you to put into your product. However, you can't rely on those customer insights to drive the bottom line results that your company is looking for.

I learned this the hard way myself. On one of the first products I worked on that was aimed at a broad audience, I noticed a problem ... we were signing up new customers, but not keeping them. When the time came for them to renew their subscriptions, a large percentage of them didn't. So, I did the obvious thing – I started talking to customers, confirmed to my satisfaction that there was a problem with the quality of the product we were delivering and then ran a customer survey to get the data to convince executives that we had to do something.

They were persuaded, and we started rolling out the features they said they wanted. And it had an effect! The rate at which new customers came onboard shot up significantly and stayed that way for years. Everybody was happy, except me ... because although I had improved our customer **acquisition** rate, the changes I'd put in place had a minimal effect on the **retention** rate. But because revenue was up, and customer satisfaction numbers went up too, I wasn't able to get further investments into researching and fixing the original problem.

Now, in that case I sort of succeeded. I've seen other, smaller products I worked on simply fail to make any significant dent in the market. Every one of them had a set of customers that were loudly demanding that we build them and telling my team that if we did, they and many others would buy it. This has been called the 'Product Death Cycle',[1] and it tells you something when it's a common enough syndrome to have a name ...

In most cases, your customers won't put in a lot of time and effort into thinking about how your company could do things differently. They know where the irritants lie (if they've run into them), but their ideas are naturally going to be focused on what are, to them, the obvious problems. So you'll hear about things that they think should be easier for them to do, or features that your competitor has that you don't, but not about problems you **could** be solving but aren't. And they definitely won't be able to tell you how to turn non-customers into customers.

Furthermore, the customers you have the easiest access to, and the ones that are most vocal about your product and its direction, may not be the best ones to listen to. Often, the most vocal segments of your customer base are a minority with distinctive needs. They are likely heavy users of your product and focused on problems that most aren't concerned with, or asking for things that won't convince a single customer to switch to your product. Obviously, these things can be useful information and spark good ideas! But they aren't enough, and may not lead to growth.

When (and I mean **when**, not if) you talk to your customers, you need to structure the interview to give you the bigger picture. Always ask open-ended questions. Avoid leading questions that might inadvertently direct your customer's thoughts in a specific direction. Focus on their experiences and their situation to find opportunities that have been overlooked.

In addition to your actual customers, you need to put time and effort into learning what drives the decisions of people who aren't your customers but could be. Do you know why customers that switch to other products did so? What were the features that convinced them to switch or which drove them away? What about non-customers, the people who decided never to get your product at all?

That's a lot of people to talk to, to be sure, but that's part of your job. Of course, you don't need to talk to everyone all the time. If there's a question regarding who you should listen to, your product strategy is the place to look for the answer. (The Ansoff Matrix, which we will discuss in Chapter 3, is a particularly useful tool for this.)

---

1   The term was originally coined by David J. Bland.

FORMING A CLEAR VALUE PROPOSITION

If I had to pick just one thing that a product manager needs to understand, it's their product's value proposition. A value proposition is a short, easily understood statement explaining why customers should buy and use your product. Defining your value proposition forces you to take a step back from all the features of the product and define what's really important and unique about it. It's not a sales pitch or marketing slogan – it's a guide for you and your team. It tells you what is truly important and what isn't.

It's easier to show you what a value proposition is than to try and specify how it should read. For example, here are the value propositions of some well-known brands:[2]

- Zoom® solved a common problem with video conferencing services. It was the only service that could reliably work through corporate firewalls and prevent 15 minutes of work at the beginning of every meeting sorting out connection and login issues.

- Uber simplifies transportation for people. Rather than having to call a taxi company or flag down a passing driver, you can just put your destination into the app and someone will show up to take you there. It also removes the friction trying to pay with cash or credit cards.

- In its original version, Netflix® removed the hassle of having to go to the video store and being limited to only whatever they had in stock at a given moment. Instead you could get DVDs mailed to you and return them when you were done, without late fees.

The biggest shift people have to make when moving from projects to product management is to understand and apply the concept of a value proposition. If product managers don't know what their product's value proposition is, they will find themselves rushing to add features to their product, blindly chasing the ideas and demands of internal stakeholders, and losing any sense of what really matters. While we'll talk more about the desires of internal stakeholders later, keep in mind that they will most likely be amplifying the kinds of customer comments that we've warned you about following blindly – complaints and requests for features offered by competitors.

If your target customers are enterprises, rather than consumers, a different approach will be needed. The key to understanding the enterprise market is that the buyer and the user will usually be two different people, who may work in different departments and who may barely even talk to each other. With enterprise customers, you will need to keep in mind that the buyer and the user have different jobs-to-be-done. Buyers tend to be focused on comparing features and getting the most capability for an acceptable cost. Users, on the other hand, will be concerned most with how well the product supports their work.

In a project environment, the mindset is that more is almost always better. We agonise over scope cuts and creep. We try to reach out to every affected stakeholder and make

---

2   These aren't 'official' value propositions defined by the companies in question, but rather my own descriptions of them.

sure that their voice is heard. When we are constrained in what we can deliver, we try to find a compromise that provides every stakeholder with **something** to view as a win. We are working against known and well-defined processes. The result is a process of facilitating negotiation among a broad range of business stakeholders to try and deliver business value.

These are not the problems product managers face.

In product management, you are building for a customer who may not be easily accessible to you and who cannot easily articulate their needs. You won't and you can't speak to every affected stakeholder or stakeholder group. Making one set of customers very happy with your product is usually **better** than delivering something that has a little value for all of them. Finally, there are times when cutting features actually makes your product more valuable.

In short, as a product manager, you need to think differently about value.

WHAT IS VALUE?

The key to understanding value is understanding that it is not an absolute – it is a **relationship**. The nature of this relationship is captured in the Sammy Value Concept Model (Sammy VCM).[3] Business analysts will be familiar with Business Analysis Core Concept Model found in the *BABOK Guide*. The VCM refines that model further, simplifying it to four core concepts. In this model, pictured in Figure 2.1, we see customer value as formed as the relationship of things: customers, products and context.

Figure 2.1 Sammy Value Model

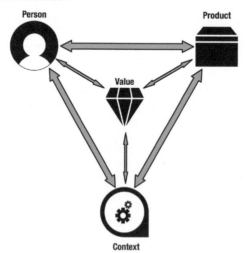

---

3   This model was developed by Julian Sammy (1970–2021) but never published by him during his lifetime. He discussed it at length with me – the material here is based on our conversations, and some of it was reviewed by him before his death. In Julian's original model, 'product' can be replaced by any 'thing', including solutions, organisations or whatever else the person might be evaluating.

The Sammy Value Model

A **customer** is any person who uses the products or services that your enterprise produces (they may or may not pay you for it; that depends on your business model). Customers have problems that they are trying to solve. Those problems may be very different from customer to customer, but the thing that makes them a customer is that you are offering them something that they see as a potential solution.

A **product** is something we offer to a customer to solve their problem. It doesn't have to be a physical object; it can be a service or even something completely intangible like an idea.

The third thing that determines value is the **context** in which it exists. A product can be incredibly valuable to a customer in the right time and place and almost worthless in the wrong one. Economists refer to this as the **diamond–water paradox**. Water is necessary for life; diamonds are not – but under most circumstances, diamonds are treated as far more valuable than water. The reason, of course, is that we place a high social value on diamonds compared to other substances. However, if you put someone in the middle of a desert, where they have no ready access to water, their priorities will change drastically.

Product managers, then, need to understand that customer value is by no means a constant and will change over time. We can also see that different customers will have different perceptions of value, based on their own differences but also changes in their context.

To define a value proposition, therefore, we need to look not just at our customer, but at the context in which they are using their product. A customer who uses your app while standing in a subway car may be very different from the same customer at home watching a streaming video, where value is concerned.

EMPATHY MAPS

A useful tool for capturing the relationship between the customer and any particular context is **empathy mapping**. Developed by Dave Gray of Xplane, empathy maps help us to explore what our customer is feeling, thinking and doing. Building an empathy map grounds your team in the customer's reality and can help you to look at your product from their point of view.

Empathy maps are best developed with a group of people in a workshop setting. While these are often built by the team, there's nothing that prevents you from doing the same with actual customers or running it past them to validate your work – that will surface many opportunities.

When using an empathy map, be careful not to simply capture the team's existing assumptions and ideas about their customer's perspective. That exercise will expose different or contradictory presumptions, and build empathy with the customer, so it isn't a complete waste of time – but it isn't telling you anything you don't already know. A better approach is to use the questions and perspectives as guidance during your customer interviews and capture what they are telling you about their context. Those interviews can then be used to build the map itself. The map allows you to synthesise your insights into a cohesive understanding, and helps you to explain that to others.

It's important to work through the map step by step and fully explore each of the sections. Each section provides information useful to the next (see Figure 2.2). Certainly, if an idea occurs to someone that fits in another section, go ahead and add it to the map rather than losing it, but an orderly approach will give you the best results for idea generation.

Figure 2.2 Empathy map

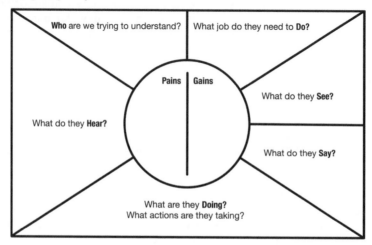

The first step in building the map is to clearly identify **who** you are building it for. Don't make the mistake of simply saying 'our customers' and moving on. Be specific about which customers you are building it for. If you have multiple customer segments, build a map for each one (and perhaps more than one for a given segment), and consolidate them later if that effort seems worthwhile. You should also consider their circumstances – where they are, what is happening around them, who else might they be interacting with and perhaps what their relationship is to those other people.

The second step is to define what they are trying to **do**. This includes the task they are trying to perform and the context for that task which you will expand on when you explore the job-to-be-done and the value proposition. However, here we would also want to ask additional questions, such as what are they doing today and why might they want to do it differently? We also want to look at the kinds of decisions they will need to make during the process, as we will ultimately want to think about the information customers need while they use it. Finally, what does success look like to them? How would they (or we) know that they have accomplished what they were trying to do?

Following this, work clockwise around the canvas, asking what the customer is seeing, saying, doing and hearing. For these sections, you are focusing on observable behaviour – **not** speculating on motives or desires (which is what separates the second 'do' from the first, which **does** capture goals). For example:

- **Seeing.** When they encounter the need for your product, what is happening? Are they at their desk, in a coffee shop or at home? What are other people doing when they encounter this problem?

- **Saying.** What are they communicating to others about the problem they're facing? What tone do they have when communicating? Are their emotions visible? Are they angry about the problem or defensive?

- **Doing.** How do they deal with the problem today? What are the actions they have to take? Are those actions working? What is making it difficult to get the result they want and how are they coping with that?

- **Hearing.** Are the people they're interacting with supportive? Frustrated? Angry? Is our user having to come up with a way to placate them, or is it something everyone views as a routine problem?

The purpose of these sections is to help you to understand what the world looks like to your customer and what they are experiencing. The focus on tangible reality pushes us to better understand their world and to see what might drive their emotional responses.

Finally, only once we understand all of these things do we start to explore what our customers are thinking and feeling. This is the point where we ask how the customer would naturally respond to all of these experiences. Look closely at each of the sections above and think about how they translate into pain points or potential gains. For instance, if they are acting defensive about the problem, why are they doing that? What's driving the emotional effect of the issue? Are they having a hard time explaining the problem, or do the people they are speaking with not care? Are the things they have to do difficult for them in some way? How much better off would they be if they no longer had to deal with those problems? We will capture the customer pains and gains here, so that we can see what motivates our customers and therefore what they might find valuable.

Unparkr's empathy map

During the early stages of development, the Unparkr team decided that they were going to target a 'bottom-up' approach to growth – develop a tool that would be demanded by users, rather than one that would be primarily sold as a product to enterprises. After all, it was going to be included in a package deal for HumberTel's customers. The challenge wouldn't be selling it, but rather getting people to use it so that it might help to keep existing customers and be adopted by other organisations.

Following that decision, they decided to build empathy maps for potential users, trying to identify the ones that might both be experiencing a painful problem and have a need for a solution. Here are the ideas they developed for project managers.

Who
- Project managers who:
  - are working with matrixed teams;
  - have many stakeholders they need to engage;
  - have limited access to the time of senior decision makers.

Do
- need project decisions made on time;
- make sure issues get resolved;
- find that people participating in the meeting don't have the authority to make decisions;
- see decisions get forgotten and endlessly rehashed;
- will know they are successful when the team moves forward with the support of all critical stakeholders.

What do they see?
- the project timeline they are having to update;
- endless emails in their inbox about an issue that was supposed to be settled;
- the project team revisiting work that was supposedly completed;
- a meeting about an issue that was supposed to be resolved months ago but everyone forgot about;
- a spouse telling them they really should log off their work computer;
- they are at their desk or working on their phone after hours.

What do they say?
- 'Who needs to be here to make a decision?'
- 'The VP needs to be in this meeting or we can't go forward.'
- 'OK, if you can't make it to the meeting I'm assuming you are OK with whatever decision the team makes.'
- 'We will have to reschedule because a key stakeholder cancelled.'
- 'OK, let's go over the background to this problem in detail so everyone understands the issue.'

What are they doing?
- sitting near an executive office hoping to catch their attention;
- looking for a time that fits everyone's schedule;
- sending out pre-meeting documents in the hope someone actually reads them;
- developing slides for a presentation that will bring all the participants up to speed.

What are they hearing?
- 'I thought we settled that issue months ago?'
- 'I wasn't in that meeting, and you overlooked this key point.'
- 'Sorry, I can't make a decision on that until I go back and review it with my team.'
- 'Why is the project being delayed again?'

Pains
- blamed for delays caused by people not making decisions;
- critical issues get missed and delay the project;
- issues turning into political hot potatoes;
- major change requests at the last minute;
- far too many meetings, which seem to go on forever.

Gains
- key stakeholders are properly engaged with the project;
- issues are dealt with early on before the project is put at risk;
- meetings are effective and decisions get reached;
- people show up for meetings because they know their time won't be wasted.

FINDING A VALUABLE PROBLEM

Once we have a clear picture of who our customers are, what they are trying to accomplish, and their experience with their existing situation, we can finally ask why they would want to use our product instead. Remember, they are finding ways to meet needs without your product (or with your current version of it), so why should they change? If they have access to substitutes for your product, why will your product be better for them?

If you can't answer these questions, it's unlikely that your product will be successful (and if it is, it'll be by accident). Yes, there are a small minority of customers who may try out new products out of curiosity, but most of them will need to be persuaded that there is a clear benefit to switching. While there are some examples of major products that succeeded because their customers found a use that the creators never intended, it's not a good way to bet. Yes, ongoing product discovery is valuable and necessary, but you can't randomly try things out until you run out of money or succeed. Effective product management is grounded in a clear hypothesis describing how your product creates value for a customer.

Why a hypothesis? Well, we call it that because you are typically making guesses regarding the value you're creating and delivering, and how your product is positioned in the customer's mind. It's impossible for it to be anything else. No product manager can perfectly understand how people will interact with their product under all circumstances, because you can't anticipate all of the things that people might do with it. You don't know their motivations for using it, or some of the creative uses that people might come up with. Even if you could know all those things, that value can change over time: a product can be an industry-shaping breakthrough one year, a commodity a couple of years later and actively painful to use a few years after that.

But you can't just throw your hands in the air and give up, either. If you do that, you'll end up being driven by factors outside your control and chasing the market. All new product features and capabilities will be based on the demands of your sales and marketing team, pushed by the needs of specific customers (potentially to the detriment of many others) or by chasing the features added by your competitors. Without a hypothesis regarding how your product can create value for your customers, you'll be driven by circumstance, and success will purely be a matter of luck.

One of the more useful approaches to identifying problems that have potential value to a group of customers is the JTBD theory. The theory achieved prominence because of Clay Christensen's book *The Innovator's Dilemma*.

There's a widely quoted saying by Ted Leavitt in product management: 'people don't need an electric drill, they need a three-inch hole in the wall'. The idea here is that the drill is a tool used to satisfy a customer's problem, which was to create a hole – but it's also true that, as Joe Leech said, 'No one wants a hole.' The hole is also needed for a reason – perhaps to hang a picture. And, of course, the picture is being hung for a reason as well – perhaps to make the room more aesthetically attractive, or for people to be able to look at pictures of their loved ones. That last motivation, the real problem they're trying to solve, is the job-to-be-done.

Your analysis starts by looking at what the customer is trying to accomplish in any given situation. What is the change in their circumstances that they're trying to create? What is their goal and how are they looking to make progress towards it? Once you understand that, you only then move to asking how your product helps them to accomplish it. That's when you go back down the chain, looking at the steps the customer takes to achieve their goal and finding opportunities for your product to help them. There may be parts of the job that just aren't a fit for what your company does. Choose your steps with that in mind.

A good example of this can be found by looking at coffee. In theory coffee is coffee, right? And yet we see coffee delivered in a number of different ways – some people prefer to get their coffee from a Keurig® machine, others insist on cold-brew, drip filters or a French press. Some buy it from a doughnut shop, others go to Starbucks™, and still others wouldn't be caught dead in Starbucks and will only go to a local place that roasts its own beans. People drink espressos in the morning to wake up and have decaf after an evening meal. What we want from coffee varies significantly based on the context we use it in.

If we want to look at coffee through a JTBD lens, we'd ask ourselves **why** people are drinking coffee at this time and place. For instance, they might be trying to:

- wake up and be able to think after a bad night's sleep;
- work at the coffee shop and see buying the coffee as the price of being allowed to sit there;
- have it as part of a quick breakfast;

- meet someone for a conversation in a low-key, informal location;
- take a short break from staring at a computer screen.

From a JTBD perspective, coffee is serving a different function in your customers' lives in each of the above scenarios. **Make me able to think** is very different from **give me a way to socialise**. They imply different things about not only the coffee itself, but the way the coffee is made and the environment in which it will be consumed.

Everything about the process of making coffee depends on the job-to-be-done. In the context of a quick breakfast, you may want to have only a few types of coffee and machines that can dispense standardised amounts of milk and sugar so that a customer can get their coffee and leave within a couple of minutes, even at times of peak traffic. In other contexts, it may be important to have a lot of seating areas with the knowledge that people will be happy to wait five or ten minutes to be served. The point is to start with what your customer is trying to accomplish by purchasing your product, so that you can optimise the product and the services around it to meet those other needs.

KANO ANALYSIS

Kano analysis is a technique used in product management to understand how product features affect customer satisfaction. It was developed in the 1980s by Dr Noriaki Kano[4] to help explain the effect that product quality had on customer loyalty. The model behind Kano analysis recognises that not all features have equal value in the eyes of the customer and, more importantly, that different features affect customer satisfaction in different ways. It's helpful for exploring how product features create market differentiation.

The Kano model describes five different relationships between features and product satisfaction. Each type of relationship leads to different results from increased quality. The model helps to explain why improvement in a product feature doesn't necessarily result in increased customer value – in some cases, it can even lead to decreased customer satisfaction, if those efforts focus on elements that are irrelevant to your customer (see Figure 2.3).

The first relationship that the model identifies is must-have features or basic needs. You can think of these as the minimal features that a product has to have to be viable in the market – often incorrectly referred to as the minimum viable product or MVP,[5] but more correctly called the minimum marketable product (MMP). These features have no real positive contribution to customer satisfaction, but they make customers actively dissatisfied if they're missing. For example, an app that doesn't protect customer information (such as credit card numbers) from being accessed by hackers would be

---

4   Noriaki Kano, Nobuhiku Seraku, Fumio Takahashi and Shinichi Tsuji (1984) 'Attractive quality and must-be quality'. *Journal of the Japanese Society for Quality Control* (in Japanese), 14 (2). 39–48.

5   The original idea behind the minimum viable product was that you would build the absolute minimum of functionality needed to put your work in front of a customer and have it actually do something. The intent was that the MVP let you test an idea to determine if it was viable. However, the term has been extensively misused to mean other things, such as the minimum needed to sell the product or the minimum needed to convince users to use it instead of an alternative.

Figure 2.3 The Kano model

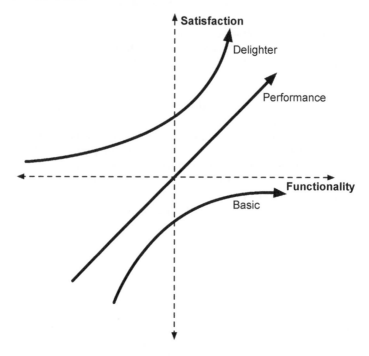

lacking a basic feature. However, extra investment in keeping that information secure above and beyond industry standards, likely won't result in customers preferring your app to competitive alternatives.

By contrast, performance attributes have a relatively straightforward relationship to customer satisfaction – with these, more is better. These qualities are the ones that customers are most likely to discuss when asked about their needs. An example of this is the search function in a shopping app. The closer search results are to what the customer is looking for, the happier they will be. Conversely, if the search brings up a lot of products that the customer doesn't want, they are likely to be dissatisfied.

Delighter attributes go well beyond this point and provide benefits that the customer doesn't expect to see in this type of product, leading to a very strong and positive response. A shopping app that tells customers that a product they're looking for will be on sale in a few days might be an example of this sort of feature. Because delights are unexpected, customers can't tell you about these kinds of needs. They have to be discovered by the product team through empathy for their customer and a deep understanding of the customer's needs. Including delighters in your product can lead to dramatic increases in customer satisfaction and the acquisition of new customers.

It's also possible that customers are indifferent to some attributes of a product – that is, it simply doesn't matter to them whether the product has that quality or not. For instance, how much storage an app consumes on your phone is likely to fall into this category, as most customers won't know what that number is and likely wouldn't care if they did. These attributes can be important to overall performance but, from a customer perspective, investment in improving them will have no perceived benefit. Product managers should aim to minimise the costs associated with these attributes.

Finally, it's possible that some product attributes may cause negative or reverse satisfaction – that is, the better they do something, the unhappier customers are. This can happen for a number of reasons, but one of the most common is that the attribute creates expectations that aren't met by other parts of the customer experience. For instance, if your shopping app search shows the exact products wanted, but those products are consistently out of stock, your customers may be more frustrated than they would be if the search was less effective but showed things they could actually buy.

PRODUCT VISION

The value created for customers is the starting point for defining your product vision. The ability to define a compelling product vision is an essential skill. A product vision tells people why they should care about your product. It spells out who the product is for, why they will want to use it and what benefits they will receive from doing so. Without a solid product vision, you are left without any clear idea of who your customers are and what the product needs to do.

Consider these two visions:

1. The app will ensure that our customers experience a digital omnichannel experience as they engage with our brand. It will ensure a seamless coffee-buying experience and allow us to participate in an ongoing, two-way dialogue with our customers.

2. When our customers go to work, they can let us know and we will have their coffee ready for them, just the way they like it, poured fresh just before they enter the door. If their schedule changes, that's on us, not them – they will always have the coffee they need when they need it.

You can judge how good the second vision is for yourself, but I feel confident that you'll agree it is much better than the first.

The product vision will be communicated to senior management, to the people developing the product and to other stakeholders throughout the company. A good product vision will be a short document – likely no more than a page or two, maybe even a paragraph. However, you're likely to find that getting that document **just right** will be much harder work than a typical requirements document or project plan because it must describe only the things that are truly important for your product to be successful, and nothing more.

There's no one industry template for defining a product vision and I doubt that it's possible to follow a good process for defining one. It might be articulated right away by a product manager or executive, or it might take months of discussion and refinement. However it's developed and presented, though, there are three things that a product vision must do:

- Explain who the product is for.

- Identify what problems these people have that you can help to solve.
- Describe how they will be better off once the problem is solved.

You may notice that these examples are entirely focused on the customer and their needs, and that's intentional. You'll know your product vision is well built when your team members can all consistently say not only what the product should do, but also identify things it should **not** do. If a proposed feature doesn't help your customer with their problem, is it something that you should be considering? A good product vision will align the organisation around a common understanding of why the product exists and what it does. Executives will see where the product fits in their strategy, and team members will understand the purpose behind their work. The product vision brings clarity to the product manager's job. It doesn't make it easy to be an effective product manager, but it is absolutely necessary for success in the role.

FINDING THE OPPORTUNITY

Obviously, though, just understanding that your customers want coffee as part of a social occasion, or as a way to wake up for work, doesn't immediately get you to a product. The next step is to look for ways to make that job easier.

The challenge you face is that your customer already has ways of doing the job that work, even if they don't work as well as they might. For example, look at the Unparkr case: there are many ways to follow up on action items, including bullet journals, task management applications and more. If you want them to adopt your product, you're going to have to give them a reason to break those ingrained habits and adopt a new approach to meeting their needs. In most cases it's not enough for that to be just slightly better either. If it's only a little better, most of your customers won't really see the need to change. Their existing habits will overwhelm your efforts to create new ones.

The good news is that you don't need to completely reinvent the way people do the job to get this kind of compelling opportunity. The improvement can be an incremental one at multiple points in the job, as long as the end result is worth it. For instance, your customer may not be that interested in an app that they can use to pay for coffee. But when you factor in a loyalty programme that provides free coffee on occasion, plus special offers you can only get through the app, plus the ability to order in advance and have your order ready for pickup when you get there, then you have something that will catch on.

Starbucks did that, and it ended up driving enough extra revenue, especially during the COVID-19 pandemic, to shift the entire corporate strategy towards closing down many stores in favour of express pickup locations. This represented a major shift in the role that Starbucks saw itself playing in its customers' lives. A big part of their offering, the 'job' that they sought to do, was to give customers a place outside the home or office where they could sit and think, work or meet with friends. Moving to takeout means reducing the importance of that job in favour of other ones, such as the ability to quickly get a drink made to your specifications on your way to somewhere else.

To find these opportunities, we need to make sure that we have a complete view of the job-to-be-done. This view includes not only the job itself, but the activities that surround it. Before the job is performed, there will be preparation steps, including identification of the need, deciding to act on the need, potentially searching for solutions and deciding on taking the action. After the job is done, there similarly may be steps, including confirming that the job is done, monitoring the results and clean-up afterwards.

Beyond that, we need to look at aspects of the job beyond the purely functional ones, such as social and emotional elements. Social elements are driven by relationships with other people. For instance, **having dinner** with the family is different from eating alone at home, or having dinner as part of a date or to celebrate a special occasion. Social elements can be vitally important. These elements are the primary reason why restaurants exist at so many different price points, from fast food all the way to places where you can pay as much for a meal as you would to buy a car. Yes, the quality of the food plays a part in that (which would be the functional job), but you can buy the ingredients for those meals for far less than the restaurant charges.

Similarly, emotional jobs shape customer decisions as well. Many people have 'comfort foods' they will turn to after a stressful day. A particular meal may remind you of home or your childhood, or a particular restaurant may be associated with happy times. Perhaps it's just that the staff know you and make you feel welcome. Perhaps buying healthy ingredients to make a meal helps people to feel like they are good parents, looking after their children's health.

MAPPING JTBD AND THE VALUE PROPOSITION

There are a number of different methods you can use to perform this next activity, including the Jobs-to-be-Done canvas[6] or Strategyzer's Value Proposition Canvas.[7] For our purposes here, though, we'll discuss using the JTBD you've identified as the backbone of a **job story map**. These are very similar in intent to the user story maps used by software teams.[8]

A job story map walks through the steps required to complete a job. For example, we might have **throwing a birthday party** as a defined customer job for a restaurant or pub (note, of course, that this is not the only job that can be performed there). It's usually best for this purpose to start with a functional job, rather than the social or emotional aspects, because an app needs to have specific functions that will be built and deployed. That said, don't forget about those other jobs, because they are vital to the overall experience.[9]

We start to build a job story map by defining each step that the customer will have to take, beginning at **their** beginning, not the point where our company comes into the

---

6   Tony Ulwick (2018) 'The Jobs-to-be-Done canvas'. Medium. Available from https://jobs-to-be-done.com/the-jobs-to-be-done-canvas-f3f784ad6270

7   'Value Proposition Canvas'. Strategyzer. Available from www.strategyzer.com/canvas/value-proposition-canvas

8   See Chapter 7 for more.

9   See the CX Pyramid in Chapter 5.

picture. The first step is therefore going to be something like **'decide to throw a party'**. From there, we walk through each major step in the planning process, such as selecting a venue, deciding on the number of guests, sending out invites, and continuing through the point where the bills have been paid and everyone has got home safely. Including these things on your story map doesn't mean that your app will have any functions associated with those steps. That's something you'll decide later. At this stage, you want a complete picture of the job so that you can explore ideas that might otherwise have been missed.

As you identify steps, put them down in a rough order. You're not trying to build a process diagram here, so if multiple steps might be happening at the same time just put them down in the way that makes the most sense to you, or just as they come up – just as you would explain it if you were telling someone how to do the job. It's good to keep them in a rough timeline, just because it will help you to figure out if any steps are missing. Completeness of the end-to-end process of doing the job is what matters here.

Now, underneath each of the steps, consider if a social or emotional element of the job comes into play. If there is one, note it below – these will be useful for the next step. Going back to our earlier example of **throwing a birthday party**, we're certainly going to have associated social jobs such as **ensure everyone has a good time** and **capture happy memories**. However, while those might apply to the JTBD as a whole, there will also be smaller steps such as **surprise the person having a birthday**, which only apply to part of the job – in this case, the planning stages.

Next, start identifying gains and pains that could be realised for the customer at each step. Note that at this stage we are not looking for features that you will build. We are attempting to find things that would make the customer happy, either if they could be made to happen or which represent difficulties that could be removed.

At the end of this process you will have an in-depth assessment of the potential opportunities that exist to reinvent the job, and the experience that your customers are currently having (Figure 2.4).

The next step is to identify the gains and pains your product is in a position to address. This is where you need to start getting selective. Start by considering which steps of the job you believe your app is best positioned to help with. This is the basis for deciding on your features.

While the jobs that a particular product addresses may remain more or less constant, the value of a feature will change over time. A new feature that exists as a delighter when first introduced will often be copied by competitors, causing it to become a performance attribute and eventually a must-have. Every so often, you will need to revisit the job that the customer needs to have done and see if or how things have changed. Don't make the mistake of thinking that a cutting-edge product will remain so five years later. If you had the impression that you can do this once, at the time a product is conceived, and then not worry about it, you're going to find that you're mistaken.

Figure 2.4 Part of Unparkr's job map for the job 'Organise a Meeting'

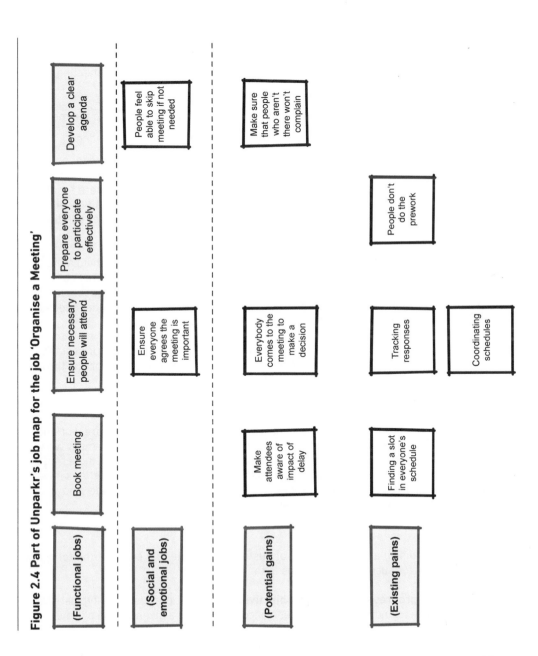

CASE STUDY: UNPARKR'S JOBS-TO-BE-DONE

To provide a working example, let's take a look at Unparkr, the fictional startup that we covered in Chapter 1. The inspiration behind that product was to develop a mobile/web application that would help teams to better manage their meeting outcomes.

For a first approach, we might look at the kinds of things that happen in a meeting and build an application centred around those activities. That would lead us to develop an application with features such as:

- the ability to capture and circulate an agenda;
- a place to capture files that will be reviewed and referenced at the meeting;
- the ability to indicate who will be attending the meeting;
- the ability to capture points of discussion and decisions made during the meeting;
- a way to capture and assign action items developed during the meeting;
- and a place to capture issues that will need to be resolved in a future meeting.

Now, there's nothing particularly **wrong** with this list of items, but there's nothing especially right about them either. You can do all of those actions with a typical office suite. If Unparkr is going to succeed, it needs to offer a substantially better solution for some set of customers.

The starting point for the analysis is to explore **why** the meeting is being held. What are some of the possible reasons for having a meeting in the first place, and what outcomes do the people calling and managing the meeting want to accomplish? That exploration can help us narrow our focus to a particular customer segment with unmet needs and find potential features that would be part of a unique value proposition.

After discussion, Unparkr decide to focus on the needs of temporary and project teams, which may include people from multiple organisations or departments. Working through those questions, they come up with the following vision:

> One of the major reasons projects fail is that project team members are working on too many things at once and every meeting requires people to remember what they were doing and why, resulting in the same topics being discussed over and over. We will help these teams be more effective by ensuring that meetings have a clear purpose, that everyone knows what decisions need to be made, and that important issues are never overlooked or forgotten.

Based on this vision and their choice of customer, they identify some of the following jobs as critical for successful meetings in that context:

- **Manage progress towards an objective.** This is the purpose of a typical status meeting – to find out what has been accomplished in a given period of time, track issues as they come up, ensure that those issues get resolved, make sure that the team is getting closer to their goals and take corrective action as needed. These meetings will be attended by a regular set of participants and an occasional guest.

- **Explore and resolve a contentious issue.** These kinds of meetings may be required on an ad hoc basis as a problem emerges. They may be called to resolve an issue around project requirements or a change in the direction or goals of the effort. It's critical to ensure that the right people attend these meetings and they are likely to involve people outside the regular project team, including senior executives.

- **Review and approve a major deliverable or milestone.** These kinds of meetings are planned in advance as the team completes a significant piece of work. Stakeholders outside the project team will be involved, but the structure of the meeting itself is likely to be carefully planned to demonstrate or review work completed by the project team. The outcome of this meeting is approval of the work by those outside stakeholders, and may also include some specific actions that need to be taken to resolve some remaining problems.

The Unparkr team decided to focus on project team meetings and the outcomes those meetings produced for the project. They might have chosen a very different approach by instead focusing on what happens in the meeting: looking for ways to help all team members contribute effectively, keeping everyone in a long meeting engaged or flattening perceived power levels to encourage a greater diversity of views. A vision built around those goals would still be focused on better meetings, but could result in a radically different product.

As you can see from the examples above, identifying a job isn't a science and there's no specific format that a job needs to follow or level of detail that it should be defined at. What I find most important is to think about the outcomes that your customer wants to accomplish, rather than how your product will be used. If your product helps customers to reach those outcomes better than an alternative, then you have something that they will value. However, we still need to determine whether they value it **enough** to make the product viable.

KEY TAKEAWAYS

- A product vision must always be centred on the needs of the customer.

- The value of a product is a subjective judgement by your customer, and will depend greatly on the context in which they're using it.

- Value is also set by expectations, which can change over time. People may see a given feature as a must-have, something that is better the more you have of it, or an unexpected and pleasant surprise.

- We can only understand a person's context by exploring their point of view and their environment.

- Customers 'hire' products to help them accomplish a job that needs doing. The value and usefulness of any product is determined by its effectiveness at that job.

- A job can have functional, social or emotional aspects.
- To develop your product concept, look at the steps involved in the job and find places where you can help.
- A clear product vision will explain who your customer is, what job the customer is trying to do and why it matters.

3 PRODUCT STRATEGY: CREATING BUSINESS VALUE

Kevin J. Brennan

A strategy essentially consists of three things: an understanding of the problem or challenge you face, a decision about what you should do to address it, and a plan of action to make that decision a reality, including dealing with the obstacles you'll face.[1] A strategy that lacks any of these three things isn't really a strategy at all. In many companies, strategy amounts to wishful thinking or a set of (usually financial) goals with no real idea of how those goals might be achieved.

Strategy needs to start with a clearly defined business problem or opportunity. This almost always relates to customer behaviour, as was discussed in Chapter 2. Even if the ultimate motivation was internal (based on lowering costs, for instance) you still will need to find a customer problem that the business objective ties to and find a set of customer needs. The product you're managing has to offer something that represents a substantial improvement in some way over whatever it is they do today to get their job done. Otherwise they won't change their habits and the product will fail or you'll force it on people and they will be frustrated with your company.[2]

The second element of your product strategy, the decision about what to do to address it, is what this chapter will discuss. 'Let's build an app' is not sufficient. You need to have an understanding of how that app drives business value, which will in turn help you to decide what it should (and should not) do. Quite often, the decision to not do something is the harder one. However, it's critical to good product management. Understanding how the product helps your organisation gives you a way to make these decisions.

The third element of a strategy, the plan of action, will be discussed in greater detail in Chapter 4, which will describe how to build your product roadmap.

Of course, there are many factors that determine which products will thrive and which will struggle. These can include executive leadership, tastes, economic upheavals, personal relationships and random chance. A good strategy is no guarantee of success, but the alternative is to leave your product's fate up to luck.

---

1   See Richard Rumelt (2011) *Good Strategy, Bad Strategy: The Difference and Why It Matters*. New York: Currency. This is (in my opinion) a must-read for every product manager.

2   For instance, using automated systems to deal with people phoning in, which often seem to result in spending an inordinate amount of time going through things that aren't what you need to figure out how to get it to let you speak to someone who might actually help.

Your job as a product manager is to maximise your product's chances of success. Enabling customers to realise value, critical as it is, is only half of the challenge that product managers have to meet. The other half is to deliver and capture business value – to make it worth the money and effort that your company has put into the design, development and implementation of your product.

If you've read just about anything else on product management or agile development, you'll have seen the term 'business value' thrown around a lot, generally without any clear definition. Of course, business or *the* business is an abstraction, just as the concept of customer is. Any business is filled with stakeholders, all of whom have their own ideas about what value is or might be, and whose views will be affected by how the work you're doing affects them.

Business value is just like any other kind of value. In the previous chapter we discussed the Sammy Value Model, and it applies here too. Just as with your customers, there is no 'business value' that can be applied to every kind of organisation. Some people argue that everything a business does has to boil down to profit – revenue. That's close enough to true to be workable in many situations, but simply focusing on revenue can lead you astray. Some choices that increase revenue may contradict the strategy your company is trying to execute.

If you work for a government or non-profit, revenue may not be a concern, and you may naturally struggle with the idea of having competition, because you usually don't have any in the traditional sense. In your case, it may be better to reframe the question. While you don't have direct competitors, you have to think about the needs of donors (who have other non-profits seeking their support), senior government officials (who may direct funding elsewhere) or members. In addition, both government agencies and non-profits are faced with the challenge of ensuring that eligible people actually use the services that they offer and that you can deliver the expected social impact that you're promising.

Looking across industries and sectors, then, every enterprise needs to deliver some form of value to key stakeholders, distinct from its customers. That might be shareholders, donors, specific groups in society, taxpayers, the general public or all of these at once. As a shorthand, we will refer to that value as business value in this book. Given this, we can reasonably define business value as **progress towards the enterprise's strategic objectives.**[3]

As a product manager you will have to understand your organisation's strategy and how its performance will be measured by key stakeholders. You need that understanding because you will have to translate them into product strategy, roadmaps, and features.

---

3 Many writers will equate business value with money, which is a mistake. Money has value but is not itself value. In a for-profit organisation, making money is presumably one of your business objectives, but it is certainly possible for other objectives to be as or more important. In non-profit or government work, generating money may be necessary but it is not the end goal.

PRODUCT STRATEGY

The product positioning statement

An effective product manager must be able to explain who their product is for, how it helps those people and why it's better for them than other alternatives in the market. The product positioning statement is a tool for communicating those things quickly, even if you only have 30 seconds to explain what you do. The classic positioning statement[4] looks like this:

- for (target customer);
- who (statement of the need or opportunity);
- (product name) is a (product category);
- that (statement of key benefit – that is, compelling reason to buy).
- Unlike (primary competitive alternative);
- our product (statement of primary differentiation).

Let's look at what you need to fill in the blanks.

For (target customer). Chapter 2 delved into the needs of your customer and how to tie those needs into application features. However, in most cases you will not have the resources to chase after every possible customer who might want to use your product. Filling in this part of the positioning statement requires you to make a choice about who your product is for.

Who (statement of the need or opportunity). Why would your customer be willing to use your product? If the existing solutions in that market are completely satisfactory, it's likely that they won't. In this part of the positioning statement, you're being asked to set out the unmet need that your target group has that the product will satisfy. You don't have to come up with something life changing – it might be as simple as customers wanting to order your products on a mobile device – but it does need to clearly state the existing gap in available solutions.

(Product name) is a (product category). When defining the category,[5] try to avoid the obvious, such as 'app', or at least be specific about what kind of app it is – mobile ordering, customer self-service or some other type. A clear definition of this point helps you to identify who else is competing in this space and what other products your customers will compare your offerings to.

(That). Describe your value proposition here. What does the app do for your customer? This doesn't need to be a differentiator from your competitors, as we get to that shortly. This is about the core of the job-to-be-done that you have identified, and how the app helps people with that job.

---

4   Originally formulated by Geoffrey Moore (1983) *The High-Tech Marketing Companion*. Boston: Addison-Wesley.

5   The name is up to you or perhaps your marketing department.

Unlike. Identify your primary competitor or competitors by name if you can. When people open your app, who will they compare the experience of using it with?

Our Product. What makes your product different? Again, try not to answer this with 'allows them to shop from us' – that may be true but it's not providing any useful information. Is there something about your app that makes them more likely to be your customer? Better yet, is there anything unique about it that your competitors don't do?

Having a clear positioning statement means that you've taken the time to think about what makes your product stand out and you have an idea of what really matters. Most importantly, it forces you to summarise those things so that they can be communicated to other people. Ultimately, that's what your product vision and strategy are for: to help you determine what's important, and help you to understand if you're succeeding.

Of course, it takes more than a few sentences to create a viable product strategy. Let's take a deeper look at the elements in that sentence, and some tools you can use to explore them.

Who is your customer?

In Chapter 2, we discussed approaches that you can use to better understand your customers and what their needs might be. In practice, though, you can never target every potential customer as each has unique needs and jobs-to-be-done. While some companies are able to address their entire potential target market with a single set of products, it's very likely that they will instead break their market up into segments that have similar product needs.

The process of statistically identifying and defining market segments is complex and data-driven. It's also not something that you as a product manager will be responsible for; the definition of market segments, and the decision about which ones to target, are made at the executive level. However, understanding what a market segment **is** will be helpful as you make product decisions. Fortunately, even if the process of determining what the market segments are is complex, the concept behind market segmentation is fairly straightforward.

Companies perform market segmentation to better understand and market to their customers. It involves dividing your customer base into distinct groups, or segments, based on things that they have in common with one another. Knowing what these groups have in common helps you to find an appropriate hook to make them aware of your product and to pique their interest in it. Some of the lines along which companies typically segment their market include:

- **Geographic:** breaking customers into groups based on the region in which they live and work. Geographic segmentation is appropriate when you are trying to direct companies to a local business where travel distance matters, or by marketing to them in a language that they understand. You might also use this form of segmentation for climate zones (no point in selling air conditioners in the Arctic Circle).

- **Demographic:** breaking customer segments out by personal characteristics such as age, ethnicity, gender or the number of children they have. The assumption behind demographic segmentation is that your customers have similar needs at a comparable point in time in their lives or you are selling a product that appeals to a particular cultural group.

- **Psychographic:** breaking customers into groups with similar lifestyles, aspirations and tastes. Psychographic segmentation has traditionally been difficult to accomplish but is becoming increasingly common with the ability to build customer profiles out of internet surfing habits, purchases and the use of machine learning to identify statistical correlations.

- **Behavioural:** based on actions that a person performs. This might include the frequency of visits to certain stores, their use of apps or websites, or other directly observable patterns of behaviour. Most often, behavioural segmentation is based on data that you can correct directly, such as how often they use your application or what features they access. Chapter 6 will discuss this sort of data collection in greater detail.

There is some overlap between these. For instance, a particular geographic location can be home to an ethnic group with different demographic, psychographic and behavioural characteristics from the people nearby. However, most companies will choose a single approach to segmentation, so this is rarely an issue.

Market segmentation is valuable to a product manager because it gives you insights into who your customers are, their tastes and their interests, and will give you keener insights into their jobs-to-be-done. For instance, market segmentation may give you insights into what digital platforms your customers are most likely to use and their overall comfort level with and expectations of technology. It may inform decisions about which languages to support or even what features to prioritise.

Market strategies

Once a company has determined the best segmentation of its customers, it has to determine which segment(s) to target. The Ansoff Matrix[6] is a tool that defines the basic strategic approaches that can be taken to drive growth in a particular target segment or market. The matrix identifies four potential growth strategies for products. It is a 2 × 2 grid developed along two axes: whether your company is trying to grow through selling existing or new products, and whether they are seeking that growth in existing or new markets (see Figure 3.1).

While the Ansoff Matrix is still widely used and well-regarded, it's important to understand that it is designed for corporate strategy across a product portfolio, **not** an individual product. However, it remains useful for understanding the context in which your product operates, and the approach you will likely be expected to take to developing your product strategy. The distinction is important to keep in mind – your company may

---

6   H. Igor Ansoff (September–October 1957) 'Strategies for diversification'. *Harvard Business Review*, 35 (5). 113–124.

Figure 3.1 The Ansoff Matrix

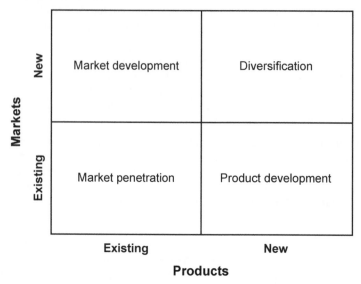

be focusing on growth with its existing products, without much intent to invest in major changes, but still view a new digital product as a key part of that growth strategy.

The first strategy, **market penetration**, focuses on expanding the sales of the organisation's products to customers similar to the ones it already serves.[7] Market penetration is viewed as the least risky form of growth, as no major changes to products need to be made and the market should be well understood. Strategies used may include deep discounts or promotional offers, acquisition of competing companies (or their digital products) or adding limited new product features.

Growth in this scenario can come from two sources. The first is to make more money from the people who are buying from you today, by selling them more services and encouraging them to buy from you more frequently. The second is to reach the customers who are very similar to your existing customers, but who don't buy from you or use your services. These may be potential customers who were previously unaware of your organisation's product (particularly in emerging markets) or customers who previously bought from a competitor.

The second approach for targeting customers is **market development**, where an organisation takes existing products and sells them in a new market, which might be a distinct geographical location, speakers of additional languages or customer segments that are otherwise distinct from ones you have served in the past. This is viewed as riskier than market penetration. Your product may be mature and well understood, but there is no guarantee that the new market will have the same needs as your existing markets.

---

7   In government and non-profits, 'market penetration' might include working to make more people aware of services they can access.

Here, again, the investment in new product capabilities will be limited, although those products may be packaged and marketed quite differently. This approach can be successful if your organisation benefits from economies of scale, the new market has very similar characteristics to your existing ones, or the new market segment is willing to pay a higher price for what is essentially the same good.

So, how might a digital product help to increase demand for a company's other products? Most likely, your product strategy will be built around marketing to the customers your organisation is targeting. That may lead to it being designed to support loyalty programmes, enabling greater self-service, increasing convenience around product pickups or delivery, or potentially enabling access to the organisation's products in additional languages or offering other forms of localisation.

On the right side of the matrix, we have strategies built around growth through new products, whether through existing markets or new ones.

Product development drives growth by creating new products that you can sell to the customers already buying from you. It is considered to be about as risky as market development. To make this approach successful, you have to both identify further unmet needs in your customer base and find opportunities to create new products and services that address those needs, and which also make sense for your organisation to offer.

These products will have to be aligned to your existing business capabilities and fit in with the expectations around your brand. For instance, a wireless carrier will understand the desires of its customer base around phones very well, and can probably assess which features and price points align with that customer base, but they are unlikely to be successful at building and selling their own phones. On the other hand, a game company will likely have relatively little trouble convincing their customers to at least consider playing another game that they publish.

Finally, there is the riskiest approach to growth – **diversification**, or growth by acquiring new customers in new markets. When Dr Ansoff developed his matrix, this approach was more common than it is today. Large multinationals would routinely enter markets where they had no prior experience, based on where they saw the biggest opportunities for growth. For example, in 1982 Coca-Cola® bought multiple movie studios in its efforts to drive growth. They would reverse that decision later in the decade, selling those studios off to Sony. This approach has fallen into disfavour, as companies recognise that success in any given industry will require skills and expertise that may not translate well.

Apple® is a company that has been extremely successful implementing a more modern approach to diversification. From a base in personal computers, they were able to expand into personal music players, music sales, phones, audio products and general entertainment. This may seem inevitable now, but definitely didn't seem to be at the time. Apple was successful in large part because it was relatively careful in its growth strategy. It moved step by step into markets that were at least adjacent to the ones it previously sold into, ensuring that the customers in those markets would be familiar with its reputation, and focused on product segments that fit well with its existing competencies in hardware design and user experience.

In one key respect, the Ansoff Matrix has a 'blind spot' that you need to keep in mind. With digital products, it's virtually impossible to succeed with a product that isn't under continual development. You will always be adding new features, improving existing ones, or keeping pace with shifts in hardware design and UX paradigms. If you stop developing a digital product, it will fade away – maybe quickly, maybe slowly, but sooner or later it will lose all of its customers. Additionally, many startups should logically fall into the diversification quadrant, as they have neither an existing product nor an existing market – but they clearly aren't diversifying, as they only have the one product.

Startup strategy is heavily influenced by examples such as Facebook® or Google®, and is funded by investors willing to accept a significant risk of losing their money in return for the possibility of ending up with a very large stake in a multi-billion pound company (known in startup parlance as a 'unicorn'). These companies may offer their service for free or at a loss with the goal of getting most of the potential customer base in their market to use their platform, knowing that the economics of purely digital businesses will then reinforce their market dominance.[8] In many cases, they aim to get customers first and figure out how to make money off them later.

If you are developing a digital product as part of a diversification strategy, then the startup approach is the one that will give you the best odds of success. Since the market is new to you and your company, startup practices including early exposure of your product to actual customers, rapid development and release cycles, and a willingness to make a 'pivot' and significantly change or update your business model will push you towards finding your market, if there is one. These practices are useful in other contexts, but they are vital in this one.

Government and non-profit considerations

The Ansoff Matrix is focused on company growth as an objective, and so it won't be a good fit for a lot of government and non-profit work. However, it's still possible to draw some useful lessons from it if your organisation is looking to increase the number of people it can effectively serve. In these contexts, you can replace 'existing markets' with 'existing communities served'. You can look at the question of whether you should increase your focus on current beneficiaries or potential future ones, and whether the services and help you offer are what you should continue to offer. Your organisation's vision and mission should help to guide these choices.

Unparkr's market

So, how would our team at Unparkr address their challenges around market segmentation? Remember, HumberTel's goal was to market Unparkr as a bonus for its existing enterprise customer base, with the idea that over time it would become a viable standalone product (and, it hopes, potentially a highly profitable spin-off if things go **really** well). This strategy means that Unparkr is going to be addressing multiple market segments in different ways.

After discussions with HumberTel's marketing department, the team is told that HumberTel's current strategic focus is on companies that need to support a large

---

8   See Peter Thiel (2014) *Zero to One*. New York: Currency.

number of remote teams and work-from-home employees, and that they have identified two major segments among that group:

- large companies who will directly supply their employees with company-purchased technology, including computers, peripherals and phones;

- small-to-medium companies that require their employees to use their own devices. They will specify minimum requirements and allow the employees to expense some of the cost back.

However, this poses something of a dilemma for the Unparkr team, as their strategy is built around bottom-up growth, and not on enterprise sales. After some discussion, they recognise that in the longer term they will have to focus on the needs of the enterprise buyer, which will mean being able to demonstrate value for money with a comparable feature set to other software in this space.

But what should they do in the short term? Going back to their product vision, they recall that their focus was on project teams and particularly project managers who were being forced to split their attention across multiple projects. They conduct some interviews and reach the conclusion that this is more common in small-to-medium companies, as their larger customers have projects that can keep entire teams working solely on a single project for long periods of time.

However, they also recognise that this decision makes the project more risky for them. A review of their vision against the Ansoff Matrix shows that they are building an entirely new type of product for HumberTel, and targeting the product at a new market as well (since HumberTel's prior experience has been built on enterprise sales). After some discussion, though, they agree that the risk is necessary to fulfil the product vision and the strategic goal set for them.

Coming back to 'for' and 'who'

As we've seen, there's a lot that goes into deciding exactly who your customer really is. In Chapter 2, we explored your customer largely through the lens of jobs-to-be-done. In this view of the world, your customer is anyone who is facing a particular type of problem or challenge, and what they have in common is the thing that they are trying to do. That is the most important lens for a product manager to use, but you also have to keep the marketing lens in mind as well, which is likely to segment customers through a set of characteristics that they have in common.

You may find that the customer segments have little to do with the job you identified, or that customers who are not considered part of your company's target market still face the same problem. As a product evolves and becomes more mature, a critical decision to make will be whether to pursue customers with similar jobs-to-be-done, or continue to focus on a particular market segment and think about other jobs you might be able to take on to drive growth and adoption. There is no default 'right' answer to this question: it will depend on your company's capabilities, its understanding of the market, the nature of the different customer segments, and the intensity of competition, among other things.

What **is** vitally important is that you and your company do make a clear choice, and align your efforts to that choice. The product strategy should capture that decision and follow through on its ramifications.

Competing products and the market

Most companies will be able to tell you what kind of business they're in or what market they serve. You'll hear this expressed by phrases such as 'we're in the grocery business' or 'we serve upscale customers'. It may, or may not, surprise you to know that there is no strict definition of which markets exist. Governments may in some cases define things like industry codes, but there is certainly nothing that requires a company to 'stay in its lane' and stick to one market or industry.

Even so, as a product manager, it can be helpful for you to have a clear understanding of your industry. In most cases, those competitors are serving the same market or are in the same industry as you. We need to understand who our competitors are and what they're offering to customers. As you explore these questions, you may find that customers have a different idea of who your competitors are than you do. They will see your competition from the perspective of their jobs-to-be-done and, from that perspective, there may be alternatives that you had never thought about.

To keep things clear, we will use different terms to differentiate the kind of market competition you face. The term 'competitor' refers to the more obvious case, companies who produce a very similar product to yours. Other products that meet similar needs are referred to as substitutes. For example, Netflix and Disney+® are competitors, as they both provide streamed online entertainment. XBox® and Playstation® are substitutes for online streaming, as they are an alternative form of entertainment (but are, of course, competitors to one another).

Firms within a given industry tend to have many things in common. They face very similar competitive pressures and will tend to gravitate towards similar business models. This happens because there is usually one model that is better at generating profits or sustaining itself than the alternatives. Their products usually have significant similarities or may even be interchangeable. They may well hire from similar pools of people and have similarities in business culture. And quite often, despite all the effort put into strategic planning, their actual business strategies end up being very much alike as well.

WHAT ABOUT NON-PROFITS?

If you work in government or in the non-profit sector, these tools are still going to have some relevance for you. The big difference is that business value for a non-profit organisation isn't measured in profits, it's measured in the social impact that your product creates. With that said, you can likely skim bits of this chapter that may have less application for you, such as the next section. There will be callouts throughout the text that touch on the differences.

Intensity of competition

The primary theory for explaining industry attractiveness comes from the work of Michael Porter.[9] The Five Forces Model (Figure 3.2) suggests that profitability has less to do with the performance of individual firms than it does with the industry in which they operate. There are five forces, each of which tend to drive down profitability if they are strong because each of them will increase pressures on a company.

Figure 3.2 The Five Forces Model

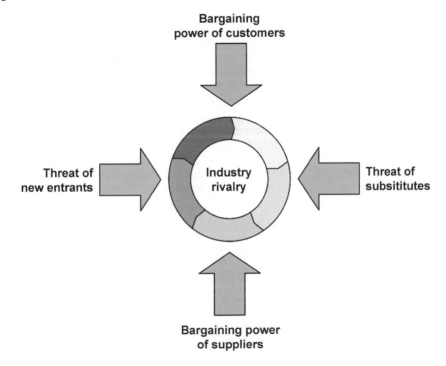

As we've noted earlier in this chapter, of course, profitability isn't the only measure by which a product's success should be measured. Additionally, if you're not an independent startup, the industry you're in is already determined. However, although Porter developed this model to explain why some industries are more profitable than others, he also determined that profitability is largely driven by the intensity of competition for customers. The more competition there is, the lower prices are likely to be.

From your perspective as a product manager, the more intense competition is, the more likely it is that your team will have to deliver increased value rapidly and repeatedly. This is where we should consider the concept of clockspeed – the pace of ongoing change

---

9 Michael Porter (1980) *Competitive Strategy*. New York: Free Press. This book also included the four types of competitive strategies, which will be discussed shortly. His next book, *Competitive Advantage* (1985) New York: Free Press, introduced the value chain. Porter's work remains foundational to much of corporate strategy and it is very likely that executives will be familiar with it.

in a given industry.[10] How long can you afford to stay put on a product release? How quickly will new competitors emerge and how long will it be before they duplicate your best features? Will those competitors come from inside your industry, from adjacent industries, or seemingly out of nowhere? What kind of pricing models will be viable? The Five Forces Model helps you to explore these questions and their effects on your strategy.

Bargaining power of customers

The first force is the **bargaining power of customers**. How easy is it for a customer to change their purchasing to another company? If customers can easily switch, then this force is considered to be high. These factors aren't limited to actual contractual penalties and the like; the difficulty of moving over customer records, loss of utility from integrated products and software, and even brand loyalty or strong relationships with an account manager can all create relatively high perceived switching costs. A digital product can serve to decrease the relative bargaining power of customers through locking in useful data and benefits. For instance, a loyalty programme may discourage customers from moving to a competitor because they don't want to lose their points.

A good example of a programme designed to increase switching costs, and therefore lower the bargaining power of customers, is Amazon Prime®. It started as a simple programme where customers could reduce shipment times by paying an annual fee, but Amazon® has since loaded up Prime® accounts with many other benefits, including its streaming music and video services, and special offers. The expectation, which has proven to be accurate, is that once customers pay the fee to access Prime they will be less likely to shop elsewhere.

Unparkr

What is the bargaining power of Unparkr's customers? At first glance, it would seem to be low – HumberTel signs big multi-year contracts, and it provides enough IT services that a switch won't be easy. So at first glance, this would seem to be relatively low. However, on closer examination the Unparkr team realises that this isn't the case. The project teams working at HumberTel's customers don't have to use Unparkr – they can use another tool that they've bought, or nothing at all.

Eventually, Unparkr hopes that they can build up enough functionality and add enough value that teams will resist switching to another service, giving them more control over pricing. Unfortunately for them, that's still some time away. Right now, the bargaining power of their customers is **very high**.

Bargaining power of suppliers

The second force, which parallels the first, is the **bargaining power of suppliers**. If a supplier is the only source of something that you must have, they can increase the price of that good or service and there's not much you can do about it. On the other hand, if

---

10 Charles Fine (1998) *Clockspeed: Winning Industry Control in the Age of Temporary Advantage.* New York: Basic Books.

there are many similar suppliers, they have much less ability to drive prices higher and therefore demand a cost premium.

Returning to Amazon, we see programmes like Amazon Marketplace® that effectively drive down the ability of suppliers to bargain. Many companies really cannot afford not to be listed on Amazon, and so Amazon is able to set the terms of the relationship as it sees fit. Many digital products take a similar approach to their markets by presenting consumers with multiple offers to meet their needs and forcing suppliers to compete for their business. That is, in fact, the business model for many startups – if they can get a large enough percentage of consumers (or a sufficiently valuable niche) using their product, they can effectively force suppliers to that customer base to sell through them.

If your product is an offering of a company that sells other products and services, then the strength of this force is likely to be similar to its strength across that industry.

Unparkr

Unparkr runs off of HumberTel's cloud offerings, which can use any of the major providers. These providers are competing with one another and largely offering their services as a commodity – with the right architecture, Unparkr can move among service providers with relative ease. Unparkr doesn't have any other suppliers, since it's not repackaging any other third-party services and or aggregating business providers. It will accordingly rate this force as **very low**.

Barriers to entry

The third force is **barriers to entry**. The term 'barriers to entry' refers to the difficulty any new entrant will face trying to launch a successful business in that market. In some industries a startup can reasonably jump in with a small investment and some determined people (for instance, restaurants). In others, starting a new company may require the expenditure of millions or even billions of pounds. Money may not be the only barrier; intellectual property, trade secrets or regulation can also be barriers. With this force, it's important to remember that when the barriers are high, the force is **low**. If it's easy to start a new business in a particular industry, you can assume that many people will and the resulting competition will drive prices down.

With many digital products, a key barrier to entry is the data held by earlier entrants. Social media companies such as Google and Facebook have years of data on the habits, likes and dislikes of billions of people, allowing them to drive advertising to those audiences with far more efficiency than any company that would try to supplant them. The sheer scale of advertising these companies sell also allows them to offer targeted ads at a lower cost due to economies of scale, which further lowers the potential profits of other companies that might seek to offer advertising. The result is a market that is only attractive to companies that can offer advertisers a specific, valuable niche audience.

Unparkr

The Unparkr team gets into a debate here, as the team is divided between two perspectives, One group argues that barriers to entry are **low**, given the number of startups focused on the enterprise productivity space and the low cost of launching a cloud-based product. The second group feels that barriers to entry are **high**, due to the potential risk of competition from the big software vendors and their existing collaboration software. Ultimately the first group wins the argument when they point out that existing tools don't offer the features they have on their roadmap, and so there is no need to 'replace' these tools in the mind of the customer.

Threat of substitute products

The fourth force is the **threat of substitute products**. These are products that may not appear to be in direct competition with yours, but which can still perform the customer's job-to-be-done or remove the customer's need to do that job. For example, a fast food restaurant and an expensive formal dining establishment are unlikely to attract the same customers, or even think much about one another, but both can fill a hungry stomach and might be appealing to those customers at different times. For your digital app, the substitute products you should be considering are the ways customers can do what they need without opening or using the app. It may also include other applications that serve a similar purpose, or apps that solve the customer's problem. A substitute product can do a different job or be targeted at a different market. What makes it a substitute is that as people use it more, they will use your product less.

Unparkr

When the team moves on to this force, the group that lost the last debate points out that companies have many existing tools from large vendors that can be used to manage meetings and track tasks, even if they are currently less than ideal for the job. Further, if Unparkr does establish a truly compelling offering some of these vendors may consider adding similar features to their tools. Given these factors, everyone agrees that this force must be considered to be **very high**.

Industry rivalry

The final force is **rivalry between competitive firms**. When thinking about this force, ask how much attention your company pays to its competitors and how much effort is typically made to attract customers away from them. For example, consider the 'Cola Wars' between Coke® and Pepsi®, where the companies went head to head, ran ads comparing their taste to one another's, and enlisted high-powered celebrities to endorse their products. In an industry with high rivalry between competitive firms, you will see your app benchmarked against and compared to other similar apps all the time, with feature-by-feature comparisons. You may see promotional offers for customers willing to switch to your competitor's product, or other aggressive marketing moves, and it will be much more critical to frame your value proposition in ways that highlight your product's relative strengths against others, rather than in terms of the job-to-be-done.

Unparkr

As the team moves to the final force, they pull up the websites of other companies in this space and look at their positioning. While none of them offer the exact set of features they are considering, they see over and over again that each company's site includes a feature-by-feature comparison of that company's product against the other tools in that space, with each company obviously focusing on the features that their product is best at. In addition, several of these companies have been aggressively funded by venture capitalists who are hoping that the company will emerge as the dominant player in this space and be the next tech unicorn. Clearly, the rivalry between these companies is **very high**.

With the exception of the bargaining power of suppliers, Unparkr is in a space where every single competitive force is bad for them. With a low set of barriers to entry and a very high threat from substitutes, they must be prepared for competition to come from surprising directions. It's clear that the company is going to face tough competition and must be ready to respond quickly to shifts in the market, up to and including a major pivot in its business model, if a new opportunity arises or its current direction becomes no longer viable.

Considering 'product categories' and 'unlike'

It's important to keep yourself informed about what is happening in your market at all times. Without a well-developed awareness, you risk your product team being blindsided by a new competitor or a sudden shift in customer demand. Remember that competition can come in many forms, not all of which will be obvious. The value of examining your target market from a number of different perspectives as set out in the five forces is that it will help to develop your awareness regarding these potential shocks. While your direct competitors deserve special attention, as they will be seen as the obvious point of comparison, you may also face surprises from other directions such as new startups with a radically different solution or changes elsewhere that eliminate the problem you've been working to solve entirely.

While you can never be aware of every potential threat and risk, a survey of your environment will help you to identify many of the challenges your team will face and consider how best to design your strategy and your product roadmap to overcome those challenges. If your industry is relatively stable, and new challenges are unlikely, you can think in the long term about that roadmap and plan quite far ahead. If industry change and unexpected shifts are a regular occurrence, you should be aiming for a shorter horizon on your roadmap to allow for rapid and frequent shifts in priority.

KEY PRODUCT BENEFITS AND DIFFERENTIATION

The four basic strategies

One of the most significant influences on your product strategy will be your company's overall strategy. A starting point for that understanding can be found in the four generic strategies first described by Michael Porter (see Figure 3.3).[11] Porter's insight was

---

11 Michael Porter (1980) *Competitive Strategy*. New York: Free Press.

Figure 3.3 Porter's generic strategies

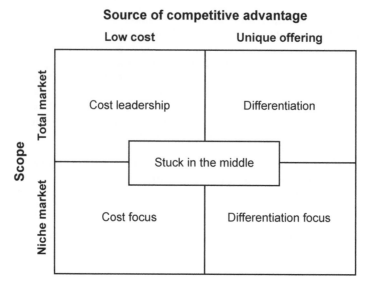

that every meaningful company strategy can be described as one of four alternatives, which drive a set of decisions about the activities that the company will execute. This company-wide strategy will set the context for your product strategy and will help to direct you as you seek out opportunities to find points of differentiation from other competing products.

Some larger companies are in a position to target a wide range of products, services and markets, as they have the size and resources to do so and will generally benefit from economies of scale. Most companies, however, will have to focus their efforts on a niche market, one that has unique needs not shared by the rest of the market and which would likely not be worth the cost or added complexity for a larger, more broadly oriented competitor to address. The unique expertise that these companies develop can serve as a barrier to potential competitors.

Industry-wide low-cost provider
The first is to be the **low-cost provider** for a given market. There can only ever be one company in a given market that follows this model, by definition. If a competitor has lower prices than yours, you aren't the low-cost provider.[12] The low-cost provider focuses above all else on taking costs out of their value chain. All unnecessary expenditures must be eliminated. It tends to be most effective in markets where customer needs and the products sold in a particular market are relatively stable. That stability allows for the supporting processes to be refined and costs to be driven out.

---

12 If you see a large number of competitors that are offering similar products at similar prices, none of them are pursuing a low-cost strategy. These firms may be pursuing a differentiation strategy (the coffee shop on your block is different from one 500m away in that it's right there) or just be stuck in the middle with no discernible strategy. A low-cost strategy doesn't mean just being in a low-margin business, it means doing everything possible to eliminate every last penny of avoidable expenditure.

A likely use for digital products for a company focusing on this approach is self-service, allowing customers to directly order products and resolve issues without the need for (more expensive) human intervention. That often means looking for ways to get customers to execute parts of the business process through your app. For instance, price checking, addressing questions or even purchase and payment may be done through the app – although that last might be limited by the payment policies of Google or Apple.[13]

Industry-wide differentiation

The second generic strategy is **differentiation**. Every company in a given market that is not the low-cost provider must be competing on some other attribute of value to customers. In JTBD terms, there's some part of the job that they are exceptionally good at, so that they provide greater value to customers who care about that element. An industry-wide differentiator is a company who has found ways to provide that unique value to a broad group of customers.

For instance, Apple products emphasise industrial design, user experience and Apple's brand appeal. Those qualities attract a broad group of customers who have little in common in other respects. The most successful social media apps differentiate on the types of social interactions they support, but otherwise try to appeal to customers across a great many demographic categories.

Companies that seek to be industry-wide differentiators will seek out opportunities to build unique, hard to replicate capabilities that provide a competitive advantage across a broad range of products. One example of such an approach is a focus on service excellence, where they provide products at a higher quality, more features or with better service than others can match. Another might be innovation and product leadership, focusing on offering new and exciting features to the market on a regular basis and forcing competitors to constantly try and catch up, or they might aim to have a better understanding of each customer's specific needs and desires by building a strong relationship.

Low-cost focus

A company that chooses a low-cost focus strategy aims at providing the lowest-cost service possible to their target market. Unlike an undifferentiated low-cost provider, which will drive out cost everywhere it can, a focused company following this strategy will have to pick and choose its targets. Because it's focused on a niche, its customers are likely to see some elements of the product as vital to their jobs-to-be-done and demand superior service and quality in those areas, even as they are willing to eliminate everything else. From a Kano analysis perspective, they will aim to invest just enough into the performance attributes of their products to ensure they meet their niche's expectations better than any alternatives, and invest in other attributes just enough to avoid dissatisfaction.

Differentiation focus

A differentiation focus means that your company has chosen to target a certain type of customer above others, and create additional value for that group that gives them a reason to buy from you rather than someone else – in other words, your company

---

13 Companies pursuing excellence as part of their differentiation strategy can be as ruthless at cost-cutting as a low-cost provider. The key difference is that those savings aren't passed on to customers, but retained by the company as profit.

satisfies one or more jobs that others don't, or that they don't do as well. Looking back at our discussion of Kano analysis in the previous chapter, this likely means that you excel on some performance attributes or provide delighters of some kind to customers.

One approach to differentiation is to focus on one product or a very small group of related products. Product development here will focus on ensuring that your product offers superior performance to its competitors. What superior performance means will depend on your customer base. From the perspective of Kano analysis, this product should sit at the high end of the performance line. This development will keep the product as the leader in its market.

Another form of differentiation is an adaptation strategy allowing a company to move quickly in markets where customer needs and tastes change frequently. In this scenario, it's vital to ensure that your product is frequently refreshed to be in line with the current market demand. While this can sometimes be done with industry-wide differentiation, it is more likely to succeed if executed by a niche company, just because it's easier to monitor changes in taste among a smaller, more homogenous group.

Fashion is one industry that demands adaptation, as what's considered fashionable can change from season to season and year to year. Entertainment is another adaptive industry, as people's tastes change over time and older forms seem old fashioned. This kind of strategy can be seen in digital gaming products as well. If you are managing a digital product that has to be adaptive, you should look for ways to invest in building a platform of reusable assets that can be used to develop new products quickly in the same space. Games, for instance, are typically built on various engines, developed in-house or by third parties, that implement many of the common elements needed in particular game genres.

Stuck in the middle

Finally, there is the fifth 'strategy', stuck in the middle, which describes companies that essentially follow industry trends without any clear vision or direction. They don't really try to do anything in particular differently from their competitors. I imagine you can easily think of a number of companies that fall into this category. These companies may succeed and even prosper for a time due to residual brand loyalty, being in the right place at the right time or simply being lucky.[14] This is really a non-strategy, but honesty compels me to admit that a lot of companies operate this way.

If you happen to be working for one of these companies, the good news is that the company strategy won't really constrain you. That's also the bad news, as it will make your strategy harder to formulate and to get approval for.

Unparkr

Based on the decisions made already, Unparkr will clearly pursue a differentiation focus. While at the beginning it will have to keep its costs low simply because it isn't bringing in direct revenue, its long-term goal is to increase the value offered to its target niche to a level where it will have some power to set its prices.

---

14 If I knew how to be in the right place at the right time, or to be consistently lucky, I wouldn't need to be writing this book.

In its initial list of candidate jobs-to-be-done, the Unparkr team identified three that they thought looked promising:

- 'Manage progress towards an objective.'
- 'Explore and resolve a contentious issue.'
- 'Review and approve a major deliverable or milestone.'

Reviewing these problems, the team identify potential alternatives and sources of competition that might apply to each of these, such as project management applications, brainstorming and whiteboarding apps, and document workflow management. They discuss at some length the possible evolution of each of these, the opportunity they see and the risks each entails. Again, there is no objectively right answer. The choice a product team makes will depend at least as much on the insights and inspiration found among the team members. If someone has a compelling new approach to solving a particular class of problems, that could outweigh stronger competition in that sector.

One interesting consideration for the Unparkr team is that their corporate parent, HumberTel, is also a focused differentiator, albeit with a larger niche. This isn't a concern for the Unparkr team right now, as they need to get traction with their initial chosen target audience before they can worry about expanding their focus. Assuming that they do, though, the time will eventually come where they have to determine whether to align themselves with their parent's strategy or pursue a different direction.

- If they stay aligned to HumberTel, future product development should focus on addressing the needs of other kinds of teams. For instance, they might choose to identify and solve problems found in large meetings (at the departmental or company-wide level), or for committees that convene on a regular basis to discuss ongoing business.

- Alternatively, they might choose to continue focusing on problems found in remote project teams and move beyond meeting management to other, similar issues, such as risk management, requirements management and task tracking.

These are not the only two options, of course – there are many others. The strategic choice they face, as most digital product teams will, is when to expand the scale of their niche versus dealing with additional jobs-to-be-done.

Choosing what to do best ('that' and 'our product')
In practice, almost every digital product will at least start out as a focused differentiator, and the vast majority of them always will be. This isn't a bad thing – the same is true of most companies! If you want to serve a particular group of customers well, and help them with their jobs-to-be-done better than any alternative, you absolutely should be a focused differentiator. The issue is what to focus **on**.

By the time you've reached this point, you should have a solid idea of who your customers are and what jobs-to-be-done you can help with. The decision to be made for this final part of the strategy is where to draw the line – what can you uniquely do that nobody else is doing, at least not for this group of customers?

Expressing your strategy

Product strategy, as you've seen, is an art rather than a science. There are things that you can do to make your strategy more likely to succeed, which largely boil down to exploring multiple options, selecting one that seems most likely to work and then making sure that the rest of your choices support that option. That means:

- Ensuring that you know who your customer is and have found jobs-to-be-done that are valuable to them.
- Exploring those jobs to understand what pain points your customers are experiencing that would genuinely make them want to switch.
- Looking for ways to do that and validate those ideas with your customers to make sure they really are valuable and your solution really does make them better.
- Assessing the market for that customer group carefully to understand who else is working on that problem and whether they might effectively compete with you.
- Narrowing down your customer niche and the job you work on until you have something that nobody else can offer.
- Executing on that and staying focused. Expand it over time in ways that increase the value you can offer without losing focus on your customers.

The positioning statement is a succinct way of capturing all of that and communicating it to others, but a catchy positioning statement is useless if you haven't done the work to make sure your position is strong.

When product strategy is rooted in a clear theory of customer value, it becomes possible to identify other new and innovative features that can delight your customer base and enable you to outperform the competition. A useful theory lets you explore additional unmet needs that may result in new products or partnerships. Sometimes, more importantly, it helps you to figure out when a proposed idea is actually detrimental to many of your customers and may belong in a different product entirely.

Unparkr's positioning statement
- For project managers working with remote distributed teams
- who are dealing with project cost and budget overruns because their teams are overloaded,
- Unparkr is a meeting facilitation application
- that helps remote teams to work through complex and contentious issues.
- Unlike whiteboarding applications,
- our product ensures that everybody comes into the room with the knowledge and willingness to find a lasting solution.

CREATING AND CAPTURING BUSINESS VALUE

Like your customers, the business is using your product in a specific context to perform a job. How well it performs those jobs determines the business value of a product. Of course, the jobs it needs to perform for the business and the jobs it performs for the customer aren't the same – and that's the balance you have to strike. Well-designed products bring those jobs into alignment, while poorly designed ones have them working against one another. That job might be revenue generation, but it will likely include other goals and objectives as well.

In this chapter, we're focused on what business value is, rather than setting specific performance targets for specific periods of time. We've defined business value as progress towards an enterprise's strategic objectives, and I assume that you've discussed those objectives with the people you report to and your key stakeholders (if not, go and have that conversation right now). So, how does your product capture value, whether financial or otherwise, and deliver it to the enterprise? That's where your product's business model comes in.

If the product is what your customer buys, the business model is how that purchase converts into business value. A sound business model generates additional value to the business, just as the value proposition describes how extra value is created for the customer. There will be times during the life of your product, particularly when it is in the early stages of development or following a major release, when you don't fully understand sections of your business model because things are still in flux. That's normal, and you will generally have to be sure you have the right value proposition for the right customers in place before the rest will come together (commonly known as product-market fit).

Many discussions of business models imply that a company has only one business model. That may be the case, but it also may not. It's not uncommon for a company to have several different business models. They may pertain to different products, or how products are bundled and sold to different customer groups. As a product manager, you can't assume your product has the same business model as the rest of the company, or the same model as other products. Even if it does, you'd better understand exactly how that business model works.

The Business Model Canvas

The most common approach to describing a business model is the **Business Model Canvas**.[15] The Business Model Canvas describes a company's business model as a combination of nine different elements (see Figure 3.4). The canvas roughly parallels the company's value chain, with suppliers and partners on the left and the customer on the right. We'll discuss the model from right to left, because we want to start with the customer. The sections are:

- Customer segments;
- Channels;
- Customer relationships;
- Value proposition;
- Key activities;
- Key resources;
- Key partners;
- Revenue structure;
- Cost structure.

---

15 Alex Osterwalder and Yves Pigneur (2010) *Business Model Generation.* Hoboken: Wiley.

Figure 3.4 The Business Model Canvas

Key partners	Key activities	Value proposition	Customer relationships	Customer segments
🤝	↱□↴ ○↰△	💎	💗♡	👥
	Key resources		**Channels**	
	👤💲 ⏰💡		🚚	

Cost structure	Revenue structure
💷🧾	📈📊

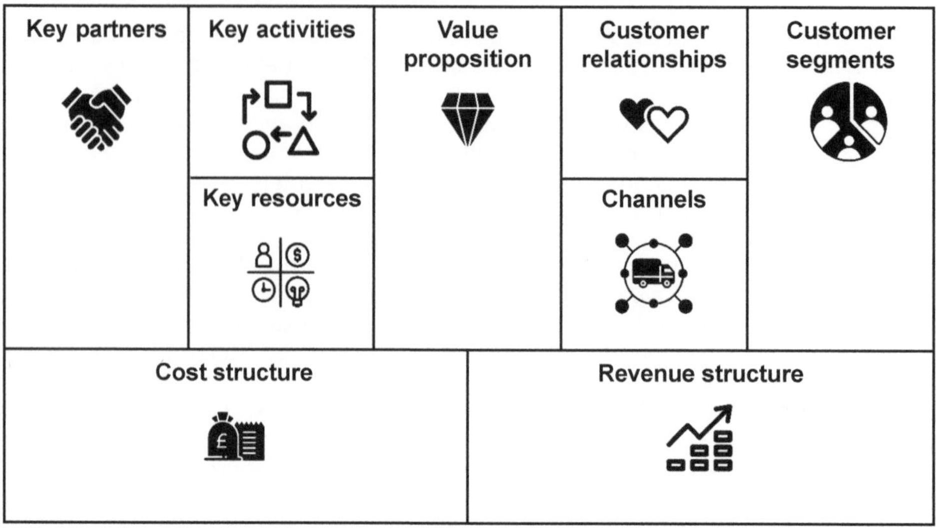

Here, we're going to talk about the business model of your **product**. And yes, each and every product comes with a business model around it, even if you can download and use it for free. The purpose of developing a Business Model Canvas for your product is to understand how that product drives revenue for your company.

If you're working for the government or in a non-profit, the business model is still relevant, although you may prefer to use a variant that has been modified to be more suitable, such as the Mission Model Canvas.[16] As we walk through the Business Model Canvas, I'll discuss some changes you might make that would help it to better suit your needs. Overall, though, the logic is still the same. Your product strategy won't be optimised for revenue generation, most likely, but the principles behind the canvas still apply. You may have **clients** or **beneficiaries** rather than customers, you may track outcomes or impact rather than (or in addition to) revenue, but you are ultimately still delivering a product or service that creates desired results and which needs an organisation that is able to do so.

The Business Model Canvas has nine sections. As you work through it, keep in mind that the Business Model Canvas is intended to highlight the most critical parts of your business model, and it isn't necessary to capture every detail. It is designed to help you visually depict what's truly important about your product. As a general rule, try to keep each section to no more than five-to-seven elements, and it's perfectly OK to only have one. Similarly, keep the descriptions short, usually short enough to fit on a sticky note.

---

16 Alexander Osterwalder (2016) 'The Mission Model Canvas: An adapted business model canvas for mission-driven organizations'. Strategyzer. Available from www.strategyzer.com/blog/posts/2016/2/24/the-mission-model-canvas-an-adapted-business-model-canvas-for-mission-driven-organizations

The first element you need to assess is the **customer segments** you intend to serve, as discussed earlier in this chapter and in Chapter 2. If you are developing this in a group setting, it may be a good idea to give each segment its own colour, so that you can easily link customer segments to other parts of the business model that only apply to them. For instance, a particular customer segment may have a distinct job-to-be-done that others don't – so that job should be shown in the value proposition as only relating to that segment.

Non-profits and government agencies frequently don't have 'customers' as such. Your organisation may prefer to use other terms, such as members, clients or beneficiaries. Further, the beneficiaries of your product may not actually use it, as long as they receive some form of value from the adoption of your product.

In addition to end users, beneficiaries may include groups such as donors or other organisations with a common interest, and may or may not provide funding. Because the value received may be radically different for each beneficiary type, you should make sure to assess that value and the jobs done for each beneficiary group. For instance, the donors to a charity may find value in being altruistic, solving a problem they are passionate about, or good publicity, while the recipients of your services have entirely different needs. This distinction will lead to distinct elements for each group.

The second element to define is the **value proposition**. This, too, is addressed in Chapter 2, and consists of the jobs-to-be-done that your product helps with (and, at a very high level, **how** the product helps). This element only needs to include the critical jobs – if you have a lot identified, try to assess the most critical ones and list them here.

In the non-profit world, some of your beneficiaries may not receive any tangible benefit from what you have to offer. Don't be too concerned if that's the case, as it's pretty normal. For instance, donors may be motivated by the social prestige of hosting a charitable event, or by the altruistic desire to help others. Ensuring that everyone has a good education doesn't directly help those who could afford to send their children to public schools, but it results in a more just and equitable society. Social and emotional benefits are still things people want and still qualify as jobs-to-be-done. In effect, the donors and the recipients can be treated as distinct customer segments with a distinct value proposition.

The customer segments (or beneficiaries) and the value proposition are the two most important elements of the Business Model Canvas. Everything else flows from these two elements. Your channels and relationships will deliver the value proposition to your customers. The key activities, key resources and key partnerships identify the things you need to create that value. And of course, the cost and revenue structures are dependent on your product creating value for the customers and for your company.

Once the customer segments and the value proposition are clear, we then need to explore the **customer relationships** we are seeking to establish or reinforce through the product. The primary questions you need to answer are how you will get customers, whether they're new ones or existing business customers who will move over to your app, and how you expect to keep them once you have them.

A purely transactional relationship (cash for goods) is the most basic, but rarely worth developing an app for. More likely, you are looking to build a longer-term relationship with your customer. Will the app experience be customised or customisable? Is the app just part of their interaction with your company? If not, how do those other parts of the experience work and how do they link up? It's important to capture this, as it provides a critical context for the app design. Is the app where customers start interacting with you, or are you providing an alternative to the primary form of interaction?

Again, you may not have customers, but you will still have relationships with your beneficiaries. Each of the major stakeholder groups have to be given reasons to support your mission or use your product. Donors or other funders still want to be assured that their money is making a difference and having the desired effect. You may also have critical stakeholders outside your organisation who have to be convinced to allow you to move forward with the product. In these cases, a critical consideration is **when** their support is necessary. Engaging some groups too early may cause you to get so caught up in change management that you aren't able to actually deliver, but waiting too long can also backfire.

The next element is **channels** – the means you will use to reach your customers and make them aware of your product. Obviously, app stores or your website will be a primary channel. Beyond that, though, you should focus here on what you will do to get customers to start using your app. Will you use advertising? Promotions? Does your app solve a set of current problems for your customers, driving them to use it? Or will you need to persuade them in some way?

You may not need marketing, but you will still need some way to make your beneficiaries aware of your existence and get them to engage with your organisation. How will you get beneficiaries to use your app? What support or encouragement might they need? Do they even have the means to go online for products or services? Age, lack of computer literacy, or disabilities may also present challenges for key beneficiaries. These barriers should be part of your thinking here, and may require that you include alternative ways to access your product.

As we move to sections on the left side of the canvas we shift from a customer focus to exploring the internal operating model required to support your product, including key suppliers, partners, activities and resources. The typical product manager is likely to give much less thought to this side, as it falls outside the product itself. That attitude is risky. If you don't have the internal processes in place, the right resources available and stakeholders lined up to support them, you may see your beautifully designed product fail catastrophically as it turns out that the enterprise is poorly equipped to deliver on the value proposition promised by the application. Even though you will have less responsibility for these elements, you need to ensure you have thought them through and understand what's involved.

One major decision that will shape this section of the canvas is how your development team is structured. Are they an internal team (in which case they are **key resources** and **activities**), external (**key partnerships**) or a mix of both? As a quick aside, while outsourcing development work can be an attractive proposition, there is the inherent risk of a breakdown in relationships leading to development expertise and product knowledge being lost.

The list of key activities should identify the business processes that are needed inside the company to support your value proposition, and the related elements that are needed to deliver it. Poor performance in these processes will damage the overall customer experience, and harm your product (and conversely, if done well these processes make a product seem better to the customer).

Key resources are the assets or capabilities required to deliver on your value proposition. Assets are things that your company can own or purchase (and which can, in principle, be resold – this is why people aren't resources), while capabilities are skills and technology that can be applied through activities to produce a business outcome. Assets may also include trade secrets, patents or other intellectual property that is embodied in the product. Again, keep in mind that these are not simply the resources needed to build your product, but include the ongoing operational resources needed to deliver on your value proposition. As with activities, identifying resources is necessary to ensure that you have them available for future use.

Finally, we have **key partnerships**. This captures the other organisations you will need to work with to deliver on the value proposition. These will always be external – we're not looking to define internal stakeholders here. They might include cloud providers, tool vendors, external developers and more. The value of highlighting these is to ensure you're aware of the relationships you will need to give your product the best chance to be successful.

The third section of the Business Model Canvas, found at the bottom, are the **cost and revenue structures**. These are used to give you an understanding as to whether your product is valuable to your company. The default Business Model Canvas captures the answer to that question in purely financial terms. The Mission Model Canvas frames these differently, in terms of the organisation's mission, and opens the way to a broader range of metrics. We'll focus on the financial aspects here – not because they are necessarily the most important, but because other metrics are explored in detail in Chapter 6.

Costs and revenue

At the business model level, you're not trying to account for every penny spent or worry about general ledger allocation. Rather, you need to have a sense of the costs involved to make sure that you're spending time and resources in value-generating areas. Ultimately, the goal is to make sure that the product is delivering enough value (financial and otherwise) to justify the expenditures on it.[17] Financial metrics can help in this regard, allowing you to track costs such as development time and customer service representative training.

Despite what people outside the public and non-profit sectors think, controls are, if anything, tighter in these environments than in most private companies. Most non-profits are constantly hunting cash and looking to keep spending under control, and may well have to go up to the board of directors for any significant spending decision, including any decision to develop a new product.

Costs break down into two major categories. Fixed costs are those that don't change based on sales. In other words, selling one (or a hundred) more items doesn't affect them. In general, a fixed cost applies to things that last for years at a time. They cover things like leases for warehousing or office space, equipment purchase, maintenance and repair, and other assets. For the most part, these won't make up much, if any, of the cost structure of a digital product, even if they are relevant to other products your company offers.

The second category, variable costs, do change as you sell more of something. These include raw materials, staffing, hosting and bandwidth, and other resources that you consume as part of the product development process. You'll note from this that most of the actual costs associated with your product are going to be variable. Many of these won't change that much as your product scales. You might hire some new developers, or pay more in hosting fees, but if you're not in a startup pushing for rapid scaling you won't see them change much from day to day.

When looking at the cost structure, what you want to focus on are cost drivers. These are variables that can go **significantly** up or down as the product scales. For instance, if your product is cloud-hosted, additional users, even a lot of them, will add very little to marginal costs.[18] However, if the product interacts with your own self-managed data centre, then it's possible that you will face increasing IT costs as app usage increases. Most likely, though, the critical costs will come from one of two things: the cost of manufacturing, purchasing and shipping of any physical products customers purchase

---

17 This is not the same question as 'is the product making a profit?' The key concern here is the opportunity cost of the money spent – would the investment in this product do more to help your organisation achieve its goals if it was spent on something else?

18 Marginal cost is the cost of selling one additional unit of a product. A lot of new users may increase costs significantly, but a single user won't.

through your app, and any related services, such as technical support or other points where workers are required to provide services or process information in the back end.

Part of the *raison d'être* of a digital product may also be that it lowers costs that have traditionally been incurred by other parts of the organisation, through enabling customers to directly interact with your systems and processes, rather than have to go through your staff or third parties. Allowing customers to purchase services or check on the status of an existing interaction can simultaneously increase customer satisfaction and lower costs.

Revenues, similarly, break down into two categories, one of which is easier to measure than the other. The first is direct revenue – money paid by customers through your app. These may be generated through:

- sales of the app;
- sales of goods and services through the app;
- brokerage fees (where your company takes a cut of third-party transactions that you made possible);
- selling data or advertising.

The second is indirect revenue. Indirect revenue can be tricky to measure, because it represents revenue that was generated because of the app but not **through** the app. Indirect revenue occurs when a customer sees something on the app and goes to a store to buy it, for instance. While you can't know for certain how much of this revenue is due to your product, you can approximate the contribution your product is making to it through indicators, such as app usage, increases in overall sales or customer surveys.

Membership organisations, charities and many other non-profit organisations still have the need to generate revenue. They may not be concerned with profitability, but there are still many costs they need to cover, including staff, rent and the services they need to function. Other organisations may be funded in ways that don't involve revenue generation, such as through grants or government funding.

Whether or not revenue is a concern, though, it can't ever be the only concern – there should always be a greater overriding mission and delivering on that is the highest priority. In these cases, you should seek to measure the changes in behaviour that result from usage of the app – the outcomes that will lead to the impact you are trying to create. For instance, a medical app's success might be reflected in decreased pressure on emergency rooms. These changed behaviours should be selected by considering the social impact your organisation is looking to have, and then asking what measurable actions would be expected if that impact was occurring and looking for ways to assess how the app affects those.

Whether you choose to capture these metrics as 'revenue' or give them their own section, make sure that these key metrics are listed as part of your business model.

THE UNPARKR BUSINESS MODEL

Unparkr's business model is still a work in progress (Figure 3.5). The team know that this plan will change, possibly drastically, as they get Unparkr out and being used by real teams and they learn more about the problems those teams are facing. However, documenting their first-cut pass at a business model and working through the pieces is a good way to validate that they haven't missed anything important.

Customer segments

Going back over their strategy, the team has some discussion over whether they have one customer segment or two. They are depending on project teams to adopt their software, so arguably it doesn't matter that much whether that team works for a HumberTel customer or not. However, HumberTel's enterprise customers are paying for their early development, so ultimately, they settle on two. The project teams are the more important of the two, everyone agrees, but if enterprise customers start asking HumberTel sales reps 'why am I paying for this' or 'can I get a discount if I leave this Unparkr thing out', the product will meet an early and ignominious end.

Value proposition

The value proposition is an easier discussion, because of all the work the team has done to figure out the project team jobs they will target. Better, faster decisions; faster closing of action items, and ultimately making meetings useful rather than an ordeal are core to what they are trying to do. Similarly, since HumberTel is adding it in as a bonus, increasing the value of its bundle of services to clients is part of it.

As the team meets with potential customers to explore their needs and let people try the prototype, however, they note that one big concern is that confidential project data is just going to be sitting on their servers. There is a fear of hackers or competitors being able to access that data and see the current status of any company's current efforts, including the challenges they've been facing and the potentially proprietary solutions they've found. The team adds 'data confidentiality' as a key part of the value proposition.

Customer relationships and channels

Unparkr anticipates working through two channels: sales by HumberTel and sign-ups on its website. In future, it will probably have to add Google Play and the Apple App Store to that list, but mobile apps aren't on the development roadmap until the team are confident that they've nailed their product/market fit.

With those as their channels, it's clear that the customer relationship with enterprises will be controlled by and through HumberTel sales. Where project teams are concerned, they feel that the problems they're helping with will require them to build a number of automated services that will help with meeting management work to encourage people to offload their work. Once they do so, Unparkr expects that switching away will be somewhat difficult, but more importantly it needs to focus on making the product solid enough that teams won't **want** to go back to the bad old days.

Figure 3.5 Unparkr's Business Model Canvas

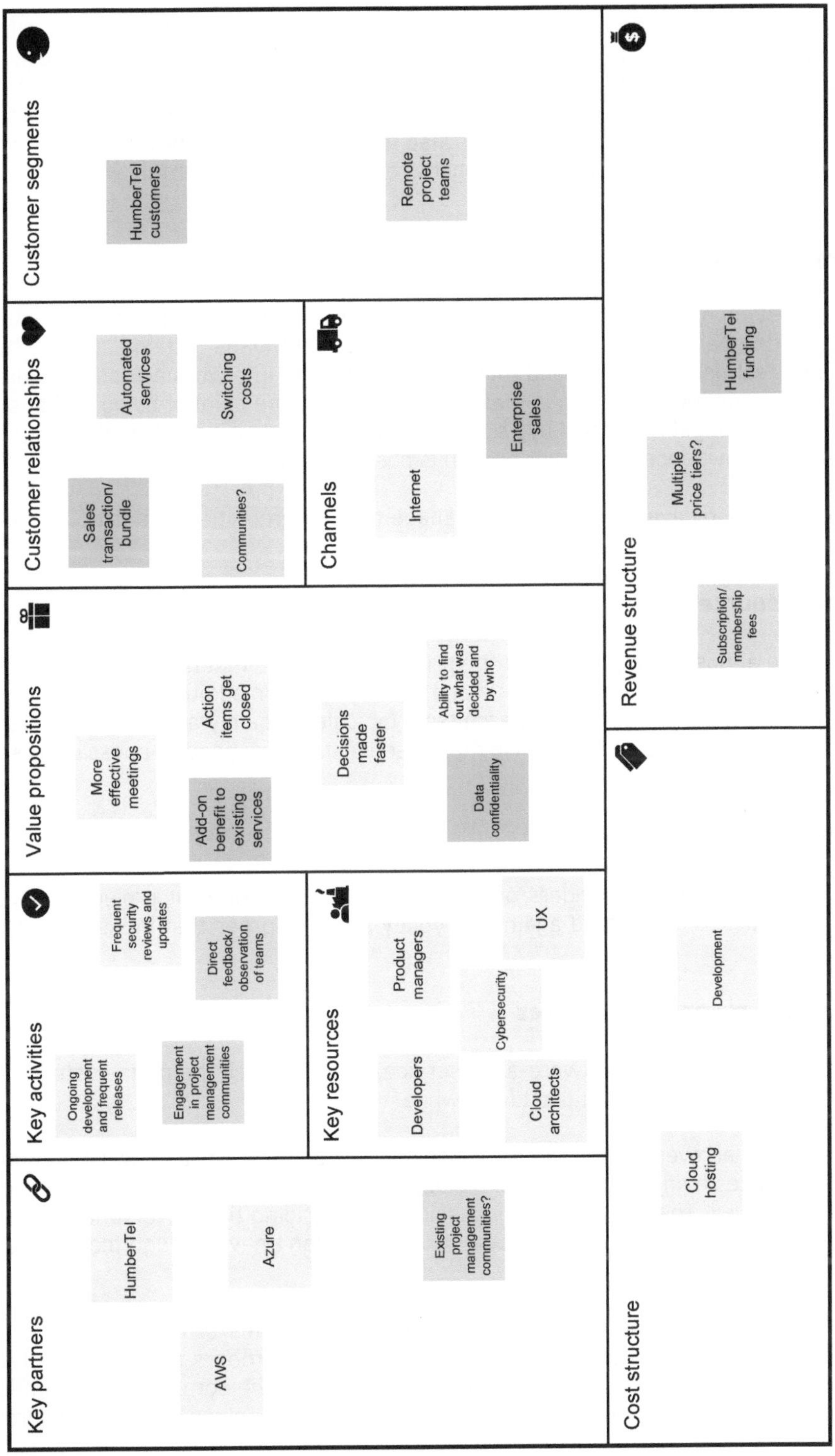

Key partners	Key activities	Value propositions	Customer relationships	Customer segments
HumberTel	Ongoing development and frequent releases	More effective meetings	Sales transaction/ bundle	HumberTel customers
AWS	Frequent security reviews and updates	Add-on benefit to existing services	Automated services	
Azure	Engagement in project management communities	Action items get closed	Switching costs	Remote project teams
Existing project management communities?	Direct feedback/ observation of teams	Decisions made faster	Communities?	
	Key resources	Ability to find out what was decided and by who	**Channels**	
	Product managers	Data confidentiality	Internet	
	Developers		Enterprise sales	
	Cybersecurity			
	UX			
	Cloud architects			

Cost structure		Revenue structure	
Cloud hosting	Development	Subscription/ membership fees	Multiple price tiers?
			HumberTel funding

Finally, there's some discussion as to whether it's worth the time and effort for HumberTel to try and build a strong user community or to actively participate in project management communities instead. Realising that this particular issue isn't at the top of its priority list, it cracks open Unparkr and notes it as deferred, scheduled for review in six months. (The product manager also makes a note that they need other ways of resurfacing deferred topics, since nobody really knows whether this will be relevant in six months.)

Key activities

The most important activity for Unparkr right now is to get its product to the point where customers want to use it as quickly as possible. That means getting out of the building to do direct user research, and turning those insights into working code as quickly as possible. Unparkr's thinking is that it needs to get to the point of being self-sustaining before the budget is slashed by its corporate parent. Even if it can't get there right away, it will have evidence that major growth is possible.

The issue of involvement in project management communities comes up again, and is deferred again.

Key resources

They are almost purely digital, so the primary resources that matter are product team members (product management, UX and development). In addition, the team knows that they will need a few good cloud architects to scale up safely and securely. Given their focus on data confidentiality, it also makes sense to have a good in-house cybersecurity team.

Key partners

HumberTel and cloud providers, of course. Although someone put 'project management communities' on the board again, everybody silently agrees that the issue is dropped for now.

Cost and revenue structures

Since they're using a software-as-a-service (SaaS) model, the main costs should be hosting and developers, at least for a while.

The two initial revenue structures are also obvious. Unparkr has already been committed to its services being sold as part of a package deal, and it plans to sell licences to other teams as well. There is a lot of discussion about pricing tiers. Everyone agrees there should be more than one tier, but right now they don't have enough features to make multi-tier pricing workable.

The team takes some time to do some rough estimates of revenue growth under pessimistic, expected and optimistic scenarios. The numbers aren't great – they are going to have a tough time getting to the point where the company has a sufficiently solid customer base that they no longer need investment unless they can onboard many project managers in the first two years. Given that data, they make a note to look into the needs of adjacent customer segments – if everyone on the team wants a licence, and not just the project manager, the numbers start to look a lot more attractive.

KEY TAKEAWAYS

- As a product manager, you need to understand how your product supports your organisation's overall strategy.

- Strategies are most effective when they can be communicated clearly and succinctly. A strategy should be concrete and avoid meaningless jargon.

- Your strategy must articulate which customers you are trying to reach, what your product will do for them or help them do, and why your product is better for those customers than the alternatives.

- Your strategy will evolve as your product does. Over time, you may need to target additional customer segments or find a new way to separate yourself from your competitors.

- Every product has a business model that describes how the product creates, delivers and captures value, and is a subset of the company's overall business model.

- Understanding your product's business model is vital to ensuring your product's success.

4   PRODUCT ROADMAPS

Sallie Godwin

Of all the artefacts and deliverables you'll be responsible for as a product manager, the **roadmap** is the one that seems to be the hardest to develop and which causes the most grief. This chapter will explore what a roadmap really is, how to go about creating one and how it differs from other artefacts, such as project plans and release plans. Once you have assembled your roadmap, it will need to be continually updated and reprioritised, as well as communicated and explained to your audience. The later part of this chapter will discuss different ways of doing this, depending on who you are presenting to and how much certainty you and your team have about your priorities and goals.

WHAT IS A ROADMAP?

Simply put, a roadmap is a document that captures the priorities of the product team. It shows what the product team will be working to deliver in a given timeframe. First and foremost, it is a communication tool. If well executed and maintained, a successful product roadmap helps to keep various groups in your organisation in alignment. And so roadmaps require product managers to carefully play the expectations game and understand how to manage changes in scope and timing. Because a product roadmap is intended to reflect priorities as they are understood at a given moment in time, not the work that is needed to create a fixed-scope deliverable, they can and should change on a regular basis to reflect market requirements. Your job isn't to deliver features, it's to deliver business outcomes. The roadmap is a way of communicating what you think is the most effective path to accomplishing that, given what you know right now.

ROADMAP AUDIENCE

As with any communication tool, the most important consideration in developing a roadmap is to understand who it is for and how they will use it. Every group of stakeholders will have different expectations from the roadmap and may interpret it in different ways. These demands are one of the reasons roadmaps cause so much angst. For your first step, then, consider your audience. Some potential audiences for a roadmap include:

- sales and marketing teams, who will use the roadmap to plan campaigns around a feature and who will want to shape (or even control) the roadmap;

- customers, who want to know when features they need will be implemented and who may decide whether or not to buy something based on that information;
- resource managers, who will want to know when their key team members may be required to support specific features;
- operational staff, who need to know when they can advise customers to use your app to solve problems;
- senior executives, who will want to know when key features will be implemented so that they can assess the revenue and cost impact, or make progress on other strategic goals, and so that they can budget for future years;
- the product team, who will want to know what is coming up so that they can plan their work accordingly.

It's very challenging to meet all those information needs in a single document. You may even decide that it's better to have multiple roadmaps for different audiences. For example, you may choose to have a roadmap that you are happy to publish externally and show to customers and competitors, in addition to your internal roadmap. However, it is best to avoid having different roadmaps with different items for internal teams, as you run the risk that those different versions of the roadmap will get out of sync with one another, or that readers will think they're being told different things. It's hard enough to keep everyone aligned with a single document, let alone multiple different ones.

Ultimately, you'll have to find the right balance regarding what and how much information to share on your roadmap. Digital product managers typically want to maximise their flexibility and minimise the risk of being locked-in to unrealistic, unachievable or unnecessary commitments. However, the rest of your company and your customers have needs of their own, and that may require you to be more specific about stating your plans.

BUILDING THE ROADMAP

With that in mind, you can start thinking about what kind of information needs to go into your roadmap. That involves considering what your possible audience needs to know, what they want to know, and how to resolve the matter when the two don't match. Most roadmaps will focus on the outcomes you are looking for, alongside the order or timeframe they will be delivered in.

Any discussion of outcomes will inevitably lead to the question of exactly when they can be achieved. However, digital products are almost always built by teams using agile methods and approaches. The benefit of those approaches is greater flexibility for the team and an improved ability to adapt to changing business needs and customer feedback. The challenge is that agile teams don't (and shouldn't) be spending days in a conference room building long-term plans that are probably going to change anyway.

That's why we started this chapter discussing stakeholder communication needs, as those needs are going to drive the roadmap content. However, even if your team isn't going to plan every feature in advance, it's likely that your stakeholders are going to view the roadmap as reflecting some degree of team commitment. At a minimum, if something is on the roadmap, that means you and your team think you can deliver that feature in the given timeframe if nothing happens to change your plans. No matter how agile you are, your roadmap needs to be credible.

Goals and objectives

In Chapters 2 and 3, we discussed goal-setting and how you link your strategic goals to the why of your product and your business strategy. As we move towards delivery and a more tactical focus, we similarly have to break our goals down further and define the objectives we intend to meet in the relatively near term. Building out your roadmap from a defined set of objectives relates the activities you are doing right now to the bigger picture. It shows your stakeholders how everything you and your team plan to do builds towards an objective that, in turn, helps your product to realise a strategic goal (see Figure 4.1).

Figure 4.1 Goals and objectives

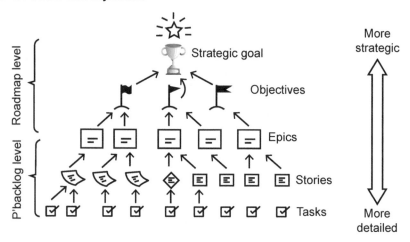

Levels of detail

An essential part of ensuring your roadmap works as a communication tool is getting an appropriate level of detail for the people who are going to read it.

Generally, it's easier to start with the high level, zooming out as much as possible. If people want more detail, they will usually ask for it. If they are overwhelmed by too much detail, they will probably not ask you to summarise. Instead, they are likely to stop listening, so you may miss an opportunity to communicate what's next for your product.

Most roadmaps only show items at epic level and above – something it will likely take at least a sprint, possibly more, to deliver. Stories and tasks that break things down below this are too detailed and belong in your product backlog. The roadmap is not the place to show how something will be achieved. Particularly for the later items in your roadmap, you may not know the approach you will take anyway, as there are likely to be several different ways of solving each problem.

The roadmap will need to articulate the benefits delivered once each goal is achieved. This will be different depending on your audience. For users, make sure the focus is solely on what each item allows them to do now that was not possible previously. Business users will be more interested in how your roadmap helps them to move towards their business objectives, such as achieving compliance or increased sales. How will revenue have increased, or costs decreased? Some product managers take this further by creating an entirely outcome-orientated roadmap. Most stakeholders are more interested in the consequences of each item on the roadmap than what you plan to do to deliver it. It is also possible that you and your organisation may discover that the epic or feature originally proposed was not the best way to achieve a desired outcome. With an outcome-based roadmap, this doesn't matter – the roadmap item can still be considered completed. See the end of this chapter for an example of an outcome-based roadmap.

When presenting a roadmap to the product team and other technical teams, you can include more information on technical enablers and dependencies, as this will be more relevant. However, it is always worth considering whether some of this is better covered off in the product backlog, as it may not be suitable for a wider audience.

Even at a high level of detail, this might seem rather a large amount of information to be able to summarise coherently on one page. To make it easier to organise, many roadmaps group objectives and epics into themes.

Developing your roadmap using themes

Developing your roadmap by thinking about the key themes that make up your product strategy helps to ensure that you have all of your main objectives covered. If there's nothing on your roadmap that moves your product towards one of your organisation's overall goals, it's clear you've missed something. Showing your roadmap broken down into themes also provides a shortcut for your audience. It prevents them from having to try to digest the whole thing in one go. Instead, they can focus on what your team is doing next in the areas most relevant to them. This is useful when you have a diverse range of stakeholders from different business areas, who will all be looking for something slightly different from your roadmap. The themes will help to cut across departments and roles to show that your product improvements will be beneficial to more than one group.

Having the right number of themes is important. Have too few and your audience may think there's nothing on your roadmap for them. Your roadmap may also not reflect all of the work your team is actually doing, prompting your stakeholders to add more things, or suggest you do more of them at once. But have too many themes and your roadmap will be very hard to read, limiting its usefulness as a communication tool.

Through experimenting with the number of categories people can reliably sort information into, psychologists have concluded that most of us can handle sorting things into about six different categories before we get confused.[1] This makes six a useful number to aim for when you are developing your themes. Anywhere between four and six will work pretty well – if you have more than this, the level of detail you are working at is too granular and some of them should be combined.

To be effective, themes need to be intuitively understood by your audience, so developing good ones will involve some audience participation. You can apply the same principles of rapid testing and iteration that are useful in testing your product with users. Some potential ways of doing this include:

- **Card sorting:** writing out all the candidate items for including on your roadmap on cards or sticky notes, then organising them into categories and naming the groups.
- **Rapid prototyping:** sketching out a draft of your roadmap using paper and pens or a whiteboard, then asking participants what's missing, or what doesn't make sense to them.
- **Affinity mapping:** asking participants to suggest themes (without talking to one another) and then highlighting where the same or similar items come up repeatedly.
- **Impact mapping:**[2] breaking down each goal to show the actors involved, the impact it will have on them and the deliverables needed to support it.

At the end of this process, you should have an idea of the themes that will resonate the most with your audience. Some common categorisations include:

- User segments, for example if your product is used by consumers, businesses and educational institutions, you might have a theme for each type of user.
- Different business goals, such as increasing new users, improving the experience for existing users and increasing the time users spend logged in to your product.
- Very high-level customer goals, for example registration, checkout, delivery.

It's also common to have a theme for enablers – things like technical setup, provisioning environments, even sorting out where you work and setting up collaboration tools. These are unlikely to belong in any one theme, but support all of them. Your audience will need to know when you are doing them and why, otherwise they won't recognise what the team has been spending time on, leading them to question why there has been no progress!

---

1   G. A. Miller (1994) 'The magical number seven, plus or minus two: Some limits on our capacity for processing information'. *Psychological Review*, 101(2), 343–352.

2   See https://www.impactmapping.org/example.html

Prioritising your roadmap

Once you have a good idea of your themes and the objectives within them, it is time to put them in order. This is never as simple as it sounds. Inevitably, everyone with any stake in your roadmap will expect to see what matters most to them in the top spot.

There are a number of different techniques for taking the items that you have within each theme and working out what needs to happen in what order. Which will work best for you will depend both on your product and the way your organisation makes decisions. In this section, we will look at some common techniques and the situations in which they are more (or less!) useful in prioritising your roadmap.

MoSCoW prioritisation
You have probably heard of this one already and it remains the obvious place to start. In focusing on the true importance of each item on your roadmap, it makes you consider what would actually happen if you placed each feature outside the 'must have' category – or even in the 'won't have' category. What would not be possible? What would be achievable without it?

> **M**ust have: Without this the product will just not work.
>
> **S**hould have: These things will be important, but could be done later or in a different way.
>
> **C**ould have: These things would make it even better, but are not necessary for success. They are sometimes called 'nice-to-haves'.
>
> **W**on't have (right now): These are ideas for the future; there is no money or time to look at them at the moment.

This is effective when your stakeholders understand that there is a limit to the number of things you can reasonably do, for example when you need to get to market within a specified timeframe. But there will come a point in your roadmap when the 'Must Haves' are done.

Then the arguing can really begin.

To differentiate between Shoulds and Coulds, it is helpful to compare the benefits with effort expended in getting them (see Figure 4.2). Ideally, you should do the things first that deliver the most benefit. Mapping the impact (benefits to your users or improvements in efficiency) on a graph like this can help to identify opportunities and to rule out things that do not effectively pay for themselves. It's a good way of agreeing to start first on anything that falls into the top left-hand quadrant, while saving for later anything that drops into the bottom right. It is much harder, however, to order items that fall into the other two categories. If you find that many of your roadmap items fall into these categories, the RICE Model provides a more specific measurement of the various benefits and is discussed further on pages 107–110.

Scoring items using these models is often used in creating a prioritised list. It is also referred to as 'stack ranking' and can be helpful in determining priorities between numerous items where a natural order is not obvious. It does, however, have one large

Figure 4.2 Impact versus effort

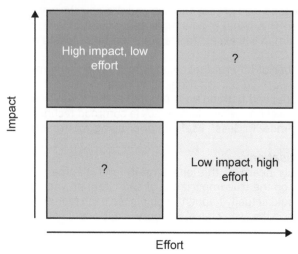

limitation. It relies on your organisation having a single strategy, or at least a common understanding of the overarching objective it is trying to achieve. If your organisation is trying to be several different things at once – with several different customer segments and goals – and they want your roadmap to serve them all, stack ranking sometimes fails. It will descend into horse trading, as each one of your stakeholder groups insists that their users should take precedent, or that increased revenue in their business area will make the highest impact.

What to do if there is no strategic alignment

If you are struggling to prioritise, it is worth considering if this is not a roadmap problem, but an organisation strategy problem. Each of your stakeholder groups may be right in the context of their own goals, but they won't be recognising that their competing strategies are playing havoc with your roadmap. They are also probably focusing on specific features, rather than the outcomes that they support. Shifting the emphasis back to the problem they are trying to solve can help to move the conversation back towards the objective – and highlight if there are multiple competing ones.

Ultimately, your product will need a coherent company strategy to succeed. You can't have a roadmap with multiple different destinations in mind. However, if this is the issue, it takes time to resolve – and your team will still need to decide what to work on next. In this situation, you can try to identify common needs. Even where aims are very different, some items are no regrets, because:

- they will speed up everything that comes after them;
- they genuinely meet a common need;
- most other items are dependent on them.

Examples of this might be technical enablers, such as setting up collaboration tools, or features that all customers will have to use, such as registration or password reset capabilities. If you can determine what these are, it can help you to agree priorities in the short term. However, this only buys time – use that time wisely to resolve the strategy problem and clarify your organisation and product goals!

ROADMAPS AND OTHER ARTEFACTS

Roadmaps differ significantly from traditional project plans. Because they are primarily a means of communication, product roadmaps have to be created at a much higher level of abstraction and are typically designed to fit on a single page. Where a project plan is intended to capture the tasks that the project team will execute so that you can track what work still needs to be done, the product roadmap is intended to communicate what the product team will deliver and the resulting business outcomes.

Even in agile delivery teams, roadmaps are not the only artefact that shows what the product team needs to achieve over time. Your team will usually have a backlog and may also have a release plan. The roadmap will need to work alongside these, but they will hold greater detail on what work will actually be undertaken to achieve an outcome.

Project plan

If you are firmly committed on both timelines and on the features to include, you're managing a project and not a product. In that situation, you should follow project management best practices in developing and managing your work.

A project-like approach is appropriate when you can clearly define scope, and updates are likely to be minor after the app is made available, most likely focusing on bugs and operating system update compatibility.

If you're in this situation, there's no particularly good reason to develop a separate roadmap, as it won't and shouldn't contain any information that isn't also captured in whatever project management tool you may be using, and there's no good reason to have to update two documents. You may find other BCS books such as *Project Management for IT-Related Projects*[3] or *Project Manager*[4] useful. For the purposes of this chapter, we will not be diving deeper into the intricacies of project planning.

Release schedule

There are many cases when a regular release schedule might be needed in addition to a product roadmap. If your app is part of a subscription business model, where customers are paying for support over a period of time and expect to see regular improvements, or there are major seasonal business cycles or other product launches to consider, you may have to hit a date, or a regular series of dates, that have been decided in advance.

---

3   Bob Hughes (ed.) (2019) *Project Management for IT-Related Projects.* Third edition. Swindon: BCS Publishing.

4   Elizabeth Harrin (2018) *Project Manager.* Swindon: BCS Publishing.

Even if there are no such constraints on when you release, having a regular pattern of releases can help customers and internal teams, such as marketing and sales, to understand when changes will be made and to plan for them. Since the release date will not move, the content of each release should be flexible, with the potential that some features simply won't be fully ready for release and may have to be delayed to a future release. Your roadmap will show in which order you will tackle each objective, while your release plan will show when the features that you need to meet them will be shipped. As a result, a release plan usually shows a shorter timeframe than a roadmap and has more detail.

Most of them look something like Figure 4.3.

Figure 4.3 Release schedule

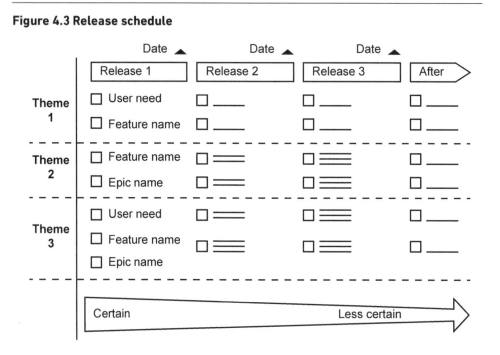

It's a good idea to highlight that while you might be certain about the next release, there is a degree of flexibility in future releases. It's common to display this with a colour scale or simply an arrow denoting the degree of certainty.

Naming releases is a challenge in itself. It's quite common for releases to be named simply after the month or quarter they are planned to happen in, for example Q1 YYYY or YY.MM. This is extremely clear and easy, until the unexpected inevitably happens and a release is delayed. Then you can end up explaining to people that the July release is actually now in September, while they scratch their heads in puzzlement and you wonder what you will do when September arrives. A common way of dealing with this is to pick a category and give each release a name. This is why Google released

Android Gingerbread, followed by Android Honeycomb and then Android Ice Cream Sandwich. This has the benefit of being easy to understand, but as I once found when explaining to some concerned stakeholders that their most desired feature had missed Fox and was now in Badger, it has the potential to sound ridiculous, so choose wisely. A sensible option is to name the releases after the goals or objectives they try to achieve, which helps everyone to focus on the outcome. For example, if the main purpose of your release is to help users to customise notifications from your app, you might call it 'Manage notifications'.

Backlogs and roadmaps

If commitments are loose on both timeframes and features, then releases to production should be frequent but, unlike with a release schedule, new features will be released when completed rather than in a predefined order. The product team will regularly gather feedback from customers and the feedback process will be critical in guiding the product development process and deciding what to focus on next.

In this case, your roadmap is effectively a highly summarised product backlog. Detail will need to be kept at the level of epics (a set of user stories or a sizable chunk of work), or be presented as the outcomes that should be achieved once the work is completed. This serves as a starting point for ongoing conversations with key stakeholders regarding development priorities, and will be subject to change as needed. It allows for maximum flexibility and learning at the expense of being able to communicate a long-term plan. However, in rapidly evolving markets, a long-term plan may be a liability.

One important note: don't be tempted to combine the roadmap with your backlog, which will be discussed in Chapter 7. While the product backlog and the roadmap are related, they serve different purposes and audiences. The backlog usually contains many features that may not be reflected on the roadmap (or ever be completed!) and captures information at a lower level of detail.

PRESENTING YOUR ROADMAP

Once you have identified the content for your roadmap and prioritised it, it's time to present it. You can find wildly divergent practices around presenting roadmap content, with some product teams keeping their roadmap a closely guarded secret and others publishing it for the world to see. Neither of those approaches is inherently wrong. What works for your product will depend on your team, your industry and your organisation. Here are some common ways of getting started.

First, next, later

If you want to present the order in which customer or business problems will be worked on, but the timelines themselves are not yet clear, it's common to show something like Figure 4.4.

Figure 4.4 First, next, later

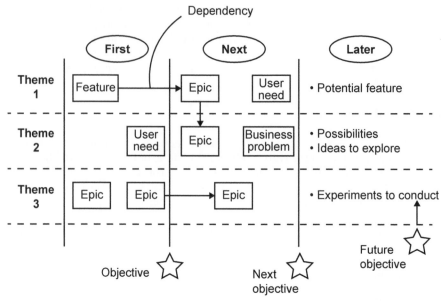

As you move from first to next to later, there is less detail and less certainty. For some teams, 'later' is in essence a high-level backlog of items that may be prioritised at that point in time, but that equally may never be looked at.

An even simpler way to show this is just as a list. It can even be a spreadsheet. This can be especially useful if you have taken a stack-ranking approach to prioritisation, as it can contain the reasons why the items are in that order, in the form of your scoring criteria.

There are a number of more sophisticated (but not necessarily better) ways of displaying your roadmap. Workflow tools such as Trello® and JIRA™ allow you to display your epics in a high-level view that can be presented from within the tool. Some even allow you to toggle between a 'backlog' view as a list and (once you have estimations) a timeline-based view.

However, you should consider carefully if this is the right approach for your audience. It can be tempting to zoom into the details, which may risk losing people's interest. On the upside, it can be a good insight into the way your team works, particularly if you are able to relate the more granular chunks of work such as stories and tasks to the higher-level epics, objectives and goals. Your stakeholders will then start to understand the work that goes into delivering each epic, which can in turn help to manage their expectations on what can be achieved and when.

There are also an increasing number of specialist roadmapping tools that are designed for roadmap creation and come with built-in templates for creating your roadmap. The good thing about this is that any changes you make are made in real time, which reduces the possibility that people can be looking at old versions of your roadmap. Some of them even allow different views of the same data for different audiences. However, it is always worth experimenting with what you already have first before deciding that something else is needed – if a one-page PowerPoint roadmap is working for you and your team, the cost of additional software is probably not money well spent!

MANAGING EXPECTATIONS

As discussed in the introduction, roadmaps need to change over time. They will evolve, based on changing priorities, competitor actions and the data you gather on user behaviour. For many organisations, though, this comes as a bit of a surprise. Particularly where financial or programme plans may have once been detailed years in advance, the concept of constant ongoing change can be hard to digest. It's a good idea to be very frank about this fact upfront and remind people of it every time you present the roadmap.

In particular, if priorities have changed, be sure to explain why things have moved and what has driven the decision. If you start by reminding people of what the roadmap was like, then take them through the new data you have and what this means, you will have a much better chance of bringing people on the journey with you. When you present the updated version, they will share the conclusions with you and be less likely to question your thinking. Over time, they may even start to anticipate or even recommend such changes themselves.

Scheduling in regular times to review the roadmap can help to create some rhythm around this, or you might decide to publish a new version of the roadmap at regular intervals, either internally or externally, with commentary on what has changed. Regular sessions such as show and tells or product demonstrations can also be used to present the current view of the roadmap. Look out for any regular company updates or all team sessions your organisation has that can become opportunities to display the roadmap. With a captive audience, you can cover what your team has delivered in the last month or quarter, and link what's up next to the organisation's overall strategy and vision.

ROADMAP TIMESCALES

As the roadmap will show what your team is going to deliver over time, you'll need to decide how long a time period you want to visualise. Too long, and it will be hard to present. The items on the far side will likely be meaningless anyway, as they are likely to be superseded in importance before you need to deliver them. But a roadmap with too short a timescale won't be of any use as a guide to your next priorities, as it will just show what's currently being worked on, or will be picked up next. In general, three months is a sensible minimum and 18 months a sensible maximum. Most teams fall somewhere in the middle. It's also common to show the later time periods in much less detail, so even if your roadmap shows a full year, most of the visualisation may be of the next three to six months. If you are struggling to reconcile the need for firm dates and detail in the next few months with showing your longer-term strategy, consider having a release plan as well as your roadmap.

Roadmaps can be physical or digital

Most of the time, having an online, easily shareable roadmap is an advantage in communicating it. Some teams even publish these online, on company websites or on open versions of tools such as Trello, for maximum transparency and visibility. An online product roadmap is easy to present and send people links to. You can also refer to it wherever you are, which is essential when working remotely, travelling or with geographically distant teams. However, some teams also still use physical versions of the roadmap. This might be:

- a wall in the office, where cards are used to represent epics or outcomes;
- a whiteboard or writable wall;
- a large scale printout of the current iteration of the roadmap.

This might seem a bit old hat, but there are some benefits. Particularly for organisational roadmaps, it helps to make the roadmap extremely visible, so it's impossible to miss. This helps to catch any misconceptions early, because everyone has to walk past a single version of the truth! Some teams also use a physical wall somewhere prominent in their office space as a meeting place for conversations between teams. It can become a focal point for discussions around prioritisation or dependencies, where you can physically move and compare different items as you discuss them.

INTEGRATING ROADMAPS ACROSS TEAMS

In larger organisations, it's likely that you will not be the only person with a roadmap. There may well be other product managers with roadmaps, objectives and strategic goals all of their own to worry about. Their roadmap may not look anything like yours, which is absolutely fine – until someone in a senior position starts to wonder how all of these roadmaps fit together. Then you and the other product managers may need to consider creating a 'roadmap of roadmaps', sometimes known as an 'organisational roadmap'. In a Scaled Agile Framework®, this is known as the portfolio roadmap. It brings together the solution and product increment roadmaps to communicate how the portfolio vision will be achieved over time, usually one to three years.[5]

Quite often, you will not be entirely in control of creating this artefact. It may be a strategy team, somebody in a more senior product lead role, or possibly even your chief executive officer (CEO). It may also be a group effort by multiple product managers. However, you should have the opportunity to make sure the key improvements you have planned on your own roadmap are reflected. The chance to have a discussion with other

---

5   Scaled Agile Framework (2010–2022) 'Roadmap'. Available from www.scaledagileframework.com/roadmap

product managers can also help to highlight any misconceptions about what is being delivered when, or the direction of dependencies.

Probably the simplest way of doing this is to take each roadmap and zoom out to the very highest level. Each product manager would contribute the highest-level items or objectives to the organisational roadmap. Instead of displaying each theme, you would display each product and highlight the key improvements you are making at each point. At this level, you can also point out any connections between items, or the strategic objectives that rely on elements delivered by different teams.

As noted previously, keeping multiple roadmaps up to date can be hard work. This is true to an even greater degree with organisational roadmaps, because you are unlikely to be able to update them yourself. You will need to keep a beady eye on the organisational roadmap and make sure that changes you make to your own roadmap are reflected and vice versa. Not doing this regularly can mean your team becomes blocked, due to relying on items other teams have decided to de-prioritise, or your stakeholders become confused about what is being delivered next, because your product roadmap is out of alignment with the overall roadmap. A good place to have these discussions with other product managers and catch any miscommunications early is as part of a community of practice, as discussed in Chapter 8.

YOUR ROADMAP WILL NEVER BE PERFECT

Creating a roadmap can be a time-consuming and emotionally draining process. Not only do you have to develop the content, agree on prioritisation and find a way to present it, it needs to be constantly tweaked and updated to reflect the decisions that you will be making about your product. Particularly in the first few iterations, you will be nervous about how it will be received. The best thing is to release it into the wild, accepting that it will never be 'finished' and will always be slightly out of date. It certainly won't be perfect, but it also won't get any better as a communication tool if it isn't shared. Communicating something also helps to identify any misunderstandings that might have been spreading while you were developing your roadmap.

Over time, you will learn more about the level of detail that works best for your audience. You'll find what themes resonate best with them and learn whether it will be useful to have a physical version of the roadmap or not. If you're unsure about what will work, the best approach is to start as simply as you can, with a spreadsheet or even a whiteboard drawing, show it to people and iterate onwards from there.

CASE STUDY: EXAMPLE ROADMAPS

Taking the example of our fictional startup, Unparkr, a theme-based roadmap could look something like Figure 4.5.

Figure 4.5 A theme-based roadmap

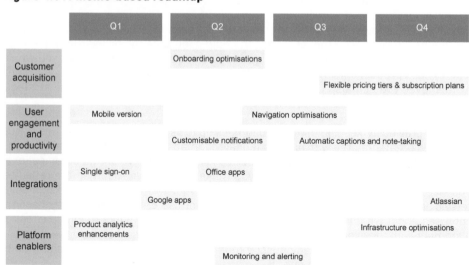

If we imagine this was shown to a sales team, a product support team and the product team, each group can see how the themes cut across business areas:

- Sales will understand when key user productivity tools and integrations will be available, allowing them to develop materials to promote premium subscriptions.

- Support will see reduced time to help new clients, enabling them to focus on helping existing users with their new devices and integrated apps.

- Infrastructure and platform enhancements will make things easier technically, but they will also enable scalability, allowing sales to add more customers over time.

The same roadmap items could also be presented to focus on outcomes. For example, rather than saying that the team are going to create new pricing tiers for clients to select from, you might show the aim of moving more of them on to a premium plan (see Figure 4.6).

KEY TAKEAWAYS

- Roadmaps are in essence communication tools, so take time to understand what will work best for your audience.

- If your roadmap isn't resonating with your audience, consider whether it contains too much or too little detail.

- Roadmaps are always a work in progress and should never be finished – don't let the fact that yours will always be slightly out of date stop it from being shared.

Figure 4.6 An outcome focused roadmap

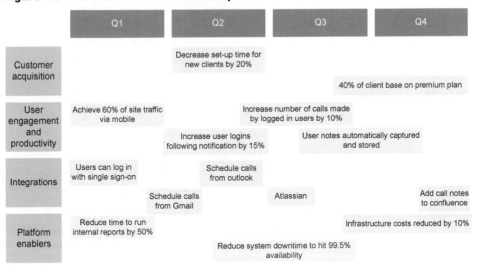

5 DISCOVERING AND DESIGNING A VALUABLE CUSTOMER EXPERIENCE

Filip Hendrickx

A good customer experience can make or break a product. Especially with digital products, competition is often just around the corner, so getting the customer experience right is crucial.

But what is a good customer experience? How can you design it and identify the most important features, and the ones to leave out? And how do you ensure that your product is ethical by design?

WHAT IS CUSTOMER EXPERIENCE?

When talking about customer experience, especially in a digitally enriched or enhanced world, it's useful to distinguish three levels of experience:

- **usability** refers to how a system, product or service handles the human–machine interaction and how safely, effectively and efficiently that system or product can be used through its user interface;

- **user experience** refers to how the user experiences their interaction with a system, product or service, including the user's perceptions of that interaction, their emotions, physical and psychological responses, and so on, that occur before, during and after the interaction;

- **customer experience** refers to the overall experience a customer has while interacting with one or more businesses or organisations and their systems, products and services. Customer experience spans multiple user experiences across multiple systems, products and services over a longer period of time.

For example, running apps and devices to track your runs are widely used these days. You may be using one yourself every now and then. A good **user interface (UI)** design considers the placement and size of the on-screen buttons and perhaps a smart use of your device's physical buttons so that the app is comfortable and reliable to use while exercising. Usability then is a quality attribute of the UI, covering whether the system is easy to learn, efficient and pleasant to use, and so forth.

UI design also includes the look and feel of the product. A run tracking app may use colours expressing energy, while a yoga app will have a more relaxing colour palette.

User experience is a broader concept. While your tracking app may provide a vast number of routes in an easy to search and navigate way, if information about road types is missing, you may find the user experience poor.

Usability and user experience both focus on the digital or physical product. **Customer experience** looks more broadly at how that product fits into the overall customer context. Suppose you have built the world's best run tracking smartphone app, but the customer has no place to put his smartphone while running; the customer experience will not be great. In fact, failing to understand the context in which the customer is using your product may very well lead to an unsuccessful product, no matter how good the user experience of that product in and of itself is (see Figure 5.1).

Figure 5.1 The relation between usability, user experience and customer experience

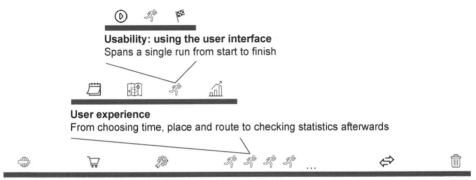

Usability: using the user interface
Spans a single run from start to finish

User experience
From choosing time, place and route to checking statistics afterwards

Customer experience
Spans pre-purchase → purchase → setup → consumption → post-consumption
Spans multiple uses

Why is this distinction between UI, user experience and customer experience important? Because considering the entire customer experience enables us to discover and focus on those parts that have the biggest impact on what's most valuable for the customer. These may or may not be the original problem and solution you've had in mind.

To understand why the customer may be interested in using your product, you need to understand what they are trying to achieve. Is your target customer starting out and trying to get fit? Are they running to relax and clear their mind? Are they training for their first marathon? These goals are very different and require very different product features.

To create a good customer experience, you need to consider all stages of the consumption process:

- **Pre-purchase.** How do you attract potential customers?

- **Purchase.** How do you trigger them to check out or try out your product? What's the sales and delivery process like?

- **Setup.** How do you help them to get started and make the best use of the product. Provide guidance and tips, in-app and through newsletters?

- **Consumption or use.** The actual, usually repeated use of your product.
- **Post-consumption.** What happens when a customer stops using your product (like recycling for physical products or enabling migration of personal data to another app or service for digital products)?

During consumption, the customer is usually doing much more than simply using your product. They may schedule exercise time upfront, check their agenda and perhaps chat with a friend to find a suitable date and time for their activities; they may look up interesting routes; they may check the weather forecast upfront online and by going outside shortly before hitting the road. Similarly, the customer experience of exercising typically extends beyond the actual exercise activity.

Throughout their journeys, customers will often come into contact with multiple touchpoints of an organisation. These can be digital touchpoints such as the smartphone app, the website, newsletters and other emails, and so on. They can also be service touchpoints where the customer is receiving some non-digital service, like a coffee or a haircut that previously has been ordered or planned digitally. So, most digital solutions only touch the customers in parts of their journey. Moving to digital always requires a good look at the non-digital parts of that journey, as is the case with the run tracking app. At each touchpoint, digital or physical, the customer experience can improve or worsen.

Another good example is when Mexican food chain Chipotle realised their fledgling mobile app would improve the entire customer experience only when mobile customers would be able to skip the line. So they reconfigured their restaurants to enable this by setting up grab-and-go shelving next to the cash registers. Furthermore, non-mobile customers waiting in line did not like it when employees stopped serving them to put together an online order. So Chipotle created separately managed, second kitchens at the back of their restaurants.[1]

Customer journey mapping is a great way to get better insight into the overall context in which customers use a product or service and to check if your product pushes the right buttons at different steps along the journey. It helps you to understand the overall context in which a customer problem occurs, and triggers you to think about the role you can play to help solve that problem throughout the entire journey.

You can ask yourself several questions to get a better grip on the customer's problems and the context in which they arise throughout their journey:

- Who experiences the problem?
- When does the problem occur?
- Where does the problem occur?
- What is the customer doing when the problem occurs?

---

1   Brian Niccol (2021) 'The CEO of Chipotle on charting a culinary and digital turnaround', *Harvard Business Review*. Available from https://hbr.org/2021/11/the-ceo-of-chipotle-on-charting-a-culinary-and-digital-turnaround

- Who is with the customer when the problem occurs?
- What other problems occur in this context?
- Is the customer having fun, or do they simply want to get their task done?
- What thoughts, feelings, actions and words is the customer having or expressing?

The last bullet can be analysed more thoroughly with the previously discussed empathy map (pp. 25–29).

It is important to stress that while you can to a large extent control the usability and the user experience through a well-thought-out product design and user tests, you usually have much less control over the customer journey. The customer decides whether or not they interact with the different touchpoints you offer, or with alternatives that are just one click away. You may be able to influence the journey, but you do not own it. So it's important to understand the channel preferences customers have when designing your channels and when deciding which use cases you'll support at each of them and how (for example human or automated or a combination thereof). Even with conscious touchpoint and channel design, it's important to realise that, ultimately, the customer owns their journey: it's the customer's journey.

Because of this, it's useful to take two viewpoints when mapping a customer journey:

- one focusing on how the customer approaches things independent from your or your competitors' specific solutions;
- one showcasing your specific implementation approach.

WHAT IS DESIGN AND WHY DO WE NEED IT?

> Most people make the mistake of thinking design is what it looks like. People think it's this veneer – that the designers are handed this box and told, 'Make it look good!' That's not what we think design is. It's not just what it looks like and feels like. Design is how it works.
>
> Steve Jobs[2]

Have a look around you. Every object you see, touch or hear has a specific design. It works in a specific way, whether that's intended by the creators or not. A good example is the 'auto-pause' functionality of run tracking apps, which automatically pauses the tracking timer when the user is standing still for a number of seconds and resumes when they start moving again.

The same is true for interactions, for example with a service desk. The standard interactions behind a traditional phone menu, the predefined questions of a chatbot or the scripted conversation of a service desk employee are all examples of designed interactions.

---

2   Steve Jobs quoted by Rob Walker (2003) 'The guts of a new machine'. *The New York Times.* Available from
    https://www.nytimes.com/2003/11/30/magazine/the-guts-of-a-new-machine.html

However, even if how something works is not consciously designed, you do end up with a design. The product will still work in a specific way, though it may not be the way your customer likes or the way you expect the customer to apply and interact with your product. This is true for the first version of a product, so teams usually take some time to consciously reflect on how they want their product to work. However, digital products typically evolve continually in small steps. User feedback triggers the team to add or change features every sprint or release. If no one takes the time to consciously watch the overall design throughout this organic process, the result may be as bad as Frankenstein's monster. So you'll want to consciously and continually design at least part of your product and the services around it.

Of course, analysing every design detail would be too time-consuming and costly, so a product manager will need to ensure the product team focuses on the key design elements.

- Which parts of the customer journey will you participate in, which will you not?
  - Where are the moments that matter? Where are the moments where problems manifest for customers in their journey, which you can choose to solve?
  - Where are the potential moments of magic? Where are the moments where you can delight your customers and differentiate your offering?
  - Across these moments, where can you make a difference for your customer with your product and the services around it?
- When do you want the customer to be aware that you are or could be doing something for them? In which parts of the customer experience do you want to be visibly present?

At a more detailed, solution level, you'll start thinking about the user interaction and user experience:

- When do you want or need the customer to interact with your product and provide their input? Do you need the customer to actively provide their input, like their age, height and weight, or can you/should you get the input in some other way, for example from the customer's social media profile? Should the customer be aware of what data you are using?
- When do you want to be present without active customer input, like the run tracking auto-pause feature, or like running a progress report behind the scenes and feeding it into the customer's training schedule?

It's important to note that a lot of work in the world of digital services is invisible to the customer unless we explicitly make it visible. For example, if a customer uses a search engine to find a definition of 'interval training' and your website is designed so well that the definition on your website is shown directly in the search results, the customer may not need to click that search result. That's great from a customer experience perspective, as the customer (efficiently) has found the answer they were looking for, but you may have missed the opportunity to connect with that customer, or to make them aware that it was you providing the answer.

A service blueprint is a good place to start and consciously select the steps and touchpoints where you want to make a good impression, and thus where you need to think about the product design. It allows you to see how different touchpoints and frontstage and backstage activities interact to create a good user experience. Such a service blueprint can be created for different key moments or usage scenarios in the customer journey where there is an unsatisfied customer need (see Figure 5.2).

Design process

In the previous section, we've covered the customer experience, which can be analysed using tools like customer journey maps and empathy maps. We've also briefly touched upon the solution design when discussing the user experience, usability of a user interface and service blueprints. All of the above is part of a design process.

One of the most widely used frameworks of a design process is the Design Council's Double Diamond, originally published in 2004 and updated in 2019.[3]

At its core, it deconstructs the design process into four seemingly consecutive steps:

- **Discover.** The first diamond helps people to understand, rather than to simply assume, what the problem is. It involves speaking to and spending time with people who are affected by the issues. In this first step, you diverge from your initial idea and consider other related problems and opportunities so that you can pick the ones with most potential.

- **Define.** In this step, you converge towards the problem you'll focus on. The insights gathered from the discovery phase can also help you to define the challenge in a different way, for example using the customer's language.

- **Develop.** The second diamond starts again with a diverge step, encouraging people to come up with a wide range of answers to the clearly defined problem, seeking inspiration from elsewhere and co-designing with a range of different people.

- **Deliver.** Delivery involves testing out different solutions at a small scale, rejecting those that will not work and improving the ones that will, converging into the solution you'll deliver to your customer.

The Discover and Define steps help to design the right thing, whereas the Develop and Deliver steps help to design the thing right. During Discover and Define, you increase your understanding of the customer and their problems and you decide which problems to tackle. This is where customer journey mapping and empathy mapping come into play. During Develop and Deliver, you experiment with multiple solution options and deliver the ones that work, guided by your service blueprint.

In reality, it's not a linear but rather an iterative process, as learnings from a later step can send you back to an earlier step. One of the strengths of a process like this is that you can consciously check if you are taking the time to perform each of the steps, and are not just rushing toward the end (see Figure 5.3).

---

3   Design Council (2019) 'Framework for Innovation: Design Council's evolved Double Diamond'. Design Council. Available from https://www.designcouncil.org.uk/our-work/skills-learning/tools-frameworks/framework-for-innovation-design-councils-evolved-double-diamond/

Figure 5.2 Example service blueprint for one of the run tracking app usage scenarios

Run tracking app
Service blueprint for a single run

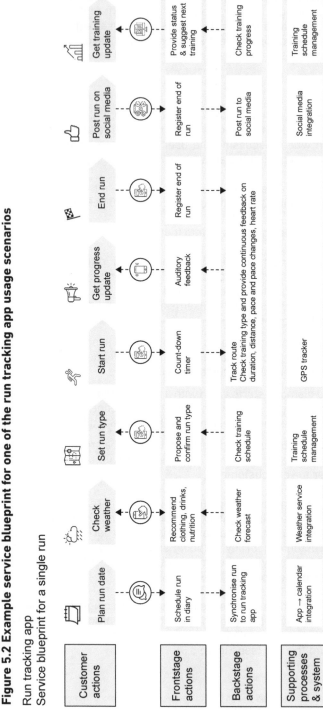

Figure 5.3 The Double Diamond design process[4]

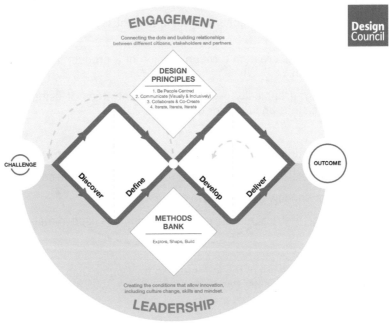

© Design Council 2019

A key reason why this Double Diamond design process works well is that it emphasises first taking a step back from your original idea, whether it's a problem or opportunity, or a specific solution you are already thinking about. By looking at the bigger picture, you can come up with other problems or opportunities that are more worthwhile for your customers and for you.

There's a wealth of techniques and approaches available that you can apply at each step. For example:

- **Discover:**
  - Interviewing: asking questions to get a better understanding of what customers think and (say they) do.
  - Observing or shadowing: closely following and watching what a customer does.
- **Define:**
  - Root cause analysis: finding the true or fundamental reason a problem occurs, for example using the 5 Whys or Ishikawa/Fishbone technique.
  - Affinity diagrams or card sorting: techniques to organise ideas, problems and so on into groups.
  - 'How might we ...' questions: phrasing a problem as a question to trigger solution ideas.

---

4   Design Council Double Diamond, created in 2004. Available from www.designcouncil.org.uk

- **Develop:**
  - SCAMPER: a brainstorming technique to come up with many potential solutions.
  - Wireframing: creating a schematic or blueprint laying out the skeleton of a solution.
  - Rapid prototyping: creating a rough version of a product that users can hold and interact with.
  - Storyboarding: graphically organising different steps of using a solution to explain those steps and uncover gaps.
- **Deliver:**
  - Surveys: collecting data from a group of respondents in a structured way.
  - Think aloud: participants say whatever comes to mind while completing a task.
  - Observing or shadowing: see above.
  - Product usage metrics: measuring how a product is used in reality.

> You'll notice that in three out of the four steps in the Double Diamond, learning is a key aspect. Chapter 6 goes into detail about why and how to do this.

Whatever tools and techniques you use to design the user experience, you must be aware that you cannot fully control how the customer uses your product. This is an important point: going through a conscious design process tends to create the feeling of being in control. You're not.

For example, when energy-saving light bulbs came onto the market, carefully designed to reduce power consumption in already lit places, people actually started lighting more places for longer periods, since the cost of doing so was low. Customers took a product and started using it in such a way that it defeated the purpose it was designed for. This example demonstrates the importance of asking yourself how your solution could be used in unexpected ways, and of learning from real-life usage of prototypes and products.

PROBLEM AND FEATURE IDENTIFICATION

To identify relevant customer problems and potential solution features, the first step is to select which customer journeys you want to appear in, which customer segments you are targeting and what is driving their behaviour.

Below is an example for our run tracking app (Table 5.1).

It's clear that the key solution features will be quite different depending on the target segment. A single solution **could** in theory work for each of these segments, but will it work well enough? It's tough to develop and maintain a product that solves many problems for many people with somewhat different expectations or reasons for using your product, even when those problems are related and a single solution seems to be reusable. You risk

Table 5.1 The behaviour drivers for different customer segments for the run tracking app and their key customer journeys

Customer segment	Behaviour driver	Key customer journeys
Occasional runner	Wants to relax	• Single run
Getting (back) in shape runner	Wants to get (back) in shape	• Single run • From 0 to 5 kilometers
Pushing the boundaries runner	Wants to run a first marathon	• Single run • Milestone to milestone
Community runner	Wants to meet (new) people through a shared activity	• From finding someone like-minded to friendship

developing a product that is just okay for most but good or great for no one and therefore fails to make a lasting impression or to have a real impact. On top of this, supporting multiple segments and journeys at once takes time and will probably slow down your learning process and thus increase your time to market. So, focus is key, and the first step is to identify the customer segment, their behaviour driver and their key customer journeys.

Once you have identified and selected one or more customer journeys, you can map the customer's key moments (positive and negative) and use a tool like the Value Proposition Canvas[5] to identify pains and gains, and corresponding pain relievers and gain creators. The Value Proposition Canvas also distinguishes between different types of customer jobs-to-be-done (see Chapter 2):

- **Functional jobs:**
  - When your customers try to perform or complete a specific task or solve a specific problem.
  - Example: find a new route.
- **Social jobs:**
  - When your customers want to look good or gain power or status.
  - Example: post a training achievement on social media.
- **Personal/emotional jobs:**
  - When your customers seek a specific emotional state, such as feeling good or secure.
  - Example: get positive feedback on training progress.

Going through these different job types is a good way to come up with potentially interesting customer problems and product features and check if they link to your customer's behaviour driver.

---

5   Alex Osterwalder, Yves Pigneur, Greg Bernarda, Alan Smith and Trish Papadakos (2013) 'The Value Proposition Canvas'. Strategyzer, Wiley. Available from https://www.strategyzer.com/canvas/value-proposition-canvas

Two other frameworks that you can use are Bain's Elements of Value Pyramids. There's a B2C[6] and a B2B[7] version. This framework also puts a strong emphasis on the perceived value of product features, tying into what the customer is trying to achieve and how this will make them feel. If you succeed in helping the customer achieve their objectives and make them feel good, you have a good chance of making a lasting impression.

These approaches have a clear link with customer value. They make you think about what value the customer could get when using your product to solve their problem. The bigger the value the customer experiences, the more they'll be willing to invest in that product, be it their money, time, personal data and so on. This is the driver of your business model: the customer gets value from using your product and gives you something in return that is valuable to you.

A final, more practical technique to identify potential customer problems and product features, and their importance, is asking the customer how they solve certain problems today.

- Maybe the customer has already found a good solution and is actively using it. Then you probably don't need to focus on it right now, though you may consider integrating it into your product at a later stage. For example, the 'community runner' may have joined a local Facebook group of like-minded people sharing their running experiences, or the 'pushing the boundaries runner' may be actively managing their diet in some way.

- Perhaps the customer hasn't found a good solution but has discovered some workaround that they actively use. For example, the 'pushing the boundaries runner' may be keeping a physical diary to monitor their progress. This is a strong indicator of an unsolved need.

- Perhaps the customer is not dealing with a certain problem right now. This could be a strong indicator that the problem is not that important and perhaps does not deserve your product development focus, time and money.

A common myth about developing or improving products is that features and solutions have to be very innovative to be successful. Often, the opposite is true. It's often difficult to time the market well when launching a very innovative product or groundbreaking new features. It's very likely that possible customers aren't ready yet for such a novelty, as it's a big change. Small improvements requiring only little change from the customer often have a bigger chance of adoption.

Also, there's a lot of low hanging fruit: many products are good enough, yet can be improved when looking at existing solutions through a mindset of quality and with a bit of creativity. For example, have you ever had the problem of a bunch of bananas becoming too ripe? Here's how they solve this problem in Korea (Figure 5.4).

---

6   Eric Almquist, John Senior and Nicolas Bloch (2016) 'The elements of value'. *Harvard Business Review*. Available from https://hbr.org/2016/09/the-elements-of-value

7   Eric Almquist, Jamie Cleghorn and Lori Sherer (2018) 'The B2B elements of value'. *Harvard Business Review*. Available from https://hbr.org/2018/03/the-b2b-elements-of-value

Figure 5.4 A solution for the problem of having a bunch of bananas becoming ripe at the same time[8] (Note: product image shows ripe bananas on the left hand side of the image, semi-ripe in the middle, and unripe on the right hand side)

Is this innovative? Is it a big or only a small improvement? It doesn't matter. As long as it's valuable for a large enough group of people by solving a problem that is relevant and important to them, it's a useful product (improvement) to develop and release.

Sometimes less is more

> Perfection is achieved, not when there is nothing more to add, but when there is nothing left to take away.
>
> Antoine de Saint-Exupéry, Airman's Odyssey[9]

For a long time, stabilising wheels were added to small children's bikes so they could safely learn how to ride a bike. It took decades for someone to think of removing the pedals, rather than adding stabilisers. Nonetheless, a pedal-less balance bike is simpler and cheaper to build and enables children to develop the coordination and balancing skills needed to ride a normal bike more quickly. The breakthrough solution is **removing** a feature rather than **adding** one.

---

8 Sabrina Barr (2018) 'Korean store unveils 'genius' banana packaging to avoid overripe fruit'. *Independent*. Image by ssg.com. Available from https://www.independent.co.uk/life-style/food-and-drink/banana-packaging-ripe-hack-korea-supermarket-e-mart-ssg-plastic-waste-a8485066.html

9 Antoine de Saint Exupéry (1939) *Terre des hommes*, Ch. 3: L'Avion, p. 60.

Consider, for example, how you would fix the bridge in Figure 5.5, which is not horizontal. The first solution most people think about is adding a block on the bridge's right side. However, removing one on the left would equally work and spare you a building block!

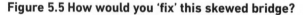

Figure 5.5 How would you 'fix' this skewed bridge?

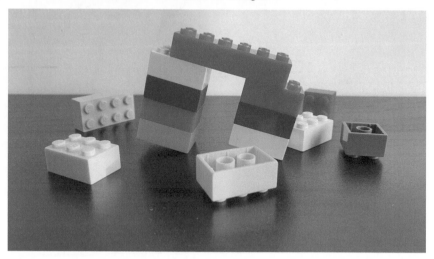

It appears that our brain is biased towards solving problems by adding features, as discovered in research by engineer Leidy Klotz and social psychologist Gabrielle Adams of the University of Virginia.[10] People tend to think of additive changes quickly and easily. Generating ideas for subtractive changes requires more cognitive investment. Our busy schedules and multitasking habits make coming up with subtractive solutions even harder. However, by accepting the first ideas that come to mind, people often miss out on opportunities to improve the world by subtraction.

So, when brainstorming solutions for a certain problem, explicitly remind yourself and your team of the option of removing features and the potential design improvements and cost savings, both in creation and maintenance, this may bring about. Take some time specifically to come up with subtractive changes and see how far they get you.

THERE'S MORE TO A PRODUCT THAN ITS TANGIBLE FEATURES

A product's features, their completeness of implementation and their ease of use are obviously key elements for how a product is perceived and will determine the product's success. A product's price and revenue model are just as much part of a product's

---

10 Erin Tor (2021) 'Why our brains miss opportunities to improve through subtraction.' UVA's Frank Batten School of Leadership and Public Policy. Available from https://batten.virginia.edu/about/news/why-our-brains-miss-opportunities-improve-through-subtraction

design. A product's price point will set expectations in the customer's mind, as it will trigger comparisons with any reference or price anchor they think of (or you trigger them to think of). It may create (a perception of) commodity versus exclusivity. Think for example of expensive Champagne versus cheap Cava. So setting the price is definitely one of the product manager's jobs.

Determining a product's price requires you to think about and research a number of things, like:

- What is your customer segment willing to pay?

- How does the price affect the product's perception and the customer's expectations of the product?

- Should you opt for a cheaper product with lower margin and higher reach or a more expensive product with higher margin and lower reach?

On top of that, the product and/or service's revenue model also has a big influence on your potential target market, your revenue stream and the balance you'll have to strike between acquiring new customers versus retaining existing ones.

Price setting

One method for researching price is Van Westendorp's Price Sensitivity Meter.[11] It uses a four-question survey:

- At what price would you consider the product to be so expensive that you would not consider buying it? (Too expensive.)

- At what price would you consider the product to be priced so low that you would feel the quality couldn't be very good? (Too cheap.)

- At what price would you consider the product is starting to get expensive, so that it is not out of the question, but you would have to give some thought to buying it? (Expensive/High side.)

- At what price would you consider the product to be a bargain – a great buy for the money? (Cheap/Good value.)

With enough respondents, the Van Westendorp pricing model reveals an acceptable range of prices, based on the customer value perception of your product. A detailed explanation of how to apply Van Westendorp's Price Sensitivity Meter can be found at surveyking.com.[12]

---

11 Peter van Westendorp (1976) 'NSS-Price Sensitivity Meter (PSM)- A new approach to study consumer perception of price'. *Proceedings of the ESOMAR Congress.*

12 Peter van Westendorp (1976) 'Van Westendorp explained'. SurveyKing. Available from https://www.surveyking.com/help/van-westendorp-analysis

Another price setting technique is the Gabor–Granger method.[13] Where Van Westendorp's pricing model is useful for new products, Gabor–Granger is another survey-based technique for finding the optimal price point for established products when researching a price increase, possibly after a product improvement. Through asking respondents to evaluate specific price points, Gabor–Granger lets you find out the price point that gives you maximum revenue and the price point at which product demand will drop significantly. A more detailed explanation can again be found at surveyking.com.

Revenue model

Thinking about revenue models (see Chapter 3) brings up a number of questions:

- Will you sell your product or service, or combination thereof, for a one-time fee, through a subscription model or through a combination of both?
- Will you have different price levels or price tiers, depending on the functionality they offer?
- Will you have a freemium model to acquire new users that could turn into paying customers and/or provide you with a large user group that gives you network effects (whereby a larger number of users increases the value of a product or service, like telecom services)?
- Do users pay for your product or service, is a third party paying for it, or are you using a revenue source like advertising?

It's clear that whether you offer a product and/or a service, with or without a physical and/or in-person part connected to the digital part, and whether your product or service is offering one-time or recurrent value will influence its features and how you 'package' the product and/or service.

For example, the run tracking app could offer:

- a free basic version for the Occasional runner;
- a more extensive one-time fee paid version for the Getting (back) in shape runner;
- value-adding subscription services like a personalised training and coaching programme for the Pushing the boundaries runner;
- ad-supported community features for the Community runner.

There's a difficult balance to strike between:

- attracting a large enough user base to get going and capture real-world-use feedback;
- building a user base that repeatedly uses your product or service (if it's not a one-time thing);
- getting your revenue model right at an early stage to ensure you are building something that structurally brings in revenue.

---

[13] André Gabor and Cliver Granger (1960) 'Gabor Granger pricing model explanation, survey template'. SurveyKing. Available from https://www.surveyking.com/help/gabor-granger

Starting out for free seems tempting, but getting a large enough user base to becoming paying customers later on tends to be very challenging. Once people have tried a product for free, it's hard to change the perception to 'this product is worth something'. That change adds even more complexity to the work of marketing and continuing development and providing support for your initial user base.

These are interesting and challenging questions that don't have a one-size-fits-all answer, so be aware that as a product manager you should consider price and revenue model as product features just like regular functionalities.

PROBLEM AND FEATURE PRIORITISATION

The research and brainstorming discussed in the previous section, if done properly, will generate lots of ideas: lots of potential pains to solve and gains to provide, lots of potential solutions in the form of pain relievers and gain creators, and multiple ideas about revenue models. Where should you start? After both divergent steps in the Double Diamond design process, there's a convergent step to consciously select the problems and solutions with the highest potential. Which prioritisation techniques can help with these convergent steps?

Some traditional techniques like using priority numbers or MoSCoW have potential downsides:

- They tend to amplify the mindset that a product needs to have all features of a certain priority in order to become successful. At the start of a design and development process, this usually is an educated guess at best.

- They don't provide information on why certain features are important and others aren't.

Here are a few techniques that help to prioritise problems and features while providing some more background information or a rationale for the respective priorities.

Ask 'Why?'

What is the customer trying to achieve when experiencing a problem or when using a solution? How well is this aligned with the behaviour drivers you identified earlier? What 'solved problem' or feature is going to move the needle most for the customer? You can check this using several of the previously mentioned analysis techniques.

Note that this may trigger you to revisit the behaviour drivers you want to focus on. It's an iterative process.

20/20 vision game

A powerful, insightful and fun way to learn why some problems or solution features are more important than others for customers or other stakeholders is to write each problem or feature on a card and have a group of stakeholders order them from most important to least important. They are not allowed to put two cards together. This simple technique, preferably done while standing with all cards on the ground or up against a wall, quickly triggers interesting conversations between stakeholders about why they think certain problems or features are more important than others and why they believe a proposed solution feature will work.

The resulting order is useful, but understanding the reasoning behind it is even more valuable input to drive product development priorities and decisions.

> Note that it's okay to rip a card in two, either because that problem or feature appears to be unimportant or because the problem or feature can be split up into separate problems or features with different priorities.

The Customer Experience Pyramid

Forrester distinguishes three levels of experience in its Customer Experience Pyramid (CX Pyramid).[14] From bottom to top:

- **Functional:** the product feature solves a specific problem for the customer. It does the job by meeting the customer's needs at least in the most basic way.

- **Usable:** the product was easy to use, and the customer did not have to think hard to use the product.

- **Enjoyable:** the overall experience of using the product was nice and perhaps even exceeded the customer's expectations. These are the features that make a new product stand out from the competition. These are the features that trigger customers to consider trying the product and perhaps switch from their current product to yours.

You can now position product features onto the CX Pyramid.[15] Take for example the run tracking app for the 'Getting (back) in shape runner' (Figure 5.6)

- **Enjoyable:** motivational 'go run' triggers and progress updates;
- **Usable:** count-down timer; auto-pause;
- **Functional:** track distances; provide a basic running schedule.

When developing a new product, it's tempting to start by listing all the essential 'meets needs' features and developing those first. A problem with this approach is that it takes a lot of time to develop a product that initially is probably not very different from existing products. Why would a customer choose your product over any other? Why would they go through the effort of changing products?

---

14 Harley Manning (2010) 'Customer experience defined'. Forrester. Available from https://www.forrester.com/blogs/definition-of-customer-experience/

15 Aarron Walter (2011) *Designing for Emotion: A Book Apart*. Available from https://abookapart.com/products/designing-for-emotion

Figure 5.6 The Customer Experience Pyramid and where to start product development

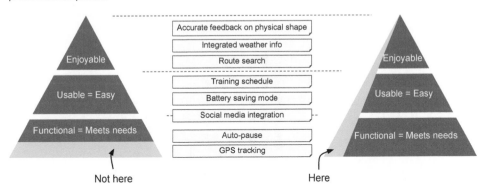

Before building a product to completeness, it's key to confirm that the features that will distinguish your product from competing ones are important to the customer. And not just somewhat important, but important enough to make them change their behaviour and start using your product. That's a tough mountain to make the customer climb!

Hence, a good point to start prioritising features is to select one or two of them that make the experience of using your product enjoyable and add features from the layers below that are essential to validate your selection. At this stage, you're not trying to build a **complete** product. You're trying to identify what is going to convince customers to **use your product**.

Kano analysis

The Kano model (pp. 31–33) can be extended[16] by classifying customer preferences into different categories and using a standardised questionnaire to measure participants' opinions implicitly (see Figure 5.7).

For a run tracking app, the Kano model in Figure 5.7 identifies three types of needs or problems:

- **Basic needs:** A run tracking app needs to have reliable GPS tracking. If it doesn't work or doesn't work very well, customers will be unhappy.

- **Performance needs:** how battery-friendly is the app? If the app completely drains the battery in 15 minutes, customers will be very dissatisfied. The less power the app consumes, the more satisfied customers will be.

- A **delighter** for the run tracking app could be matching music with running cadence.

---

16 Debapriya Chakraborty (2010) 'Kano model: tool for measuring consumer satisfaction'. Ayushveda.
Archived copy available from https://archive.ph/20120708011551/http://ayushveda.com/blogs/business/kano-model-tool-for-measuring-consumer-satisfaction/

Figure 5.7 The Kano model applied to the run tracking app

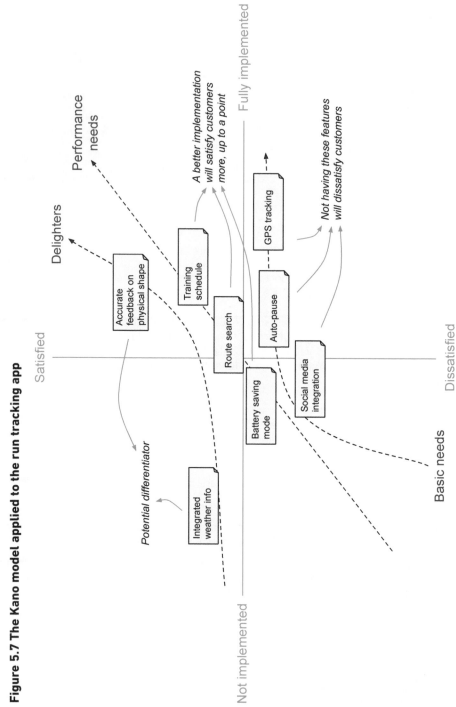

By surveying customers' opinions through both positively and negatively formulated questions you can categorise and prioritise features, or determine when a user hasn't fully understood a feature (see Table 5.2).

Table 5.2 The Kano model's standardised questionnaire[17]

	I like it	I expect it	I am neutral	I can tolerate it	I dislike it
Functional					
How would you feel if the product had …?					
How would you feel if there was more of …?					
Dysfunctional					
How would you feel if the product *did not* have …?					
How would you feel if there was less of …?					

Similar to the CX Pyramid, when developing or improving your product, you'll want to start by discovering and validating a few key delighters, before spending time and money in developing features to cover all basic needs.

Over time, customer expectations will change and delighters will become basic needs. So to attract new customers and keep existing ones, this evolution must be monitored; new basic needs will need to be added quickly and new potential delighters will need to be discovered.

RICE

The previous techniques take a more strategic and intangible approach to feature identification and prioritisation. What will make a difference for your customers? What will differentiate your product from a competitor's product?

RICE, a scoring model originally developed by Intercom,[18] enables you to turn your thoughts into actual numbers in a pragmatic way. How much will a certain feature move the needle and at what cost? Using RICE, you can move away from making priority decisions based purely on gut feeling or highest paid person's opinion (HiPPO), and instead use a more rigorous approach that at the same time doesn't lead to analysis paralysis. The RICE acronym stands for:

---

17 Wikipedia (2022) 'Kano model'. Wikipedia. Available from https://en.wikipedia.org/wiki/Kano_model

18 Intercom (2022) 'RICE: simple prioritization for product managers'. Intercom. Available from https://www.intercom.com/blog/rice-simple-prioritization-for-product-managers/

- **Reach**. How many people or events will a new feature or initiative reach in a given timeframe? How many times will a new feature be used, a notification seen, a web page visited, ... in a certain amount of time?

- **Impact**. What is the impact of the new feature or initiative on an individual person or target from your reach? This is often estimated relatively so that you can compare the expected impact of different features.

- **Confidence**. How certain are you about your Reach, Impact and Effort estimations? This is typically estimated through a percentage scale.

- **Effort**. What is the total investment needed to develop and launch a feature, for example in person-months or Fibonacci numbers?[19]

You can use absolute estimations for each of these components, but relative estimations are usually easier to make and they provide a good enough basis for comparison and thus prioritisation.

Intercom's original Impact scale was:

- 3 = massive impact;
- 2 = high impact;
- 1 = medium impact;
- 0.5 = low impact;
- 0.25 = minimal impact.

Intercom's original Confidence scale was:

- 100 per cent = high confidence;
- 80 per cent = medium confidence;
- 50 per cent = low confidence;
- Anything below 50 per cent is 'total moonshot'.

Of course, you can tweak your scales or use more meaningful numbers and calculations depending on your specific product and customer base and your existing product metrics if that helps you to make better product choices in your context.

A RICE score for each idea is then calculated:

$$RICE = \frac{Reach \times Impact \times Confidence}{Effort}$$

An example prioritisation for the run tracking app could be the following. Suppose the app has 10,000 active users tracking on average two activities per week, which amounts

---

19 A sequence of numbers 1, 2, 3, 5, 8, 13, 21, ... to relatively estimate the implementation effort of features.

to 80,000 activities, and we are checking the impact of three potential features over a period of four weeks.

- Find a new route: an estimated 5 per cent of users will try this out once over the course of four weeks → Reach = 500

- Post a training achievement on social media: an estimated 60 per cent of users are active on social media about their running achievements and will post about one-third of their achievements → Reach = 16,000 posts

- Get positive feedback on training progress: 50 per cent of users are interested in such feedback, which will be provided for each tracked activity → 40,000 feedback moments.

This is summarised in Table 5.3, adding the confidence and effort estimations, and resulting RICE score.

Table 5.3 RICE scores for different run tracking features

	Reach	Impact	Confidence	Effort	RICE Score
Find a new route	500	0.5 retention	80%	2	100
Post a training achievement on social media	16.000	2 acquisition	50%	1	16.000
Get positive feedback on training progress	40.000	1 retention	100%	3	13.333

While a method like RICE is still using estimations, it has a number of advantages over pure gut feeling-based prioritisation:

- It makes the prioritisation process more transparent.

- It enables you to link prioritisation to your product strategy: what impact(s) are you aiming for?

- It can trigger a conversation about how you may be able to increase the value of features.

- It's very flexible: you can go more or less in-depth in your estimations and calculations as you prefer.

- It triggers people to think about **measurable** impact and to start measuring the actual impact of product decisions. Especially in a digital world, many product metrics can be measured, like usage metrics but also customer feedback, for example through a pop-up asking customers to rate their experience. Even if many customers ignore such a pop-up, that tells you something about how they feel about your product.

- It triggers people to be aware of how (un)certain that impact is, and thus can lead to doing experiments to increase confidence.

Of course, you need to ensure that people are not 'estimating their idea to the top of the list', for example through a conversation with a diverse group of stakeholders and by hiding the aspects you are not discussing at any given moment. It's also not forbidden to go ahead with features that have a lower score, as long as this is a conscious decision and steps are agreed to try to increase their Reach, Impact, Confidence or Effort.

DIGITAL OR PHYSICAL OR ...? DESIGNING WITH INTENT

Technology has so much become part of our daily lives, embedded in almost everything we see, hear or touch, that it sometimes feels like there is no alternative. Will everything become digital? Could and should we turn every physical product or experience into a digital one?

In practice, most products and the experiences they are part of are hybrid. The digital run tracker is part of an analogue experience. It may enhance, enrich or even enable it, but it's not the full experience. Once more, it's clear that understanding the entire customer experience or journey in which the digital product plays a role will provide insights into the added value of that product within the wider journey.

There's often a tendency or natural reflex to replace a physical product with a digital copy: paying with coins becomes paying through an app, a paper entrance ticket becomes a QR code on your phone. The original physical product has been replaced by an almost identical digital copy and did not change much in the overall experience. The first steps when moving to digital were actually quite clumsy. You could order and pay for a cinema ticket online ('We're digital!') only to have to print it out and bring your paper ticket with you when visiting the movie theatre.

The added value of simply creating a digital 'equivalent' of a previously analogue product is often rather small. It can be quicker and more reliable (if the technology works) and perhaps hold more information, but does it provide more value? Or is it simply a gimmick (which may be fine if that's the intent of your digital product)?

A simple yet nice example is buying train tickets in Belgium: anyone can book a train trip online and link it with anyone else's identity card, which Belgians always have to carry on them. People can buy a ticket for their pre-smartphone daughter or Nokia classic-addicted grandparent just as easily as for themselves. They don't need physical access to the receiver's identity card and it doesn't require sending around digital tickets, downloading apps, creating accounts, getting weird SMSs and so forth. It's a digitally enabled and improved process that makes life a little easier, and a nice example of where **limiting** the amount of technology makes for a **better** overall experience for a wider audience.

Another example is online meetings. The COVID-19 pandemic triggered enormous growth in online meeting platforms and their features. Many of these platforms and features were trying to mimic in-person meeting behaviour, like being able to raise your hand and have breakouts. There were also quite a few gimmicks, like being able to turn yourself into Mr Potato Head. Technology providers and users tried to copy their in-person meetings and events into the digital world. Sometimes this worked, sometimes it didn't.

For example:

- People lose focus more quickly in online meetings, so the overall meeting approach needs to be adjusted. Simply replacing the in-person meeting with an online one is not going to give you the same result. What can meeting software do beyond providing video feeds that help participants to keep focus and take short and effective breaks? What can meeting organisers do and how can you support them, through meeting software or other means, like a blog post sharing tips and tricks?

- While the ability to see each other and read body language is key to communication and an integral part of in-person meetings and events, some people are reluctant to turn on their webcam, for personal or technical reasons. What can meeting software do to lower the threshold for turning on the camera or to provide clues on participants' body language and attention (or lack thereof)? What can event organisers do, through tools and other means or approaches, and how can you support them?

- Informal networking happens naturally at in-person meetings and events. Online, it's a very different story. Part of this is tool-related, but people also have different expectations from online meetings and networking compared to in-person meetings and networking. They tend to multitask or want to get some off-screen time in between presentations. So simply copying in-person networking features into a digital product is probably not a complete answer.

A good starting point is understanding the participants' intent: why are people attending the meeting or event? What are they trying to get out of it, and is it the same as for an in-person meeting or event? What is the online customer trying to accomplish and how can a digital product help them with that? A straightforward digital copy of the analogue original is perhaps not the most effective way forward. Moving from a physical only to a digitally **enhanced** experience will benefit from a rethink of the entire journey while working back from the customer's intent.

To help you think of an enhanced experience, you can ask yourself the following questions:

- Are there any opportunities to do things more simply through digital?

- What's good about the physical experience that you don't want to lose? This might provide opportunities for human interaction, for example.

- What services can we provide around the physical and/or digital product to enhance the overall customer experience and value?

While pure copy–paste from physical to digital usually is a bad idea, it can be a good starting point that gives you the first-mover advantage, paving the way to a better solution by starting out with something very close to what people already know and use.

Ethical by design

> When you invent the ship, you also invent the shipwreck; when you invent the plane you also invent the plane crash; and when you invent electricity, you invent electrocution ... Every technology carries its own negativity, which is invented at the same time as technical progress.
> Paul Virilio, French cultural theorist, urbanist and aesthetic philosopher[20]

Product designs are never neutral. Intentionally or not, a product, through its sensory and functional design, will appeal more to certain groups of people than to others, or it will work better for some customer segments than others, often unintentionally so. Consider, for example, seat belts that used to be tested by male crash test dummies only and thus were optimised for 'average' males, increasing the likelihood for females to be injured in a car crash.

As ethics is becoming increasingly topical, think for example about digital data and privacy, carefully and consciously designing ethics into a product from the start is also becoming more important. The potential reach and impact of digital products and the data that is passing through them is only amplifying this importance.

You may have seen the examples of Microsoft's racist artificial intelligence (AI) chatbot on Twitter, Google Photos mistakenly labelling a black couple as being 'gorillas', or how algorithmic bias in health care exacerbates social inequities. These demonstrate that even if the intention is good, technology can fail from an ethical perspective.

Some features are perhaps less obvious examples of potentially unethical product design, like infinite scroll or gamification, or even a simple feature such as a counter for the number of **likes** or **retweets**, which can be engaging and motivating but also addictive, as they briefly trigger small dopamine releases in people's brains. Some of the less acceptable tricks that make you do things that you didn't mean to, like buying or signing up for something, are called dark patterns. By the way, how many times have you checked your smartphone while reading this chapter?

Data capture and (ab)use cause probably the most obvious ethical concerns these days. Any data a digital product captures could potentially be used for purposes that were originally unknown and that people may perceive as unethical. For example, during the COVID-19 pandemic, some countries started using mobile location data from telecom operators for contact tracing. This is an example of function creep: the expansion of a system or technology beyond its original purposes.

---

20 Paul Virilio and Petit Philippe (1999) *Politics of the Very Worst*. New York: Semiotext(e), p. 89.

Simply adding a layer that prevents such data from getting exposed is only a partial solution. There's no guarantee this limitation will not be removed at a later stage. A better approach, from an ethical perspective, is to not collect any data that you don't really need, to delete any data immediately after using it or to transfer technical ownership of personal data to the customer. It is, after all, their data. This obviously will also impact your (digital) business model.

Ethical design is not something that can be layered on top of an existing design, or added afterwards. It needs to be part of the technical, functional and business design process from the very beginning.

What are some of the things that product managers can do to enable ethical product design?

Be aware of the ethical bias

'I AM WEIRD' describes the group of people most products are designed for. It stands for:

- I: **i**dentity
- AM: **a**ble (not disabled), **m**ale
- WEIRD: **w**hite, **e**ducated, **i**ndustrialised, **r**ich, **d**emocratic

'Identity' stresses the fact that 'normal' or 'am weird' are categories with which many people identify themselves. People search to be 'normal' and known as 'normal', there is value in being 'normal', which increases bias.[21] The 'am weird' identifier amounts to roughly 4 per cent of the world's population.[22] Use real-life examples of ethical bias in other products and industries and of the consequences thereof to raise awareness about the relevance of spending time thinking about ethics.

Use a toolkit like the Ethical OS[23] to trigger a conversation on ethics. The Ethical OS lists a number of risk zones, questions and scenarios that help to bring potential unethical product and business model aspects to the surface. These help you think about ways to safeguard your product, not only from current but also future ethical mishaps. Consequence scanning[24] is a related, lightweight practice that helps you to think about and mitigate unintended consequences before they do harm.

Be aware of the bias in your sample data

A lot of data sets are biased because historically different groups of people have not been equally represented in these data sets or because humans have been biased in the decisions they have made and that bias is now part of the data. Building new digital products on those data sets, for example using machine learning, will amplify that bias.

---

21 Alastair Somerville (2020) 'I AM WEIRD – going beyond WEIRD'. Acuity Design. Available from https://acuity-design. medium.com/i-am-weird-going-beyond-weird-958601bf5054

22 Alastair Somerville (2020) 'What if Normal is the problem?' *IAC - The IA Conference*. Available from https://vimeo. com/407879186

23 Ethical OS (2022). Available from https://ethicalos.org/

24 doteveryone (2022) 'Consequence scanning – an agile practice for responsible innovators'. doteveryone. Available from https://doteveryone.org.uk/project/consequence-scanning/

So you'll need to take steps to prevent this from happening, for example by filtering data sets to remove bias and/or make them more balanced, or by integrating human decision making into your product or service design instead of relying on the output of algorithms alone.

Ensure team diversity

A diverse team will automatically come up with solutions that work well for a more diverse audience. Take, for example, the case of the soap dispenser that only worked for people with a pale skin colour. If a dark-skinned person had been part of the team, they probably would have discovered this flaw during the development process. Skin colour is a clear example of visible diversity in product teams. Equally important is invisible diversity, like people's socio-economic background.

People with diverse backgrounds look differently at customer needs, and potential solutions and business models, which will lead to a more ethical product design.

Check for potential dark patterns

Use a checklist like that on darkpatterns.org to uncover potential dark patterns in your product and the processes around it.

It's a team sport

Business analyst, systems analyst and functional analyst, product owner, product manager, customer and user experience designer ... The list of roles in (digital) product development keeps growing and it can become hard to see the forest for the trees. Who is doing what? Who is responsible or accountable for which part of product design, development, roll-out, support ...?

While checklists of these different roles and their responsibilities are useful, every organisation and every product is different, with different roles and different sets of responsibilities and with people that have different backgrounds and levels of experience, so a standard list of roles and responsibilities is probably not good enough.

Ultimately, the goal is to launch and maintain a successful product, and it takes an entire team to do so through effective collaboration. A great approach is to sit together and discuss and agree on what product success is and what needs to be done to achieve that success. Without linking things to specific people on your team, role descriptions and checklists can be good conversation starters for this discussion. What needs to be done? What decisions will need to be made? What is a good decision-making process?

Then map this onto your team: who is able to do what? Who is interested to learn, to coach, to facilitate? How is your team and work organisation influenced by any deadlines you may have? How will the team deal with someone being unexpectedly unable to complete a task or fulfil their role? Individual responsibility and ownership are important but if they lead to a culture of blame instead of help and support, the entire team will suffer, and so will the product and in the end the customer.

CASE STUDY: UNPARKR – MEETING JOURNEYS AND VALUABLE FEATURES

Unparkr's objective is to help teams to better manage their meeting outcomes. We can distinguish the three levels of experience discussed in this chapter as follows:

- The usability of the Unparkr mobile/web application during meetings: how easy is it to go through the meeting agenda, to keep time, to create and assign action points, to configure notifications ...? If Unparkr's key features are not easy to use, users may fail to use them at all and miss out on experiencing their value.

- The user experience of preparing, holding and following up on a meeting, partially supported by Unparkr but also including, for example, email exchanges outside the meeting and Unparkr.

- The customer experience of holding multiple, related and unrelated, meetings, and following up on issues, objectives and milestones over a longer period of time.

Where in the customer journey can Unparkr make a compelling difference? Where can it offer an enjoyable experience that differentiates it from existing solutions? (See Figure 5.8).

How can Unparkr, as a digital product, offer an enjoyable experience that enhances preparing, holding and following up on meetings?

- Are there any opportunities to do things more simply through digital? For example, automatically highlighting action points that stay open for a longer than average time.

- What's good about the physical experience that you don't want to lose, for example standing around a Kanban board with the entire team? Unparkr may need to provide a large screen interface and not only a mobile interface.

- What services can Unparkr provide around the physical and/or digital product to enhance the overall customer experience and value? For example, deadlines cause tension and sometimes conflicts within teams. Could we provide a 'tension thermometer' and team coaching as a value-adding service?

KEY TAKEAWAYS

- Customer experience is much broader than the usability of a user interface or the user experience of a system, product or service. Make sure your design process triggers you to think about the broader user/customer context to discover where you can add the most value.

- Think about the potential value of products and features using a tool like job types or the value pyramids.

- Price and revenue model are also product features.

- Good feature prioritisation is key in (digital) product management. Various techniques help you to identify the basics and the differentiators needed to create a successful product.

- A digital copy-cat of a physical product is usually not the best way to go.

- Ethics and diversity are increasingly important and expected in product development.

Figure 5.8 The Unparkr customer journey

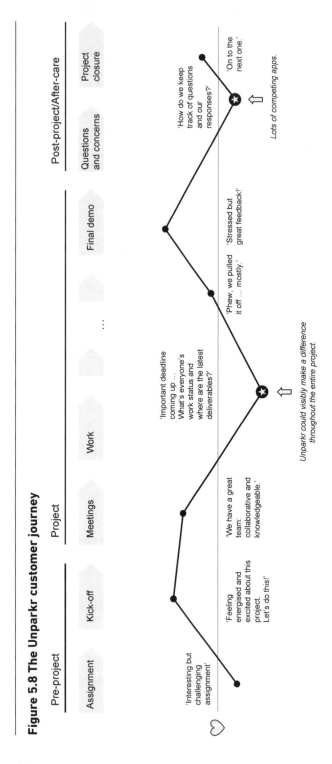

Pre-project | **Project** | **Post-project/After-care**

Assignment | Kick-off | Meetings | Work | ... | Final demo | Questions and concerns | Project closure

'Interesting but challenging assignment'

'Feeling energised and excited about this project. Let's do this!'

'We have a great team: collaborative and knowledgeable.'

'Important deadline coming up .... What's everyone's work status and where are the latest deliverables?'

'Phew, we pulled it off .... mostly.'

'Stressed but great feedback!'

'How do we keep track of questions and our responses?'

'On to the next one.'

Lots of competing apps.

Unparkr could visibly make a difference throughout the entire project.

6   DATA-DRIVEN DECISIONS

Filip Hendrickx

The visionary leader that knows exactly what customers need and how to build it for it to be a success: wouldn't we all love to be that person? Or have that person around to tell us what to do next? Reality is very different: few such leaders exist and even they all have made big mistakes throughout their careers.

While gut feeling has its place, facts from the outside world are the best input for product development decisions. This chapter covers how to find reasons why your ideas may fail and how to experiment your way to success or an early stop, which is also a success as you will have saved time and money that you can then spend on a better idea.

WHY DATA-DRIVEN DECISIONS?

'The truth is out there.'

Tagline for The X-Files

In an attempt to explain why objects fall towards the ground, the Greek philosopher Aristotle claimed that there is a place for each of the four elements – earth, wind, water and fire – to which they naturally gravitate. For the element earth, and thus all objects like rocks, people and plants, this natural place was in the centre of the Earth. Hence, consistently with our intuitive understanding and basic observations of how the world works, physical objects fall down.[1]

Furthermore, Aristotle believed that heavier objects fall faster. This philosophy, which Aristotle based on observation, reflection and thought experiments, held sway for about 2,000 years.

It wasn't until the 16th century that several scientists and mathematicians like the Dutch Simon Stevin and the Italian Galileo Galilei performed actual experiments to invalidate Aristotle's theory. Simon Stevin simultaneously dropped two equally sized balls, one ten times heavier than the other, from a church tower in the city of Delft. He heard the

---

1   Andrew Zimmerman Jones (2019) 'The history of gravity'. ThoughtCo. Available from https://www.thoughtco.com/the-history-of-gravity-2698883

balls hit the ground at the same time, experimentally proving Aristotle wrong: objects fall at the same speed regardless of their mass (except for the effects of air resistance).[2]

It may seem strange that it took intelligent people about 2,000 years before actually validating their theories. On the other hand, how often do you identify and validate your own assumptions about the products or solutions you come up with, before implementing them? And while thought experiments or upfront problem and solution analysis definitely have their value (Einstein's theories come to mind), confronting the real world is a powerful and often quick way to learn whether your ideas are correct.

A striking example of the value and need for real-life experiments is two validations done by a company that considered adding an online pay per article business model next to their long-standing yearly subscription model, which provided full access to their entire library of online articles and one year of monthly paper magazines (see Figure 6.1). In their first experiment, they added a 'Purchase article' button to some articles' preview page, next to the traditional 'Purchase subscription' button. The 'Purchase article' button was not implemented, it was a so-called 'Button to nowhere' (see the section below on 'Designing experiments' for more information on this validation technique).

Figure 6.1 Fake implementation of a purchase button[3]

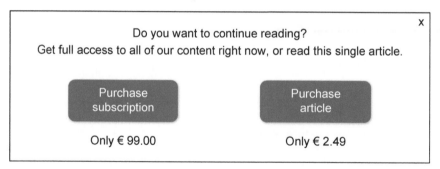

They learned that customer interest in purchasing single articles was lower than expected, based on similar business models already available in other countries. This was useful information to update their business case for the new model and refine the investment they were willing to make. But they didn't go ahead with implementing the new model right away. In a follow-up experiment, they learned that 90 per cent of customers that had clicked the 'Purchase article' button moved away from a subsequent 'Choose your payment method' pop-up without actually paying (again, the pop-up was not really implemented, but customers did not know this when selecting their payment method). For some reason, they changed their mind and decided not to buy. Clearly, further customer research was needed to determine what was going on,

---

2   Wikipedia (2022) 'Galileo's Leaning Tower of Pisa experiment'. Wikipedia. Available from https://en.wikipedia.org/wiki/Galileo%27s_Leaning_Tower_of_Pisa_experiment. 'Delft tower experiment'. Wikipedia. Available from https://en.wikipedia.org/wiki/Delft_tower_experiment

3   Inspired by an experiment by Ocu at www.ocu.org

whether or not the new business model made sense, and how the payment flow should be implemented.

> Note the use of the words 'validation' and 'experiment' rather than 'test'. For many people, a test is used to verify whether something works as expected or specified, whether something is not broken or buggy. An experiment has a very different purpose. It lets you validate whether customers are interested in your product or product feature, whether they are using and paying for that feature, whether it increases customer acquisition or retention, and so forth.

Well-designed experiments help to prevent analysis paralysis or the HiPPO effect, where the highest-paid person's opinion drives a decision. Experimental data can demonstrate whether customers will pay for a certain feature and which implementation variant is preferred. Since there are usually more ideas for potential features than you can implement given time, budget and people constraints, experiments are a great way to help set priorities.

It's difficult to find the right balance between upfront analysis and getting on with product implementation while following your gut feeling. Consciously considering uncertainties, asking hard questions like 'What might not work as expected?' and 'Why would our product fail?' will help you to find out where further analysis and small or big product design changes are needed before building the actual product to completion. Depending on where you are in the product development process, some experiments will be more suitable than others.

A JOURNEY OF DISCOVERY

In an ideal world, the journey from idea to solution to success is a simple straight line forward, as depicted in the first version of the image in Figure 6.2. You start with the idea of creating a light bulb to illuminate your surroundings.

Figure 6.2 Different journeys from idea to success

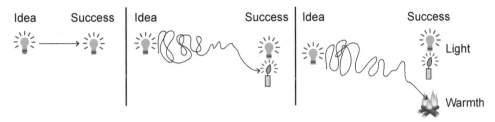

In reality, the journey is much more 'fuzzy', especially at the beginning, as shown in the second version of the image in Figure 6.2. As you're going through research and experiments, and learn about your future customer's needs, you'll fine-tune your idea and perhaps discover that a candle is a better solution to solve the initial problem of needing light in specific surroundings.

You may also discover that your future potential customer is actually not looking for light, but rather for cosy warmth, and end up creating a campfire and a business model around it, like in version three of the image in Figure 6.2.

What this picture doesn't explicitly show is that you may never get to the end, where you capture value. In fact, many, if not most, products won't become a success, and their development process is best stopped sooner rather than later. Willingness to 'kill your darlings' is a key product management skill that is valid both for entire products and product features. At regular intervals, you should ask the question, 'Is it a better investment of our time and money to continue with this product/feature, should we change it either a bit or a lot, or should we abandon it altogether?' This is a tough call to make because people tend to like their idea and because of sunk costs. Getting out of the building and performing experiments in the real world early and often helps to make the right call: if you spend much time working on your idea, you'll probably start to like it so much that it will become difficult to let go. Early and frequent feedback points you in the right direction. Furthermore, data from experiments can help to remove some of the emotive factors from the discussion.

So, continual experimentation throughout the design journey helps to answer the above question. To be able to ask the right questions **and** accept and respond to the answers you'll receive, consider the mindset you have while going through this journey:

- You know where you are going, you're convinced it's the right place and you use feedback to fine-tune your ideas. An example is the iPhone, which is the culmination of a carefully planned development process with the iPod and iPad as predecessors.

- You're open to discovering where you should be going and will change course, sometimes fundamentally, when you receive feedback. An example is the photo-sharing community Flickr, which rather serendipitously originated from a massive multiplayer online game development effort. The game never took off and its development was abandoned, while Flickr is still here.

The difference between both journeys is a difference in mindset: 'command and control' versus 'sense and respond'. To put it bluntly, the first approach is about adjusting reality to your ideas and the second one is about adjusting your ideas to reality. Do you believe you can design for (predefined) success, or should you rather be open to discovering success?

As much as we love stories of lone heroes with an engaging and wildly ambitious vision, most such development efforts fail, and if they succeed, they require very deep pockets. As a product manager responsible for a sum of money and a group of people, which approach will you be taking?

Here, the concept of working with MVPs, originated by Frank Robinson[4] and popularised by Eric Ries in his book *The Lean Startup*,[5] comes into play.

By its original definition, the 'perfect MVP' is that version of a product that gives you the highest return for the lowest investment or risk. You invest the smallest amount of money and time possible, thus taking the smallest risk of wasting time and money, to build a releasable product and then reap the highest possible benefits. The big question is: how do you know what this perfect MVP looks like? Eric Ries' definition of MVP provides the answer: 'An MVP is the least amount of work you can do to validate or invalidate a hypothesis.'

Instead of looking at **the MVP** as a release stage, you use **MVPs** as a means to continually validate whether you are going in the right direction. MVPs drive and enable the continual build/measure/learn loop and the best MVPs let you minimise the total time needed to go through that loop.

So throughout the product development journey:

- **build:** you have ideas and you will build things to validate or invalidate those ideas. What you build can be (a part of) a product but often is something much simpler, quicker and cheaper to help you experiment and learn, like an interview or a mock-up;
- **measure:** you will think about and measure the uncertainties standing between what you have now and a successful product through these experiments: what would make your idea fail?
- **learn:** you will learn from the experimental data so that you can remove uncertainties one at a time.

As you move through the product development journey, different kinds of uncertainties with different risk levels will pop up. For example, at the beginning, a key uncertainty is whether or not anyone is having the problem you are trying to solve. Many new products fail simply because they solve a problem that does not exist or is not of enough importance to a large enough number of potential customers: there is no market need. At this stage, you don't need a detailed product design or implementation, as you haven't yet clearly defined and validated the customer problem.

As your customer and problem understanding grow, you'll move towards more specific product and business model variations, and more reliable validations thereof. Once you have a live product and business, you'll keep on fine-tuning it by validating and adding, updating and removing specific features.

Giff Constable's Truth curve visualises this learning journey (see Figure 6.3 and pp. 133–134).

---

4   Sean Murphy (2017) 'Frank Robinson's minimum viable product definition'. SKMurphy. Available from https://www.skmurphy.com/blog/2017/04/24/frank-robinsons-minimum-viable-product-definition/

5   Eric Ries (2011) *The Lean Startup*. New York: Currency.

Figure 6.3 Giff Constable's Truth curve[6]

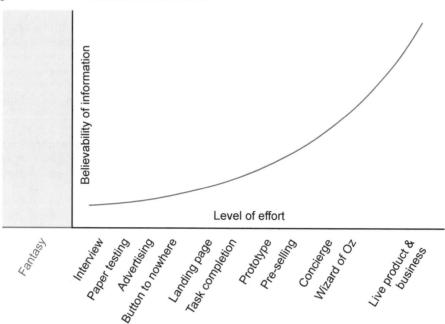

As long as you haven't been 'out of the building', confronting your idea with the real world, you're in fantasy land. Your guess on what will bring success is perhaps not significantly better than anyone else's. To decrease the level of uncertainty, simple and often more qualitative techniques like interviews, small-scale surveys or rough paper prototypes let you capture valuable insights quickly. Such qualitative techniques enable you to get into the heads of potential customers at a low investment cost, which makes them very valuable in early stages of product development. An example is the publisher mentioned interviewing a number of non-subscribers about their interest in reading and paying for single articles to find out if there is any interest, but, even more so, to learn about their needs and usage contexts. The challenge with these techniques is to execute them well, as you'll need to ask the right questions and interpret answers correctly to get to a good customer understanding. A practical tip is to perform interviews and so on, always with two people, and then compare notes and interpretations afterwards. And of course, practice will help you to build your questioning, interviewing and interpretation skills.

As you progress, if feedback is positive, experiments will be closer to the real product and thus deliver more reliable results, though at a higher cost and thus higher risk. So you'll only want to move to this stage after initial positive validation through cheaper techniques. The publisher's 'Purchase article' button to nowhere experiment already requires a small implementation effort. A next step could be a Concierge MVP: a manual payment and article procedure that delivers customers the actual experience, albeit

---

6   Giff Constable (2013) 'The Truth Curve'. Giff Constable. Available from https://giffconstable.com/2013/06/the-truth-curve/

slowly. The slowness will influence the number of purchases, as some customers will be put off by it; it will make scaling your product difficult but that's not a major concern, as you're still trying to learn whether your product makes any sense at all.

The fuzzy front-end visual in Figure 6.2 shows 'capture value' only at the end of the journey when the first real product version is released. That needn't be so. The Concierge MVP and pre-selling, where you sell a product that does not exist yet, let you capture value before the first real product is launched. The sooner you are able to capture value in the product development journey, the better, as it validates your business model and brings down your investment risk. One of the product manager's challenges is to find precisely those early experiments that enable learning **and** let you capture value early on.

DISCOVERING UNCERTAINTIES

Because you are so close to the product you're building, it's often difficult to clearly see what could possibly go wrong. If you're not able to put your finger on the assumptions you are making and your product's key uncertainties, you will not be able to validate whether you're on the right track. A few practical techniques can help you to identify uncertainties.

Why would it fail?

Most people will want to be friendly to you and positive about your idea. They don't want to hurt your feelings. However, you don't want to find out what will work. You want to find out what **won't** work. So, be explicit and ask people why they think your idea might fail. Or show them some test results, telling them it's not as good as you expected, and ask them what may have gone wrong. This will let you look at your ideas differently, and inform you of potential uncertainties and experiments to run.

Valuable/usable/feasible/viable

For your product in its entirety, or for specific features, ask yourself the following questions:[7]

- Is it **valuable** for customers?
  - Do we have a clear understanding of the problem it is solving for our customers?
  - Do we understand for which customers it's valuable and why?
  - How certain are we about this: how conclusive is the evidence?
- Is it **usable**?
  - Can users figure out how to complete their task with the product? Do users experience the time to task completion as short enough? Can/should we simplify it?
  - How certain are we about this: how conclusive is the evidence?

---

7   Marty Cagan (2017) 'The four big risks'. Silicon Valley Product Group. Available from https://www.svpg.com/four-big-risks/

- Is it **feasible**?
  - Can we technically build the product?
  - Are there any parts of the product or technology that we are less experienced with and might want to look into first?
  - How certain are we about this: how conclusive is the evidence?
- Is it **viable**?
  - Will our business model work?
  - Will we be able to capture enough value from the product?
  - How certain are we about this: how conclusive is the evidence?

Mini business cases

Business cases are a great way to structure your thoughts on potential benefits and expected costs and check if there's a viable balance between them. However, business cases often have a focus on financial expectations and tend to get rather heavy. They are mostly used when preparing for new projects.

The mindset of clarifying and balancing the benefits you're aiming for and the investment you expect will be needed, however, is relevant at any level of granularity between entire products and detailed features. This analysis doesn't have to be very detailed or rigorous to be valuable. At any moment when you are discussing a user problem or potential feature, make a quick list of benefits, costs, risks and questions you think about. Then ask yourself how certain you are about everything on your list. You'll immediately have a list of uncertainties you may need to validate before implementing the feature at hand.

Figure 6.4 The mini business case[8] for pay per article

Benefits	Costs
Additional revenue from non-subscribers New leads for upselling	Marketing the new model Development (payment, access)
Risks	**Questions**
Cannibalisation of our current business model	Technical complexity of a fine-grained article access model?

---

8 Barbara Carkenord (2018) 'Why are you NOT building business cases?', Carkenord Consulting at Building Business Capability Conference 2018. More info is available at Barbara Carkenord's blog post 'Business case analysis: a daily practice'. Available from http://blog.carkenord.com/business-case-analysis-a-daily-practice

KEY MILESTONES AND METRICS

The product development journey is complex. Chapters 2 and 3 gave you an overview of what you need to determine during the early phases. In this chapter we are going to discuss the process of getting to those answers and the milestones you need to reach.

Know your idea

Before diving into any kind of research, analysis or implementation, you need to make sure your team and any key stakeholders have a shared understanding of the idea. That may sound obvious, but many ideas start out as a few words on a sticky note and later on it becomes clear that people understand parts of the idea very differently. For example, the initial name for the pay per article product and business model was 'Pay per use', which could be understood as an alternative subscription model where customers purchase credits that they 'use' each time they read an article.

Having a focused discussion about the idea and what it does and does not entail prevents teams from jumping in head-first without having thought about where to start and at the risk of going in different directions. On the other hand, you want to prevent analysis paralysis, where you get stuck in thinking mode without moving to action.

One-page canvases are a great tool to guide this conversation.

- They provide clear viewpoints to be discussed.
- They force you to be concise and thus focus the idea.
- They are engaging workshop tools.

Some canvases that are great at this early stage are

- the Value Proposition Canvas;[9]
- the Lean Canvas;[10]
- the Innovation Canvas.[11]

This phase shouldn't take too long. If you don't have a clear, shared understanding of the idea after a few workshops, it's probably better to invest your time in something else. These workshops typically take place with (potential) team members and people close to the customer. If possible, it's definitely a good idea to include some external people as well. One agenda item in these workshops is getting everyone's thoughts on paper and converging to a shared understanding. Another agenda item is looking at everything you have written down and asking yourself, 'Are we sure about this? What proof do we have that these statements are true?' This way, you'll identify key uncertainties about your product.

---

9   Alex Osterwalder, Yves Pigneur, Greg Bernarda, Alan Smith and Trish Papadakos (2013) 'Value Proposition Canvas'. Strategyzer, Wiley. Available from https://www.strategyzer.com/canvas/value-proposition-canvas

10 Ash Maurya (2011) *Running Lean*. USA: O'Reilly. Available from https://leanstack.com/lean-canvas

11 Filip Hendrickx (2016) 'Innovation Canvas'. altershape. Available from https://altershape.consulting/InnovationCanvas

When are you ready to move to the next phase?

- When you have derived several related but different product ideas from the single, initial idea. This is a sign that you have looked at your initial idea with a challenging, open mind.
- When you have agreed on a small selection of related ideas to take forward.
- When you have a shared understanding of the ideas you selected.
- When you have agreed on the key uncertainties of each idea you will need to validate first.

Know your customer and their problem: getting to problem/solution fit

The next step is to validate the relevance of the problem that you believe exists and to identify the key elements required of a solution to solve this problem.

Through mainly qualitative customer research, like interviews and observations, you will now identify the following:

- What is the customer problem?
- What is the customer segment that experiences this problem? More precisely, what are their behaviour drivers?
- How are these potential customers currently solving their problem today and what is missing in their existing solutions?
- What is key to filling the gap between existing and ideal solutions?
- How will your solution be unique?
- How, and how much, are people willing to pay for a solution for this problem?
- What are people willing to invest apart from money that you may need or use for your business model, like personal data?

> Note that in this phase, you're not trying to define the exact solution implementation yet. You're trying to confirm a problem and one or more unsolved needs within existing solutions.

Two template sentences will help you to find your focus and describe your idea concisely.

One sentence is the Steve Blank formula:[12]

We help (X) do (Y) by doing (Z).

---

[12] Steve Blank (2011) 'How to build a web startup – Lean launchpad edition'. Steve Blank. Available from https://steveblank.com/2011/09/22/how-to-build-a-web-startup-lean-launchpad-edition/

For example:

We help	*people urgently looking for a new appliance*
do	*actionable research on which appliance to buy*
by	*providing them with up-to-date information on quality, reliability and key features for the specific type of appliance they need.*

Another sentence is the Solution Position Statement which we explored in detail in Chapter 3:[13]

> *For [target customer]*
> *who [statement of the need or opportunity]*
> *the [name of new product or business]*
> *is a [solution or business category]*
> *that [statement of compelling key benefit].*
> *Unlike [primary competitive alternative]*
> *our product [statement of primary differentiation].*

For example:

For	*people urgently looking for a new appliance*
who	*lack actionable, reliable information to help them make a purchasing decision*
the	*pay per article service*
is an	*online product review library*
that	*provides immediate access to relevant information.*
Unlike	*social feedback or customer reviews*
our product	*provides verified and comprehensive information.*

All of the above may seem quite a bit of work, and indeed it is. Going through this phase with an open mind and an approach of genuine listening takes time and effort. Your idea will go through a lot of changes and pivots before reaching a point where it is ready to move to the next stage. There's a very good chance you will even stop the idea altogether because you discover the problem does not exist or is not important enough. That's actually a good sign: you did not fall into the trap of building something that would probably fail.

Nevertheless, many people will want to jump into building something tangible, at the risk of building a solution for a non-existing or misunderstood problem. Use that energy to build experiments and perform validations instead.

---

13 Geoffrey A. Moore (2006) *Crossing the Chasm*, USA: HarperBusiness.

When are you ready to move to the next phase?

- When you have confirmed a customer problem.

- When you have identified a specific customer segment and its behaviour drivers.

- When you can describe how these customers solve this problem today.

- When you have identified the key missing elements of the existing solutions in use.

- When you have confirmation from potential customers that what will make your solution unique will solve their problem.

- When you have a confirmed price point for your product and a business model that makes sense when you do a back-of-the-envelope calculation; that is, a quick sanity check calculation that gives you ballpark figures for costs and revenue and confirms these are in balance.

How many positive answers do you need to be confident they confirm your current ideas? Rather than trying to aim for a specific number or percentage, make sure your customer input has converged into a clear and focused product. As long as additional research keeps providing input that changes the answers to the above questions, you're not done.

Know your solution's key features: getting to product/market fit

Armed with validated knowledge about an unserved or ill-served audience and what they want from your product, you can now finally start building something that actually serves your customers. This is where the rubber hits the road, as you'll find out if people actually use your solution. The previous steps were taking place in the first diamond of the Double Diamond model. Now, you are in the second diamond.

Part of this phase is turning your knowledge about the customer's journey into concrete features, using the approach and techniques from the previous chapter.

In this phase, you'll go through a process of building experiments that mimic a carefully selected set of key features. Initially, the experiments will use very rough and fake or manual implementations, steadily morphing into something that actually works. The section on 'Designing experiments' goes into more detail about what types of experiments you can run and how to set them up.

When are you ready to move to the next phase?

- When you know what the bare minimum solution implementation is to solve the customer's problem.

- When this solution is confirmed by the customer to be usable and valuable.

- When the estimated number of customers is high enough for a viable business model.

A popular metric to check whether you have reached product/market fit is the 40 per cent rule: at least 40 per cent of surveyed customers indicate they would be 'very disappointed' if they no longer have access to your product or service. They consider your product or service a 'must-have'.[14]

Scale your solution's business model: business model fit

You have a solution that people use and find valuable. Can you scale it to become viable? There are multiple sides to this challenge:

- **Technical.** Can you handle a larger number of users and a larger usage load?

- **Functional.** Does your product offer the features and level of quality expected by the early majority of users? This can be tricky, as you want to attract enough users to get to a viable solution without losing focus: more features dilute your unique value proposition and will make marketing more difficult. Building and maintaining a great product is also hard and costly and the bigger the product, the harder this becomes. When you get stuck in this situation, perhaps you moved to this phase too quickly.

- **Organisational.** Can your team handle additional workload, for example to deal with customer support requests?

- **Sales.** Do you have the marketing and sales capacity to attract and retain customers?

Throughout the journey from product/market fit to business model fit, you must be aware that you will only reach a part of the entire potential market (realistically, not everyone will use your product), and you will not reach that part from the beginning (it takes time to acquire a customer base). In Figure 6.5, your actual, real market will (hopefully) grow into your target market over time and you need to factor that time into your financial estimations. You also need to think about whether you want to build a profitable business as quickly as possible, or whether you want to take the market before your competitors do and only then start worrying about profitability.

Figure 6.5 Your real market is smaller than your target market and much smaller than your potential market

---

14 Sean Ellis (2009) 'The startup pyramid'. Startup Marketing. Available from https://www.startup-marketing.com/the-startup-pyramid/

In order to find business model fit, or discover that it's unreachable, the AARRR funnel[15] helps you to make informed decisions and take focused and effective actions. AARRR stands for

Acquisition → Activation → Retention → Revenue → Referral

and defines the steps you should try to get your customers to go through (see Table 6.1).

Table 6.1 The five-step AARRR funnel customers go through

Acquisition	Where do you find users, or where do they find you?
	Market your product to your target market and measure which combination of messages, channels, sub-segments ... is most effective in attracting new potential users and customers.
Activation	What is the first experience your users have?
	Experiment and learn what gets users to actually start using your product.
	For products designed to capture one-time value, activation is your key metric.
Retention	Are users coming back to your product?
	Experiment and learn what features get users to keep on using your product and how those features may need to be fine-tuned.
	For products designed to capture recurring value, retention is a more important metric than activation.
Revenue	Are you making money from your product and its users?
	Revenue should follow activation or retention, depending on how you capture value.
	Revenue by itself is not always a reliable form of validation in the early stages, as in the short run people may keep paying for a product they do not use, for example when someone else is paying or when they simply forgot to cancel. In these cases, retention is a more reliable indicator of product success.
Referral	Are users telling others about your product?
	Referral is a powerful feedback loop into the AARRR funnel that also should follow activation or retention. Depending on what drives your business to grow (see the 'What is your growth engine?' section below), retention may be more or less important.

---

15 Dave McClure (2007) 'Startup metrics for pirates: AARRR!' Ignite Seattle. Available from https://youtu.be/irjgfW0Blrw

To get a clear view of what actions (marketing actions, feature changes and so on) are working, you need to track how different **cohorts** of customers move through the AARRR funnel. A cohort is a group of customers who share a common characteristic. This can be the much-used customer's date of activation, which can often be linked to a specific marketing action, or another customer property, for example related to a potential market segment or pricing plan.

For the pay per article service, the cohort dashboard could look like this:

Table 6.2 Cohort example for the pay per article service

	Week 1	Week 2	Week 3	...
Marketing action	Blog post	Newsletter	Featured in magazine	
Potential users reached by the marketing action	12,000	15,000	5,500	
Acquisition: users that started browsing articles	5%	7%	3%	
Activation: acquired users that created an account	2%	8%	11%	

What is your growth engine?

In *The Lean Startup*,[16] Eric Ries mentions three engines of growth for a business:

- **Sticky = high retention**. High retention businesses rely on a high customer retention rate or low churn rate to drive revenue. In order to grow, these businesses need to have an acquisition rate that is higher than their churn rate.

- **Viral = high referral**. High referral businesses rely on a high rate of customers bringing in new customers. In order to grow, these businesses need customers to bring in more than one additional customer on average.

- **Paid = high margins**. High margin businesses can use part of their revenue to pay for acquisition activities. More targeted acquisition activities are usually more costly. In order to grow, these businesses need their customer lifetime value to be higher than their cost of customer acquisition.

Determining your main growth engine will help you to determine which actions to take in order to lead potential customers through your AARRR funnel.

---

16 Eric Ries (2011) *The Lean Startup*. New York: Currency.

Designing experiments

The main theme of this chapter is about discovering what makes your product or service and its business model successful, or more successful if it's an established product or service. This process of discovery is driven by experiments that provide measurable and actionable results, effectively replacing gut feeling as a driver for product decisions.

Many different types of experiments are possible, depending on what you are trying to validate. Before jumping into the design and execution of an experiment, though, a clear hypothesis must be formulated.

From assumption to hypothesis

Whenever your confidence in the impact of a new feature, idea or initiative is below 100 per cent (which is almost always the case), you are working on the basis of an assumption. Any amount of time or money spent on this idea could be wasted.

One of the assumptions of the pay per article service was that the impact on the sales of regular yearly subscriptions would be limited. If cannibalisation were too high, the business case would be negatively affected. In order to perform an actionable experiment, the assumption is reworded as a scientific hypothesis:[17]

We believe that	pay per article will have limited impact on new subscriptions.
To verify that, we will	offer 2,000 site visitors both options (pay for the regular subscription and pay for the single article)
and measure	the difference in number of new subscriptions compared to when offering only regular subscriptions.
We are right if	pay per article decreases new subscriptions by at most 10%.

Validation techniques

Many validation techniques are conceivable, and part of the job of a product team is coming up with good ways to validate their assumptions. Validation techniques can be roughly divided into four groups: tell, sell, fake and make:

- **Tell:** you explain your idea to potential customers and capture their feedback.

- **Sell:** you try to sell your idea to potential customers and measure conversion. You capture feedback as well.

- **Fake:** you pretend to have your idea implemented and measure if customers actually try to use it.

- **Make:** you actually implement your idea and measure usage. The implementation is the simplest or lightest version possible. After all, this is an experiment, not the real thing.

---

17 Alex Osterwalder (2015) 'Validate your ideas with the test card'. Strategyzer. Available from https://www.strategyzer. com/blog/posts/2015/3/5/validate-your-ideas-with-the-test-card

Below is a list of example validation techniques for each type:

- **Tell**
  - **Interview:** talking to people and capturing their feedback is possible from the moment you have an idea.
  - **Survey:** a more structured way of capturing what a larger number of potential customers think.
  - **Micro-survey:** a small, one- or two-question survey you can, for example, integrate in a newsletter or a website.
  - **Press release:** a written pitch or statement that news media can use which explains what your product is about, who it is for and why people would need or use it.
  - **Newsletter/blog post/etc.:** similar to a press release using other channels.
  - **Demo video:** the most widely cited example is Dropbox, a seamless file-synchronisation and -sharing service that was technically challenging and costly to implement, even in a prototype form. So, instead of taking a leap of faith and developing the whole thing, the Dropbox team created a short video explaining how Dropbox would work. The video went viral.[18]
  - **Landing page:** a one-page website that explains your product or service and has a clear call to action for visitors, like subscribing to a newsletter for updates.
- **Sell**
  - **Sales pitch:** if you can't sell your product in a face-to-face conversation, how are you going to sell it anonymously online, where <insert favourite social media channel with funny cat pictures> is only one click away?
  - **Pre-order:** a landing page where the call to action is 'buy/subscribe now'.
  - **Crowdfunding:** the crowd version of individual pre-order, where you raise small amounts of money from a large number of people to get enough funding to start (further) product development. With crowdfunding, customers know development won't start until a minimum amount of funds is raised.
- **Fake**
  - **Fake door:** the entry point to your product or service exists, but the implementation does not. The pay per article purchase button is an example of this validation technique.
  - **Concierge MVP:** you deliver your service manually and customers know this.
  - **Wizard of Oz MVP:** you deliver your service manually but hide this behind a (digital) front-end. To your customers, it appears as if your service is fully implemented.

---

18 Eric Ries (2011) 'How DropBox started as a minimal viable product'. TechCrunch. Available from https://techcrunch.com/2011/10/19/dropbox-minimal-viable-product/

- **Make**
  - **Piecemeal:** you stitch together a number of existing tools to solve your customer's problem. This solution works but is probably not maintainable or scalable. That's also not the intent: the intent is to validate customer interest and measure usage.
  - **Single-feature MVP:** you implement **the** single key feature that is the unique selling point of your product or service and measure sales and usage.
  - **Flash build:** you implement your product or service **live**, on the spot where your customer is and get immediate real-life feedback. The Nordstrom Innovation Lab sunglass app is a widely known example of this.[19]

Note that these validation techniques should not only be applied to entire products but also to single features, pricing plans, marketing approaches and so on.

A/B and A/B/n tests are often used to validate the effects of specific product changes or choices. In such tests, you offer different random sub-groups of users a different experience and measure which leads to the best results. For example, the colour or position of a button or the subject of a newsletter are straightforward examples of potential A/B tests. After running such a test for a limited but statistically significant sample of your users, you know which version works best and can deploy this version for everyone.

Optimizely offers a useful sample size calculator for your A/B tests at https://www.optimizely.com/sample-size-calculator.

Balancing cost, reliability and time needed for validations

As you move through the different validation types, your experiments typically deliver more reliable answers, albeit at a higher cost. This is similar to moving through the X-axis of the Constable Truth curve from left to right. A product team's challenge is to find the right balance between cost, reliability and the time needed to perform any given validation and go through the build/measure/learn loop. For any given assumption, you can compare different validation techniques and assess whether low cost, high reliability or a short time to results is most important.

Typically, at the early stages of a new product or feature set, you'll want quick and cheap validation to get a first feeling for whether you are onto something interesting. It's OK that reliability is lower at this stage, as you're looking for big-picture feedback on your idea.

As you make progress and confidence rises, you'll need more fine-grained and precise learnings in order to know if and how to proceed, so you'll need to invest more time and money to get more reliable learnings.

---

19 fashiontechpr (2013) 'Nordstrom Innovation Lab'. YouTube. Available from https://www.youtube.com/watch?v=2NFH3VC6LNs

Measure behaviour, not intent

A successful validation is a validation that provides valuable and actionable learnings. It's easy to fall into the trap of measuring so-called **vanity metrics**:[20] metrics that may look good but don't provide any insight into how you got where you are or how to move forward. For example, the number of likes, site visits or even downloads often doesn't correlate well with acquisition, retention and ultimately revenue. These are examples of 'HITS': 'How Idiots Track Success'.[21]

One way to fine-tune your metrics is to distinguish between metrics that measure intent and metrics that measure behaviour. Interview responses ('Yes, I would use this product.'), surveys ('How much would you be willing to pay?') and newsletter sign-ups are examples of metrics that measure intent: a positive result shows that people (say they) are interested in using or buying your product. However, they don't tell you that people are in fact really using or buying your product. At best, they are a leading indicator for later usage or purchases of questionable reliability.

So whatever hypothesis you formulate and validation experiment you set up, try to come up with a way to measure actual behaviour. In interviews and surveys, you can get closer to measuring actual behaviour through follow-up questions. For example:

- **Question 1 (intent):** Would you visit an appliance review site?
- **Question 2 (behaviour):** How often have you asked someone for a recommendation?

Experiments that measure actual behaviour, like a mock-up website, will provide even more reliable information.

Additionally, you'll also want to learn **why** people behave the way they do. Usage and sales metrics tell you **what** and **how much** but not **why**. So it's a good idea to find ways to get in touch with some of the people behind the numbers, so you can learn what drove their behaviour.

Where to start validation?

Having a range of validation techniques is great but when you've done a great job at listing your assumptions, where do you start validating? Simply put, you start with those assumptions that:

- are least certain; and
- if proven wrong, have the biggest negative impact on the success of your idea, not in terms of implementation but in terms of customer interest and value captured.

The higher the uncertainty and the higher the potential impact, the higher the need for validating an assumption. As an example, consider four assumptions about the pay per article service (see Figure 6.6).

---

20 Eric Ries (2010) 'Entrepreneurs: beware of vanity metrics', *Harvard Business Review*. Available from https://hbr.org/2010/02/entrepreneurs-beware-of-vanity-metrics

21 K. D. Paine (2009) 'Hits = how idiots track success'. SNCR's NewComm Forum 2009, San Francisco. Available from https://www.youtube.com/watch?v=IYdA_z91bYw

Figure 6.6 Positioning assumptions depending on their uncertainty and business impact when proven wrong helps to determine which assumptions to validate first

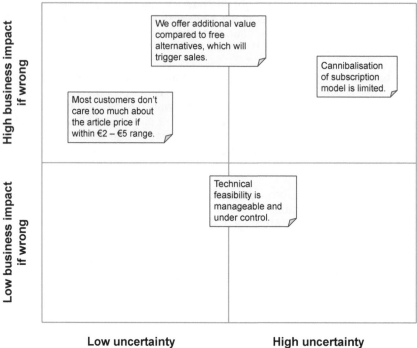

If we compare 'article price' and 'additional value compared to free alternatives', market research or an earlier A/B price sensitivity test may have demonstrated that the article price is not very important, so the uncertainty about the article price is low. On the other hand, if we don't have any information about the articles' value perception, the uncertainty thereof will be higher.

Regarding business impact, the business case may show that the number of article purchases has a bigger influence on the service's viability than the article price. Hence, we put it higher on the diagram.

Combined, the priority of validating the value perception is higher than of (further) validating the article price.

Making experimentation safe

Innovation means doing new things and that happens to be something that makes a lot of people feel uncomfortable. On top of that, early experimentation means getting out of the building with rough drafts or vague ideas, which is also something that many people find difficult, perhaps especially analysts that are used to getting all the details clarified before moving to the next stage. So early validation goes against many people's natural way of working. How can you create a safe environment in which to experiment and where people and organisations can get out of their comfort zone?

The first step is to listen carefully to people's concerns. Why do they think or feel it's not safe to perform an experiment just yet? Do they fear damage to the organisation's brand image? Do they fear losing existing customers? Do they fear promising something that in the end may not be developed? Do they fear the experiment would be too successful and the organisation won't be able to handle the customer requests? (This is actually a great indicator of success!)

Once you understand the safety concerns, you can co-create experiments that take these concerns into account. Perhaps you can experiment under a different brand or company name? Perhaps you can select customers with whom you already have a good personal or working relationship, like a partner or sister organisation? Perhaps you can simply be transparent about the fact that the experiment is about one of many ideas and that only a few will be taken forward? Perhaps you can limit the number of requests or registrations through an invite-only approach?

A powerful question to get this conversation going is, 'What would have to be true to make an experiment safe for you?' Another question that helps is asking, 'What could go wrong with this experiment and how would we handle the situation?', which makes people feel more prepared and helps you to fine-tune the experiment to make it safer.

Then it's about defining small steps that enable you to move forward and let people participate in the experiments to make them feel comfortable and to have them experience the value of validation first-hand. An example is a company that did their first 'customer' survey internally instead of with real customers. Even though the survey result was biased, they realised this experiment was not that risky and delivered interesting results.

It's also important to consider the words you are using. People may react differently when you speak about 'learning' rather than 'experimentation', or when you speak about 'improvement' rather than 'innovation', 'opportunity' rather than 'risk' or 'uncertainty', 'evolution' rather than 'revolution' and so on. This is an emotional aspect that should not be ignored and different people will find different wording engaging or frightening!

CREATING NEW PRODUCTS VERSUS IMPROVING EXISTING ONES

The approaches and techniques discussed may seem to be focusing on the creation of new products from scratch. How do you go about adding features to your existing products?

The approach is actually very similar:

1. You identify problems with the current product version for a specific customer segment.
2. You identify key solution requirements and their preferred implementation.

3. You identify the price point and business model for any additional features you'd be implementing, or for any new customer segment.

4. You scale the updated product to viable market size. This could mean selling the new features or product version to a large enough customer base or verifying that the new features offered within the existing business model are being used by a large enough group of customers.

The difference between creating a new product and updating an existing one is that in the latter case you'll probably be able to go through the validation process of each sub-problem and feature much faster, as you have an existing product and customer base to experiment with. Your goal is also different: when creating a new product, you're trying to find out if something is worth building. When updating an existing product, you're trying to optimise your product's retention or growth.

A point of attention is to ensure that your product does not lose its focus. Remember that less often is more. If you try to become everything for everyone, you'll probably end up being nothing for no one.

CASE STUDY: UNPARKR – EXAMPLE EXPERIMENTS

On the Unparkr product roadmap, we have a mobile version and integrations with Google apps and Atlassian. What assumptions or uncertainties are related to these, and which experiments would help us to find out what we should or should not develop? Here are some example experiments we could run and what we would learn from them.

Through customer interviews, we could check interest in both of these and have customers' input on priorities. While this provides input on the intent to use the proposed features rather than measuring actual usage behaviour, it gives us a chance to learn about specific use cases and user segments for each of these features and about the users' current activities and tools.

- Users may want a mobile version mainly to follow up on the progress that is being made towards an objective. This would reduce the scope of the mobile version significantly.

- Google apps may be used more intensively and frequently overall, but Atlassian is used most in the context of following up on progress, so it may be better to give this integration higher priority.

We could add a 'Get Unparkr mobile (fake) download QR code' to the Unparkr web app that leads to a mini-survey. The (fake) QR code measures actual download behaviour, which is a bit more reliable than interviews or surveys, while the mini-survey lets us check interest in different use cases.

Similarly, we could add fake 'Set up Google apps integration' and 'Set up Atlassian integration' buttons to measure interest. By positioning these buttons in specific locations in our web app, we could find out which use cases trigger the need for integration most.

KEY TAKEAWAYS

- Get out of your building sooner rather than later to learn from real people whether they will buy and use your product.

- Spend more time on experiments and learning rather than developing features that have not yet been proven to be valuable for your customer and your business.

- Consider what your organisation needs to get comfortable with performing experiments on unfinished products.

7   DEVELOPMENT

Sallie Godwin

You have identified your target market, understood your customer needs and run some successful experiments to prove your hypotheses. Now the real fun begins – it's time to start developing your product. Whatever its purpose and target market, every digital product is driven by software. The code it runs on needs to be written, reviewed, documented and tested. While initially creating something and getting it working can be relatively inexpensive, writing and maintaining software that sustains a medium to large enterprise is time-consuming, complex work – which requires significant investment. To prevent the cost of development spiralling endlessly upwards, a team must streamline their development process to minimise any rework, blockers or wasted time.

However, development is also a learning process. Your product has not been built before. Your team has not worked together before. Getting everything to run smoothly as you build will take some effort. The first couple of iterations will inevitably include some waste, which should be eliminated as you improve your ways of working. This process of continual improvement itself takes time. It's also necessary to spend some development time on understanding how best to go about constructing the product. As tools and techniques are always changing, there will always be new technical choices to explore. Decisions will need to be made on the practicalities of how the design is implemented. Your team will need to research and evaluate the options available to them – but not spend so much time doing experiments and investigations that they run out of time to complete the essential elements on your roadmap.

This leads to a complex balancing act for the product manager, who must constantly weigh the development time needed for learning, discovery and future efficiency savings against that needed for delivering value, either to customers or internally within the business. Simultaneously, they must decide how close to stay to the detail of development itself. Low-level decisions can have a material impact on a product's performance and its usefulness to customers. On the other hand, looking at every detail during development means there's less time to focus on the ongoing and essential work of maintaining the future roadmap and exploring new opportunities. And of course, development does not end once the product is launched, but continues throughout its life cycle. New features will continue to be added, bugs will need to be fixed and customer feedback acted on to ensure that the product doesn't stagnate. All of this contributes to a product manager's workload and makes delegation essential. This chapter will look at the specific challenges posed to the product manager in balancing these demands, as well as how these responsibilities can be shared with others in related roles in the team, such as product owners, Scrum masters and business analysts.

AGILE DEVELOPMENT LIFE CYCLES

Most of the time, software is built in iterative cycles that look something like Figure 7.1.

Figure 7.1 Iterative cycles

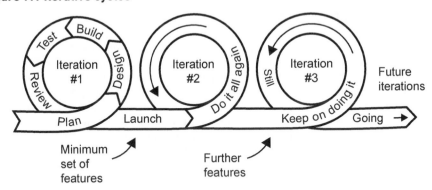

The aim of this kind of approach is to get something out into the world where it can be used as soon as possible. The quicker something can be launched, the sooner benefits can begin to be realised, offsetting the costs of further development. It also allows continual learning, because once the product is being used by customers, data can be gathered on potential future improvements. In contrast to waterfall development processes, where there are fixed stage-gates between design, development, testing and deployment phases, this approach reduces the risk that you build the wrong thing, or deliver something to a market that has moved on, making your new product irrelevant.

Working in this iterative way during development also helps to constantly review how well the team is working together. This makes it easier for the team to identify any improvements they can make to help them progress faster, saving time and cost.

Scrum and Kanban

Many teams will use either Scrum or Kanban to help them organise their work. Teams using Scrum will be working in 'sprints' – short, iterative cycles of around two weeks.[1] Each sprint will have a goal that delivers some value to the product. This might be creating a feature that solves a customer problem, or it might be learning something new, perhaps how to better develop a future part of the product. Teams using Kanban will visualise the different stages in their workflow – for example, refining a task, developing it, testing it and getting it ready for release. This shows visually where items get stuck – helping the team to identify and minimise anything getting in the way of delivery.

While Scrum helps to define the scope of each increment and is good for building in feedback cycles, Kanban works well for teams where tasks may be of varying size and

---

1   'Sprint' is a Scrum-specific term, but other forms of agile, such as Kanban or Lean, also have the concept of an 'iteration', which is similar.

where priorities can change a lot. In larger organisations, where frameworks such as Scrum are used by multiple teams, Scaled Agile Frameworks[2] are used to build very large and complex systems, without losing speed or responsiveness to change. As there is a wealth of resources on agile methodologies and frameworks, these will not be explored any further here.

PREPARING FOR DEVELOPMENT

In order to begin, your team will need to know what they are working on first. They will also need to assemble the tools they need to get started. This means the first sprint, Sprint 0, tends to look quite different from your other sprints. It's really about setting up the team for success in Sprint 1. This will usually mean getting development and test environments ready to use and ensuring that the product backlog is ready. If the team is new, it can also be time to onboard team members and get used to working with one another. One of the difficulties for product managers here is that as the work is both quite technical and doesn't often provide anything you can usefully demonstrate, it can be hard to explain what's going on to people outside the team. As discussed in Chapter 4, it can be useful to display these types of activities on the roadmap, to explain that they are essential to 'unlock' the more easily demonstrable features you are going to be delivering in future sprints.

The product backlog

By the time development begins, enough should be known about the first product increment for the team to begin work. This list of the features and infrastructure (and eventually, design changes and bug fixes) that the team will need to deliver to launch each product increment forms the product backlog.[3] As noted in Chapter 4, this is at a much lower level of detail than the roadmap. The backlog is in essence the team's to-do list, so it needs to include enough information about exactly what each task requires for it to be worked on, completed and tested. The team will only work on something if it is in the product backlog – but not everything that makes it in there will get delivered. As the team gets closer to working on each item, what actually needs to be done becomes clearer. Some items will inevitably become redundant as the best way to achieve a particular outcome is understood. The product backlog will also be continually reordered by the product owner to ensure that what the team will work on next aligns with the product roadmap priorities as they evolve. Once you have an idea of velocity (how much work your team can actually get done in a sprint), the backlog can also allow you to make some rough projections on when the next few features might be delivered.

User stories
The product backlog is commonly made up of user stories. Mike Cohn defines them as:

---

2   For more about SAFe® and Scaled Agile Framework (2017) Scaled Agile Framework – SAFe for Lean Enterprises. Available from https://www.scaledagileframework.com/

3   From the definition of a product backlog by www.agilealliance.org/glossary/backlog. A note on terminology: the product backlog generally gets referred to as just 'the backlog'. This is usually fine, but should not be confused with the sprint backlog (see below).

'Short, simple descriptions of a feature told from the perspective of the person who desires the new capability'.[4]

They usually look something like this:

As a person who will benefit from a feature

I want the feature

So that I can achieve an outcome

Stories are not really 'requirements' in the traditional sense. They are more like placeholders for discussions around how to do something, with a reminder of why that thing needs to be done, and who it is for. They act as prompts for conversations between the team on how that particular user need will be implemented. The format keeps the focus on the beneficiary of the work, whether they are the person who will actually use it, such as a customer, or an internal person, such as an admin user, or even the stakeholder who wants it to happen. They might be written on sticky notes or index cards, or directly into workflow management software before they are discussed and elaborated.

User story mapping
Once you have a growing backlog of stories, user story maps help to put them in context, organise them and divide them into increments that can be successfully released.[5] Importantly, they help to take all of your individual stories and place them in a coherent narrative about your product, where it is going and how it will help users at each stage of its development. This prevents you from getting lost in a huge pile of sticky notes and makes it easier to establish which stories need to be worked on first.

An example of a story map for a video conferencing application might start as shown in Figure 7.2.

As you develop your story map, you can start to draw lines on it to split it into releases and sprints. You might slice it horizontally – identifying the minimum functionality needed at each stage of the process to get to the end, or vertically – focusing on each stage in turn. In general, it is preferable to slice horizontally first. This is the quickest way to deliver something that can actually be used, as you cover the essential elements of each step in your user journey. Realistically, as you plan both releases and sprints, it's often necessary to do both. Figure 7.3 shows a story map that has been sliced horizontally and then vertically to give a rough outline of what will be focused on in each sprint within the first two releases.

4   Mike Cohn (2022) 'User stories and user story examples by Mike Cohn'. Mountain Goat Software. Available from www.mountaingoatsoftware.com/agile/user-stories

5   Jeff Patton (2014) is usually credited with having developed and shared this concept, and it is explored in his book *User Story Mapping: Discover the Whole Story, Build the Right Product*. O'Reilly Media. Available from www.jpattonassociates. com/wp-content/uploads/2015/03/story_mapping.pdf

Figure 7.2 An example story map: Unparkr

User activities	Register and logon		Make and schedule calls			Manage calls and contacts	
User tasks	Set up account	Change settings	Add contacts	Schedule meetings	Make a call	Get analytics & insight	Manage data and privacy
User stories **Release 1**	Registration and login; Forgot password	Add personal profile details	Upload contacts; View organisation directory	Invite call participants; Calendar integration	Start call; Mute participants		Set meeting passcode; View participants
Release 2	Manage app from a mobile device		Invite people outside the organisation	Present screen on call; Visual effects and backgrounds	Upcoming call reminders; Raise hands	See average time spent on calls daily	Record calls
Release 3	Single sign-on	Customise notifications	Create breakout rooms		Automatic captions	Automatically schedule breaks	

Figure 7.3 An example of a story map split into releases and sprints

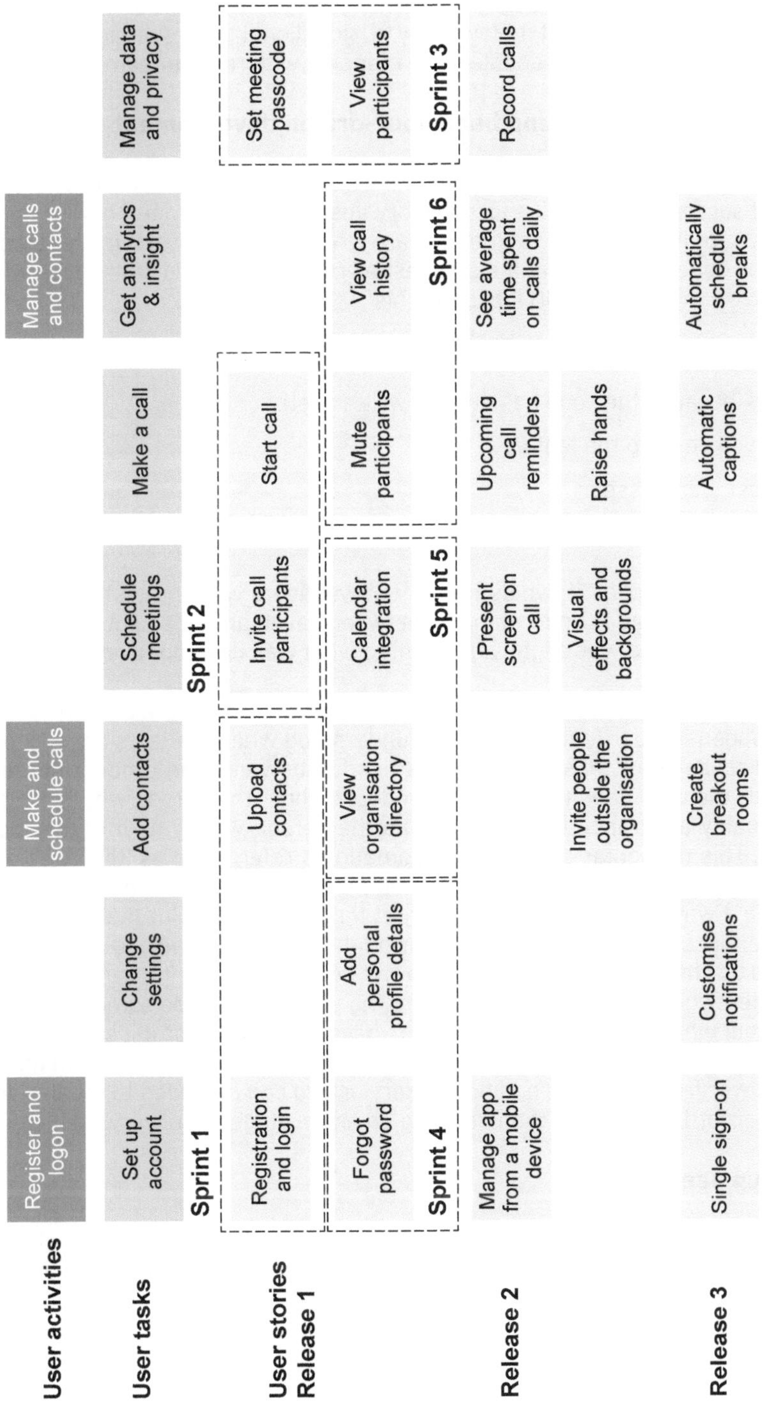

User activities	Register and logon		Make and schedule calls			Manage calls and contacts	
User tasks	Set up account	Change settings	Add contacts	Schedule meetings	Make a call	Get analytics & insight	Manage data and privacy
User stories **Release 1**	Registration and login		Upload contacts	Invite call participants	Start call		Set meeting passcode
	Forgot password	Add personal profile details	View organisation directory	Calendar integration	Mute participants	View call history	View participants
Release 2	Manage app from a mobile device		Invite people outside the organisation	Present screen on call	Upcoming call reminders	See average time spent on calls daily	Record calls
				Visual effects and backgrounds	Raise hands		
Release 3	Single sign-on	Customise notifications	Create breakout rooms		Automatic captions	Automatically schedule breaks	

Sprint 1 · Sprint 2 · Sprint 3 · Sprint 4 · Sprint 5 · Sprint 6

145

Your story map can be physical or digital – or both. But it needs to be easy to access – and robust. There's nothing worse than making a fantastic story map out of sticky notes and index cards, having excited conversations with your team around it, then opening a window and watching half of it blow away.[6] Using digital tools such as Trello and Jira can help to prevent this – and enable story mapping with remote teams.

Test-driven development and behaviour-driven development

Once the team is clear on roughly the order in which stories will be delivered, it's time to agree what success will look like for the story. Test-driven development (TDD) is where the unit tests for implementing something are written before development takes place. A unit test is done to check that the smallest element of code – a unit – does what it is designed to do. In essence, TDD looks like this:

- Write the test.
- It fails (because the code hasn't been written yet).
- Then you develop the feature.
- The test then passes.
- You know that the work is completed.

This speeds things up, as it avoids having to investigate why the test failed, which is usually caused by a gap in understanding between development and quality assurance. What was being tested was slightly different to what was developed or vice versa.

Behaviour-driven development (BDD) builds on this. It aims to ensure that every scenario that can happen as your feature is used is understood when the tests are written. This means a discussion of these scenarios is needed between the product person who understands the user need (such as the product owner), the person who is writing the test (the quality assurance (QA) person) and the person who will write the code (the developer). This triangular discussion is sometimes referred to as 'the three amigos' (see Figure 7.4). Knowing exactly how something will be tested before it is built helps to build it in a way that will pass the test first time, as in TDD. But the discussion also helps the amigos to unravel anything that might have been missed when originally writing and discussing the story, but which will become apparent during development. For example, if your story relies on a user having permission to do something, have you thought about what they will see if they don't have permission, or if it's been removed? Even if scenarios are missed, using an agile framework will generally mean that this is easy to recover from, since an additional story or two can be added to the backlog and prioritised accordingly, rather than delaying an entire stage of delivery.

Splitting up user stories

As user stories are discussed in this way, it's often found that not all parts of the story can be delivered at the same time, or that different people may need to work on different

---

6   Yes, I have seen this happen. No, we had not taken a photo.

Figure 7.4 The three amigos

parts of it at once. The story may also contain so much work that not all of it can be done in a single iteration or sprint. Inevitably, the story must be broken down into smaller parts. There are many ways to split a user story, depending on what is being done and what is most efficient for the team. Some common lines along which stories may be split include:

- Removing some more complex scenarios or steps in a workflow – for example, in a story to allow a user to log in to a service, you might initially split out dealing with anyone who has forgotten their password.

- Splitting out any different ways of achieving the same objective, such as inputting an address manually or using a lookup.

Both of these examples allow the individual stories to be 'shippable' – released and used in their own right, even if the functionality is enriched by later stories. This is sometimes known as a 'vertical' split of the story, because what is being delivered will cut through every layer of the app, from the database to the user interface. Stories can also be divided horizontally into technical components – for example work that needs to happen on the user interface versus within the data structure. It is generally preferable not to do this, as it means that a story cannot be released on its own. If you are under pressure to do this, you can always create sub-tasks for a story, so that different members of the team can work independently.[7]

Splitting stories is also a team activity. If the stories are split only by the product owner, they will often not reflect a sensible division of the actual work involved. However, it's also vital to retain the purpose behind the story – the original user need it was supposed

---

[7] For more examples of how to split stories see Agileforall.com (2022). Available from http://agileforall.com/wp-content/uploads/2009/10/Story-Splitting-Cheat-Sheet.pdf

to meet. Losing sight of this is a risk, because it may mean that what is eventually delivered doesn't add the value it was meant to. Referring back to your user story map should help to keep this in view.

Acceptance criteria

Once the team is clear on all of the scenarios that need to be covered by the story for it to be truly done, 'acceptance criteria' can be written. Acceptance criteria describe what will happen once the story is delivered. Usually, acceptance criteria for stories are written in the format:

- given (the context at the beginning of the scenario – for example, I am logged in);
- when (an event happens – for example, I select to log out);
- then (expected result – for example, my session ends and I am returned to the login screen).

Each story will likely have several acceptance criteria. Only once these are understood and refined can a story be planned into a development sprint and delivered by the team.

Definition of done

In addition to acceptance criteria, teams will often create a checklist of things that need to have happened for a story to be considered completed. While the acceptance criteria written will be different for every story, the definition of done will be common. Some common examples include sign-off by the product owner, code review completed and tests passed. A story is only considered completed when it has both met its acceptance criteria and satisfied the definition of done.

Other types of story

Not all user stories in your backlog will deliver something users would recognise as a new and exciting addition to your product. But they can still represent vitally important steps in the development process.

Technical or non-functional stories

Throughout development, there will be instances where the output of a task is a technical achievement, such as the setup of some infrastructure that is essential to enable future stories. Writing these ones is generally best left to the development team, because if you are not from a technical background it can be a struggle to make them meaningful. Their purpose can still be understood by asking what overall benefit they deliver to the product, or what would happen if they weren't completed. An answer like 'without this story we can't test any code' tends to help derive priorities!

In a similar way, it is quite possible to write non-functional considerations, such as scalability and maintainability, as user stories. In these cases, the **'As a'** part of the story may not describe an end user. It might be the chief technology officer (CTO), or the development lead – for example, you might say:

As a CTO

I want to store customers' addresses in our existing customer details database

So that my infrastructure team don't have to maintain two databases.

The advantage of this over keeping your non-functional requirements separate is two-fold. First, you can't forget about them, they're an integral part of development. Second, as with user needs, you remember why the work is important. In the example above, if the team took a shortcut and created a second data store, the CTO would be on the warpath and the product maintenance costs would increase!

Some non-functional considerations may need to be considered as part of every story – for example if every page must load within a specified time, or the content must be readable by accessibility software. In these situations, it is more usual to include these as an acceptance criterion in each story, or within the definition of done that applies to all stories. This makes sure these are applied throughout development and reduces the risk of discovering there's significant work left to do before they can be released.

Technical spikes
Sometimes, your team will be trying to achieve something that they haven't tried before. They might even be trying to do something no one has done before – and so they probably can't estimate with any real accuracy how long it is going to take. To handle this uncertainty, many teams use the concept of a technical spike. This is basically a set amount of time for research and investigation into how to go about achieving an outcome. It might include things like online research, trialling new tools, or setting up small experiments to see if a particular approach works or doesn't work.

Usually, these spikes are 'timeboxed' – allocated a specific time for exploration, after which progress is reviewed. Limiting the time spent on this helps to stop investigatory work taking over an entire development sprint. It also means that you can keep sense checking whether it is worth spending time on more investigation, particularly if the feature you are investigating isn't core to the success of the product. It's a good idea to set some clear outcomes of a spike so you have something valuable from the time spent. This might be a list of next steps you all agree on, or a review of each of the technical options you were evaluating to allow a decision to be made.

Estimating user stories

Before they can be taken into a sprint during sprint planning, stories have to be estimated, so that the right amount of work can be accepted. Teams do this in different ways. Some teams will just ask the developers and testers to give a simple time estimate in days to each story, adding stories up to the time available in the sprint (leaving some time free for ceremonies). Commonly, teams use a concept called 'story points'. This gives a number in the Fibonacci sequence (1, 2, 3, 5, 8 ...) to each story, with the larger numbers denoting more complexity. If a story has more than 8 or sometimes 13 points (this value will differ between teams), it normally needs splitting up.

Story points do not exactly correlate with time. They are just a score of how complex the development team thinks the work is. To arrive at a points value for each story, it's important that everyone who is going to work on it gives an estimate without being influenced by someone else in the team. To achieve this, teams play something called 'planning poker'. Some teams use actual cards with numbers on, or software to play this online, but the premise is the same. Everyone thinks up their own estimate and then reveals it at the same time to everyone else. If it's the same number, or very similar, then that's the estimate. If it's wildly different, someone has probably not quite understood what needs doing, so the team will discuss and clarify until a value is agreed.

Estimation is usually held as a separate session in each sprint. Sometimes it happens as part of sprint planning, although this can be time-consuming! If you are only estimating stories that will be brought into the next sprint, these estimates won't help to forecast future delivery dates, so assumptions will need to be made, for example using the number of stories in the backlog. It is best to acknowledge that these may prove to be incorrect once the stories are fully estimated. Only the development team will need to give estimates in the session itself, but product representation is important to assist with any misunderstandings about what needs to be done and why, as these may lead to differing estimates.

WHAT HAPPENS IN A SPRINT?

Assuming you have a Scrum master or delivery manager to work with (see below), you'll quickly see your calendar beginning to fill up with the following regular meetings. Is your presence at all of them essential? Over time, some of these sessions (sometimes called ceremonies) can start to blur together. Used well, they facilitate communication across the team. Having an understanding of what they should look like is important for spotting opportunities to improve the way the team works – and for managing your own time.

Sprint planning

This is where the team will decide what is brought up from the prioritised product backlog to be worked on in the next sprint, sometimes called the 'sprint backlog'. It's essential to make sure that the stories that deliver the most business value are worked on first (where technically possible). The backlog should be ordered so that if one story can't be started, the team can move to the next without much discussion. However, product representation is still fairly essential, both so you know exactly what is being tackled next and to resolve any questions on why some stories need to be worked on first.

After the first couple of sprints, the team will have an established 'velocity' – a number of story points that is achievable to complete in each sprint. As the team works together, the velocity will generally increase as communication improves. After five to six sprints it should settle down so you know the likely number of points that can be delivered in each sprint. This can be used to understand the number of sprints that will be needed to complete an iteration of the product. Understanding the development team's velocity is therefore essential in knowing whether or not your roadmap aims are achievable. Velocity can always be optimised. Common ways to do this include focusing on eliminating any wasted time in the sprint. Can you make any meetings more efficient, or reduce any manual test effort, perhaps through automation? If stories tend to cycle back through the stages of the workflow, a little more time spent on refinement may actually increase velocity. For example, stories may no longer be blocked because more information is needed, or tests will fail less often because more scenarios have been covered.

During sprint planning, one or more sprint goals will be decided on to summarise the aims of the sprint. These should be achievable and easy to measure, so they can be discussed in the sprint review. For example, a sprint goal might be that a user can do something they couldn't before, or that the team now fully understands how to resolve a technical challenge.

Stand ups

Most development teams start or end the day with a short, 15-minute or so session to focus on what has been done the previous day, what the focus is for that day and identify if any team members have blockers or issues that need resolving. Although it's not always essential for product managers to attend each day (and it might be impossible if you're looking across more than one development team – see below) doing so can help you to understand any issues affecting development that might impact velocity – and in turn, your roadmap.

Backlog refinement and backlog grooming

As stories get closer to development and near the top of the backlog, the team needs to make sure that they are ready to be taken into a sprint during sprint planning. As the 'three amigos' process described above is time-consuming, teams usually set some time aside to do this in each sprint, so there are always stories ready to work on in the next sprint planning session. This is usually an hour or two for each sprint and may involve the Scrum master and UX designer as well as the lead developer or tech lead, product person and QA (the three amigos). The UX designer checks that the screen designs are in line with the acceptance criteria and the Scrum master makes sure stories are ordered correctly, so there's nothing preventing the story from being worked on when it reaches the top of the backlog.

Sprint or iteration review

At the end of a sprint or a milestone, the team gathers to review progress so far, what was completed and whether or not the sprint goal was met. This is often held directly before sprint planning for the subsequent sprint and is used to showcase the work of the team.

Usually, this is combined with a 'show and tell' or demo, where the work that has been finished can be reviewed with the product manager and sometimes a wider stakeholder group. Depending on the size of the group interested in viewing your demo, it can be wise to separate this from the sprint review. Having a product person present at the show and tell or sprint review is essential. It is your chance to see your product evolve through the development cycle, celebrate the work of the development team to date and double check that progress is in line with the overall roadmap.

Retrospective

Usually held at the end of each development iteration, this is a chance for the whole team to look back over the sprint and identify ways to improve the delivery process or the team culture. Just as getting rapid feedback is important in understanding how well the product is working for customers, it also helps to understand and improve how well the team is working together. The retrospective shouldn't just be a space to complain without any action being taken, but instead a place to discuss what isn't working so well and to make a plan together to resolve it. Having an insight into what's going well and not so well for the team can be vital for product managers in solving any issues before they start to impact that all important product launch date.

Release

Once a story has satisfied its acceptance criteria and met its definition of done, it can be released. Releases to production should be as frequent as possible, so that what has been developed can be used. Teams may release several times during a sprint, whenever something is ready, or they may wait until the end of the increment to push to live, if it is helpful to the business to prepare colleagues and customers in advance (see Figure 7.5).[8]

Figure 7.5 The life cycle of a user story

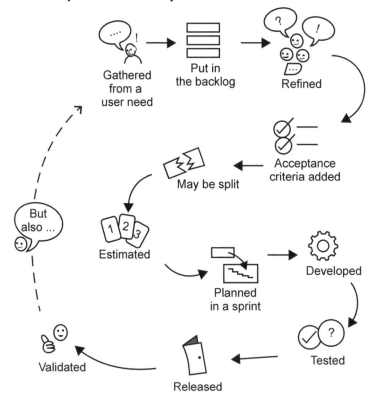

---

8   Release plans and how they differ from product roadmaps are covered in more depth in Chapter 4.

Once a story is released and being used, how effectively it meets a user's needs can then be measured. The outcome of this validation can inform the backlog priorities – for example you may discover a usability blocker that needs to be fixed quickly, or find that customers don't use a feature the way you expected. Ways of validating this are explored further in Chapter 6.

RE-PLATFORMING

Development is a continual process, so at some point during the life cycle of most digital products, the question of whether to 're-platform' – essentially, redevelop the product using more up-to-date technologies – will arise. The pressures of getting to market quickly with a first iteration of the product can mean that short-term decisions have to be made, which then become constraints when the team and the set of features they need to maintain are larger. For example, as a product scales, the original infrastructure may no longer be sufficient to handle the volume of users now expected, or the structure of the application may not support a larger group of developers working simultaneously. In order to ship new features, maintenance, documentation and infrastructure best practice may have been left by the wayside, leaving a build-up of issues – 'technical debt' – that now urgently need to be dealt with. Even if a product was built with scale in mind, new technologies are emerging all the time. They are likely to offer tempting benefits when compared with your current platform.

Signs that you should and shouldn't re-platform

The technical members in a product team generally tend to be most in favour of rewriting applications. They are the people who are most affected if the platform is creaking under the weight of additional usage and new features. When technical debt becomes overwhelming, it can be extremely hard to develop anything new, as most of the team's time is spent on fixing bugs, refactoring code, applying patches to out-of-date components or struggling with time-consuming and inefficient deployment processes. Ultimately, if you let this continue, you will reach a ceiling where you cannot safely add any more customers or features without adding some resilience into the system. Every release will soon become a tense waiting game while you wait to see whether what you have added has knocked the whole thing over or not.

If you are getting close to this point, it may be that bringing the platform you have up to date will take longer than re-building the whole thing. If a re-build will allow the business to grow, give you a chance to streamline the product and learn from its earlier iterations along the way, then it may be right to take the plunge and fully re-platform.

However, the suggestion that you re-platform can also arise because exploring new and emerging technologies is simply appealing. Learning how to manage and develop on an existing codebase takes time. If your development team are not the people who set everything up in the first place, which as your team grows, is likely, new people will bring their own preferences and previous experiences to the debate. It is worth probing to understand exactly why it's felt that a re-build is necessary. Is it simply disagreement or a lack of familiarity with technical choices made in the past? What would happen if you didn't do it? Which parts of the system would not be supportable? Re-building a product entirely is likely to be time-consuming and expensive. Does the time it will take justify the opportunity you will gain?

A middle way

Most of the time this will not be clear-cut. There are benefits of a complete re-build, but it could take a significant time – even years, during which time you will largely be recreating what you have already. This is likely to be unpalatable, even unfeasible, for the business. Then again, you can't keep piling features on to something that's not sustainable in the long term. A common compromise is to look at whether elements of the platform can be refactored or re-built, rather than the whole thing. Can you gradually replace the components that are the most out of date and at risk, re-building them in a sustainable way? A good approach is to look at the roadmap and identify which of the business goals it contains that could not be achieved without some element of a re-build. If you can tie the technical refactoring needed into the creation of some business value, explaining why it will take longer than expected, perhaps you can deliver some valuable change while gradually working your way out of the technical debt pile.

Making a decision

In the end, the decision on whether to re-build using new tools and approaches is a hard one to make. What exactly is right for each product will depend on the future roadmap, specific technical challenges and the balance of time and cost versus the future benefits. But even though it's never possible to exactly estimate the cost or feasibility of each approach, making a decision is important. Realistically, any level of refactoring – whether it's a gradual re-build or a complete replacement – is expensive and time-consuming. But so is indecision, as these problems only increase in severity over time. You might never know if you've picked the right path, but deciding means you'll be moving down it, away from ever-increasing technical debt and a product you can't sustain in the long term.

PRODUCT TEAM ROLES DURING DEVELOPMENT

As we've seen, the work of managing a digital product starts with strategic tasks, such as understanding competitors and value models. As soon as you are actually building and maintaining the product, it gets right down to the extremely detailed tasks – such as making sure each of the acceptance criteria in a user story can be used to correctly test the business logic. In very small teams, it is possible for one person to be across the whole product spectrum, managing the detail as well as the product positioning and strategy. However, the larger the product and the team get, the harder this becomes. Being on top of the amount of detail the team will need in each story in the backlog, as well as keeping an eye on the strategic horizon, can become an impossible task. You may find yourself rushing between either (1) developing the vision and strategy, or (2) grooming the backlog. But one tends to happen at the expense of the other. Either you have a great vision and strategy, but nothing that's understood well enough to work on right now, or you have the opposite – great detail on the next few sprints, but a creeping dread that in a few sprints' time, your development team will run out of stories to work on because you don't know where the product is going. To solve this problem, many teams split some of these responsibilities across multiple people, meaning that you may delegate some of the day-to-day work of grooming the backlog and attending the agile ceremonies to a product owner or sometimes a business analyst.

Product ownership

In the Scrum framework, where the term 'product owner' originates, this role is defined as being 'accountable for maximising the value of the product resulting from the work of the Scrum Team'.[9] You could be forgiven for thinking this sounds rather similar to product management. To add to the confusion, these terms are often used interchangeably, despite the fact that the product manager role is both broader than that of a product owner and predates the Scrum framework. It's also important to remember that while product owner is a role in Scrum, it isn't necessarily a job title. As a product manager, you may find yourself also doing the product owner role, or you may work with someone else who is. But their actual job title may be something totally different.

Product ownership versus product management
There are two definitions of the term 'product' in the English language. One meaning is the output of a process, the other is something that is created for sale or consumption. Broadly, product owners are concerned with the first meaning, making sure that what is coming out of the development process looks and behaves as expected. Product managers, by contrast, have a wider remit that also includes the second meaning – making sure that what is developed fits the market it is destined for, so it can generate value for the business.

Having a product owner who can stay close to the development team, ensuring that they are always taking the highest priority stories into the next sprint, can enable the product manager to continue developing the roadmap and the product vision throughout the development cycle. This split can be particularly useful in large teams or with complex products.

As you can see from Figure 7.6, many of the skills needed are very similar as you move from the detailed product activities towards the more strategic. Analysis, prioritisation and remaining focused on being the voice of the customer are always important. However, the scale is different. In organisations with larger or more complex digital offerings, where multiple development teams are needed to work on different elements of the overall product, it's quite common for each separate development team to have their own product owner. The product owner in turn may be supported by a product analyst or business analyst, who can further refine the backlog, split up user stories and support the development team with queries on the expected behaviour during each iteration. The role of the product manager then becomes more focused on aligning priorities across the different teams, checking that none of them are building the same thing and ensuring that the overall roadmap stays coherent.

---

9   Scrumguides.org (2020) *Scrum Guide | Scrum Guides*. Available from https://scrumguides.org/scrum-guide. html#product-owner

Figure 7.6 Product activities from the detailed to the strategic. Note: These are example activities, rather than an exhaustive list

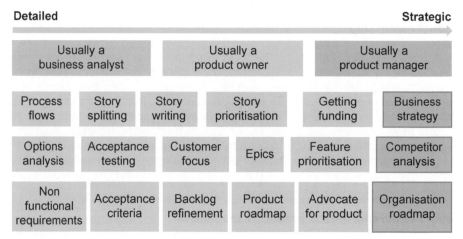

Handoffs between these roles

There are both benefits and pitfalls to working in this way. Usually, problems that occur stem from unclear roles and responsibilities between the product people in the team. As products scale, you may find that even if it was originally possible for one person to cover everything, it's now unmanageable. If you find yourself in the position of struggling to cover the whole spectrum of work, it is worth considering if there are other people in the team who could assist with some areas. Perhaps there is a QA analyst who could help to refine more of the acceptance criteria, or perhaps an additional person is needed to take on the product owner role. If there is already a product owner, perhaps the split of responsibility is not quite right between the product manager and product owner.

Some signs this may be the case:

1. **The product owner doesn't have time to support the development team.** The product owner needs to be available to the team, as their participation in the development process is key. Ownership is a powerful word. Sometimes, organisations appoint someone into the Scrum product owner role who likes the title, knows about the business and the market, but who has another 'day job' – meaning they do not have time to actually be present enough to the team. This can also happen if the product manager is trying to cover too much of the spectrum above (Figure 7.6). This starves the team of the decisions they need to move forward, leading to unsuccessful sprint planning sessions and unclear sprint goals.

2. **'Proxy' product owners.** In this situation, the product owner isn't pressed for time – they are instead not given the ownership the role requires. The development team needs timely decisions about what to prioritise in the next sprint, or how a particular feature should behave. But the product owner has to go and check first with the product manager – or the lead stakeholder, or the CEO – basically anyone else who feels it should be their decision, but isn't in the room. This again slows the team down, leading to blockers and added time and development cost.

WORKING WITH SCRUM MASTERS OR DELIVERY MANAGERS

As a product manager it is ordinarily not your role to make sure that all of the agile ceremonies and sessions discussed run smoothly, or to help unblock any technical issues the team comes across with environments or deployment pipelines. Thankfully, making sure the development team operates with maximum efficiency falls to the delivery manager or Scrum master, as this role is known in the Scrum framework. While product management is mostly about ensuring that the team moves in the right direction, delivery management aims to move as fast as possible, removing any impediments to the team's progress. While a delivery manager will take direction on prioritisation and the product vision from the product manager, they will help to manage and refine the backlog, ensuring that the team has enough 'build ready' stories to keep moving. They will also recommend improvements to product people to help keep the team efficient, for example if user stories need to be broken down further or acceptance criteria made more detailed.

Very occasionally, organisations (usually those that are euphemistically 'on a journey' towards adopting agile ways of working) try to combine this very different and extremely vital role with that of the product owner or even the product manager. This combination of responsibilities is uncomfortable and makes it very hard to succeed at either role. Trying to be responsible for both quality and delivery, aside from being too much work for one person, tends to lead to people fighting themselves as they try to go faster while not compromising on any scope or functionality. Most people don't enjoy this kind of internal conflict, so inevitably only one of speed versus quality will win – and the team will either deliver something rapidly but lose sight of customer needs, or create something that meets customer needs but takes so long to get to market that it may not be viable. Highlighting this gap – and the potential impact on the product – is usually the best way to resolve this issue before it compromises the development process.

At their heart, these problems are either caused by gaps in the support product people are providing to the development team, or by overlaps, where it's not clear who is doing what. Usually, a conversation can be had about drawing a more effective line between these responsibilities, so decisions can be made faster, enabling a smoother development process. As with any conversation about job roles, this can be divisive. All teams are different, so what works well in one organisation may not be the right fit for another. Generally, as explored in Chapter 8, focusing on the outcome for the product should help to move this beyond individual perspectives. As Roman Pichler notes when discussing this topic, what people do matters more than what they are called: 'My hope is that we will move past the divisive product manager-product owner debate and stop labelling people.'[10]

10 Roman Pichler (2017) 'Product manager vs product owner'. Roman Pichler. Available from www.romanpichler.com/blog/product-manager-vs-product-owner/

KEY TAKEAWAYS

- Balance time spent exploring new features and conducting technical investigations with developing the essential features of your roadmap.

- Expect your team velocity to stabilise and become consistent over time, as the team continues to improve development processes and ways of working.

- Consider if you have the right division of responsibilities between the product people on the team, whether there is just one person or several.

8   MANAGING FOR RESULTS

Sallie Godwin

All products are built by people. Whether the product succeeds or fails is dependent on the team behind it, whether they have the right blend of skills and how well they work together. To succeed, they will need to constantly compromise. Can they construct something that meets its business aims, delivers a great user experience and is technically feasible? Even if they're the ideal size for a product team, according to Jeff Bezos, will they still want to share those two pizzas at the end?[1] By examining the different disciplines that make up the team and their different motivations, this chapter explores the common conflicts that arise within product teams, when they happen and why, including techniques for resolving them. The later part of the chapter discusses balancing the many demands on a product manager's time in ensuring the success of both the team and the product.

Most digital product teams are 'cross-functional'. This means they are composed of specialists in different disciplines, who often think and communicate in very different ways. As a product manager, while you will be able to influence who is on your product team, most of the time you will not have complete control over who is in it. In larger companies, you may be entirely reliant on chapter heads or community of practice leads to recommend or recruit each specialist role. You may also take over an existing product team from another product manager, or join a team that has not previously had a product manager role. Most of the time, you need to work with the team you're in and make it as effective as possible, so you can focus on solving customer problems together.

As the team is ordinarily a team of peers, used to excelling in their own field, traditional management techniques, which rely on a more rigid hierarchy, are not much use. Telling people what they should do, even if you explain why, is unlikely to be very helpful. Whatever your background, it's also unlikely that you will come to product management having experienced every role in the product team. Most of the time, someone else will be better informed than you about the details of the code, the experience design, the infrastructure and so on. Rather than pointing out a direction and expecting your team to follow, you will likely find yourself managing by influence.

---

1   'We try to create teams that are no larger than can be fed by two pizzas', said Bezos. 'We call that the two-pizza team rule.' Jeff Bezos (no date) 'Two pizza teams'. Available from https://docs.aws.amazon.com/whitepapers/latest/introduction-devops-aws/two-pizza-teams.html

MANAGING BY INFLUENCE

Product managers are often referred to as generalists in a world of specialists.[2] This might seem like a disadvantage. Most product managers will, at some stage, find themselves baffled by technical detail, or accidentally frighten a UX designer with a poorly drawn whiteboard scribble. The phrase 'Jack of all trades, master of none' hovers over all of our heads.

However, having an understanding of each discipline, but not belonging within any of them, also conveys an advantage. Understanding the skills and capabilities each member of the team must have to succeed in their area is essential in resolving the myriad conflicts that naturally form part of the product development process. It gives you a degree of impartiality, a neutral place to stand from which you can observe the action. From here, you are well placed to understand your team's different perspectives and motivations and navigate a path through them.

Understanding people's motivation

Most people (we have all met the exceptions) do not turn up at the start of the work day focused on starting a conflict with their co-workers. Product teams also have the advantage of a common aim – the success of their product. So if and when conflict arises, it's usually because of conflicting motivations, or because the team members don't have everything they need to successfully grapple with the obstacles they are facing. Understanding your team's motivations, fears and blockers is key to managing your way to a successful team – and product.

As we have seen, successful teams need to compromise. But this is particularly hard to achieve in product teams, because of the motivations of the people they contain.

In thinking about this, it's useful to consider the context of the minimum viable product team, which Rei Inamoto described as 'only needing three people: a Hipster, a Hacker, and a Hustler'.[3] In essence, the 'Hacker' is the person who builds it, the 'Hipster' makes it cool and appealing to users, and the 'Hustler' sells it to them. Although most product teams will have more than three people, this does provide an accurate description of the general balance of skills you will find in most of them.

As we have seen, the motivations of these different skill sets can bring them into conflict. Unless kept in balance, they have a tendency to pull in different directions. Eventually, if left to their own devices, the Hackers will retreat into a cave and invent something groundbreaking, but that doesn't solve any problems for people – a science project. The Hipsters will create something utterly awesome looking, but that also doesn't solve any problems – an art project. In turn, the Hustlers will be busy selling people something that sounds like it solves all their problems, but either doesn't exist, can't be built or can't be used – accidental vapourware.

2   D. Epstein (2020) *Range: How Generalists Triumph in a Specialized World.* S. L.: Riverhead Books. Available from www.amazon.co.uk/Range-Generalists-Triumph-Specialized-World/dp/1509843493

3   A. Ellwood (2012) *The Dream Team: Hipster, Hacker, and Hustler.* Forbes. Available from www.forbes.com/sites/andyellwood/2012/08/22/the-dream-team-hipster-hacker-and-hustler/?sh=367e72a22c85

Of course, in doing this, each of them will be excelling in their field. The Hipsters will win the respect of other Hipsters, the Hackers of other Hackers, and so on. But they will be working as individuals, not as a team. They might win the approval of their peers, but the product itself will not meet its goals or have any use in the real world (see Figure 8.1).

Figure 8.1 Hipster, Hacker, Hustler[4]

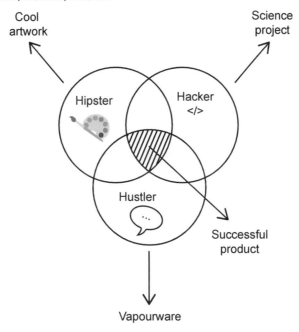

The role of the product manager is to keep these forces in balance with one another. What is eventually designed, built and sold must land in that golden middle space.

Let's take a closer look at some examples of common conflicts that arise within and around product teams and examine the motivations that lead to them.

1. The user experience team have designed a beautiful interface, but it's not technically feasible for the development team to implement.

   This is a real classic and tends to appear in some form in the life cycle of every digital product. Usually, the user experience team will have some very solid logic behind their design. This might be user research, established UX best practice or the results of A/B testing showing that their proposal does really drive more customers to do what you would like them to do, such as buying something.

   In their turn, the development team will have some extremely solid reasons why that just can't happen. Perhaps it's not possible in the current infrastructure or will just take more time to implement, and therefore cost more, than it would ever deliver in terms of user experience benefits.

4 M. Eriksson (2011) 'What, exactly, is a product manager?' Mind the Product. Available from https://www.mindtheproduct.com/what-exactly-is-a-product-manager/

Having listened carefully to each perspective, if we were to compare their motivations side by side, they might look something like Table 8.1.

Table 8.1 Comparing the different motivations of design and development

UX motivations	Development motivations
• Make sure the product provides the best experience	• Ship a working product or product iteration
• Delight the user	• Reduce technical debt so the product can be maintained
• Retain the respect of other UX professionals	• Retain the respect of other development professionals

The last point is the most important in understanding where conflict may arise. It will apply to every member of the product team. This is particularly true in organisations with a matrix structure, where people in your team are probably also part of a community of practice, guild or other network of people with the same specialism. As well as being members of your product team, your developers will also be members of the organisation's development practice and your designers part of the design practice, and so on. This sort of model allows for cross-product team training and consistency in ways of working, meaning members of each discipline can learn from one another and support one another when they need to. But it also means that everyone in your product team also belongs to – and has responsibilities to – another group of people in your organisation. This can create tension, as individuals try to navigate between recognised best practice for their particular discipline and what is actually the right thing for a specific product at a given point in time.

As a product manager your role is to become an expert in representing the views of one group to another and brokering a compromise. And this gives you a special power. By taking responsibility for the decision, you can absolve the members of your team from needing to justify it to themselves, or other experts in their field. This leaves you free to work out which path is more likely to translate into measurable improvement for the product. Perhaps there are elements of the design that just can't be compromised on, so are worth additional development time and cost. Or maybe some of the design features will need to wait for a later release, when they can be implemented. Either way, each of your experts can make their recommendation, confident in the knowledge that they've represented their discipline effectively, **even if their recommendation isn't implemented this time**.

Once this is acknowledged, the conversation gets easier. It's less about the importance or value of any individual or discipline over another and more focused on the benefits to the product.

2. The sales team need to launch – but compliance/legal/operations don't want to take any risk.

In this example, the conflict is similar, but instead it involves those outside the immediate product team, who have to accept some risk associated with the product. For example, this might be a compliance team, who have to be sure that all legislative and regulatory requirements are met. It may also be the team responsible for handling customer support, who will know that launching something too soon will drive additional issues and queries, adding to their workload.

In this example, the motivations may look something like Table 8.2.

Table 8.2 Comparing the different motivations of sales and operations

Sales team motivations	Operational/support team
• Ship a working product or product iteration	• Product stays live post-launch
• Meet deadlines	• Demonstrate we've reduced or are not taking any additional risk
• Meet stakeholder/user expectations	• Keep our issue/support ticket numbers stable
	• Avoid professional embarrassment/compliance fines/prison sentences, etc.

This time, some of the specialists are outside the product team – but they're still specialists. As in the previous example, their fears have a firm basis in reality. While it might be the role of the sales team to do everything they can to get the product ready to exhibit at the next trade show, it's the role of the operations team to make sure that once people have bought it, their queries and support requests can be handled. Does the risk of missing out on sales justify the risk of a botched launch? Does the likelihood of an operational failure justify a softer launch?

In essence, both of these examples are essentially the same dilemma: we're all experts in our own fields, so who do we listen to? The simple answer might seem to be the product manager, but the reality is a bit more nuanced.

Good product managers are facilitators. They are curious about the motivations and fears of the people in the product team, as well as those outside it. They allow team members to put their individual concerns aside and listen to one another. They are continually excited about the product's potential, allowing the team to reach a consensus on the best means of realising it.

Balanced teams make balanced decisions

In some scenarios, achieving this balance is made more difficult by the shape of the team itself. For example, if you have far more 'Hipsters' than 'Hackers', the likelihood of the design becoming too complex to implement may increase. Alternatively, if your team has some very outgoing personalities and some more introverted ones, some viewpoints may be expressed more powerfully, meaning the decisions skew towards them. Techniques that ensure that everyone has a chance to speak can help if this is the case. Some common ideas include asking everyone to contribute their thoughts on sticky notes, or passing an object, like a beanbag, around the team to denote whose turn it is to speak, minimising interruptions.

Some signs the team is suffering from a lack of balance are:

- The same type of information keeps being missed out from decisions, for example you've made some technical choices without understanding the impact on the customer experience, or vice versa.

- Tasks get stuck at the same point in your delivery process. All the tickets are assigned to one or two members of the team, or everything has become blocked at the same stage in your workflow.

Because impartiality is at the core of product management, it's important to be aware of your own bias. Check you are not leaning towards the perspectives of people you have worked with before, or who may resemble you in some way, such as in their communication style or background. Similarly, it's important to make sure you are not giving less focus to the views of people that don't resemble you. If you came to product management from another discipline, you may naturally tend towards a deeper sympathy with any constraints or blockers affecting this area because you will often have found yourself making similar arguments in the past.

One of the most obvious ways to restore balance is to add people to the team. However, this won't always be achievable. Even if it is possible, any case for change will need to clearly show the impact on the team and the product. Be creative; for example, if you have more user experience design than development time available, perhaps some design effort might be well spent on helping another area of the business, mentoring someone in another team, shouting about your great work at a conference or helping you to bring some design finesse to presenting your roadmap.

Diverse and inclusive teams are strong teams

Because all products are designed to be used by people, product teams that do not contain people with a range of perspectives and characteristics, or are not inclusive enough to listen to them, can miss important insights. There are numerous examples of products that have failed to identify important jobs to be done because the team itself did not contain anybody who needed to do those things, or where a potential customer segment was ignored because nobody in the team happened to fall into it. Even if the team itself is diverse, just as with making balanced decisions, it is still important to ensure that everyone's perspective can be heard. If your team is multilingual, this will need to be considered when communicating, for example by avoiding colloquialisms that may not be understood, or allowing those with less confidence in their language skills to contribute to discussion via email or messaging.

I once found myself discussing improvements to a banking application that allowed customers to update their personal details. Our complaints data showed that changing your name was the most complex and time-consuming process for customers, and I thought this made it a great candidate for allowing people to do this on the app. However, on presenting this to the product team and the senior stakeholder group (all male), this was met with blank looks. Why would anyone change their name? No one in the room had ever needed to. What a strange thing to prioritise, they thought.

Had the team had a more diverse range of perspectives, a more balanced decision on where to place that feature on the roadmap might have been made.

How to be wrong in a helpful way – or creating a supportive team culture

Naturally, responsibility for navigating the team – and the product – through this minefield of compromises and their potential consequences is not without risk. However well you evaluate priorities, weigh up options, listen to users and use data to inform your decisions, you will sometimes just be wrong. No one can see the future, and each judgement call is made with the information available at the time. It's inevitable that being wrong happens to all product managers and so learning from failure is an important part of the role. This means most product managers are comfortable with ambiguity, making decisions and being wrong in a constructive way that can move the product forward.

Being wrong in a helpful way tends to look something like this:

Make mistake >>> admit mistake >>> learn from it >>> tell everyone about what you learned so they do the same with their own mistakes

Feeling comfortable with being wrong in this way requires a supportive team culture, where it's not a disaster if you take a risk or a gamble and it doesn't pay off, where it's understood that mistakes are an important part of the learning process. This concept is sometimes referred to as 'psychological safety', originally defined by William Khan *as* 'being able to show and employ one's self without fear of negative consequences of self-image, status or career'.[5]

Practically, this might mean:

- taking the time to discuss as a group when things go wrong – such as after a production incident – and considering what everyone can do to contribute to a better outcome next time;
- making sure that questions about, or challenges to, the way the team normally operates (for example, from new team members) are welcomed and considered.

Without this culture, it's very hard to take risks, to innovate or to explore the new, all of which are essential in developing digital products. But as a product team, you will usually exist within a company with its own culture, which often will be very different. This is particularly true if the firm started in the offline world and has now begun

---

5   William A. Kahn (1990) 'Psychological conditions of personal engagement and disengagement at work'. *Academy of Management Journal*, 33 (4). 692–724.

creating digital products. Being wrong (or seeming to be wrong) in a large organisation can start to feel more like this:

> Make mistake >>> feel afraid to admit it >>> try to hide it >>> fail >>> try to justify why you hid it >>> fail >>> become ashamed >>> be very afraid to make any mistake ever again >>> transmit your fear to everyone around you

Human behaviour is contagious

Changing this sort of behaviour from within an organisation can look like a mammoth task. Particularly in established organisations, you will tend to hear things like:

- 'It's always been this way.'
- 'We tried that a few years back, it might work elsewhere but it doesn't work here.'
- 'It's the senior management's fault.'

All of these are myths. Team culture starts from within the team. It is also quite possible to have a radically different culture within your team than is demonstrated in the rest of the organisation. All it really requires are a few people committed to openness, sharing what has and hasn't worked, and continually trying to become better at what they do. Product managers are ideally placed to start this, because the nature of the role requires you to be comfortable with owning decisions, taking calculated risks and talking about the possibility of failure. Once people have seen you doing this, their own fear of doing the same thing will begin to dissipate. Team retrospectives are an excellent way to start and to showcase this kind of behaviour. What happens in a retrospective is explored in more detail in the previous chapter.

Because human behaviour is contagious, if enough people begin to do something, it can start to spread from small beginnings exponentially, until it has reached far beyond the original source. Once your team is seen as a good place in which to work, it will be easier for others to begin to work in the same way. Creating a supportive environment in your product team will not just help you to deliver a better product, it will make the process of delivery easier as your stakeholders become more familiar with ambiguity and experimentation. They may even begin to adopt these practices themselves.

Some promising signs that your product team culture is spreading:

- you see other teams have started standing around whiteboards;
- the volume of the discussion in the office has gone up significantly;
- all the sticky notes have mysteriously vanished from your stationery cupboard;
- people you don't know have started contacting you about licences for collaboration software.

MANAGING YOUR OWN TIME

As we've seen, being a product manager is to find yourself pulled in different directions. In order to negotiate successfully between conflicting perspectives, it helps to stay calm and rational – but at times when everyone around you is furiously disagreeing, this can feel rather hard to achieve!

As explored in the previous chapter, product managers can find themselves needing to simultaneously take charge of the product goals and strategy, as well as considering the lower-level detail of how particular epics and stories are actually implemented. This can lead to a huge amount of context switching, between very high-level aims and very granular discussions. It can feel like you are constantly taking part in a kind of mental Olympics, while those around you are free to focus on just one area.

At points, the demands on your time can begin to feel overwhelming. Brabban and Turkington's Stress Bucket Model is a good way of visualising this, to help avoid burnout and maintain a sense of calm.[6] In essence, it asks you to picture a bucket slowly filling up as you get more stressed. The taps filling the bucket are all of the things that add to your workload. For product managers, this might look a bit like Figure 8.2.[7]

Figure 8.2 The bucket model

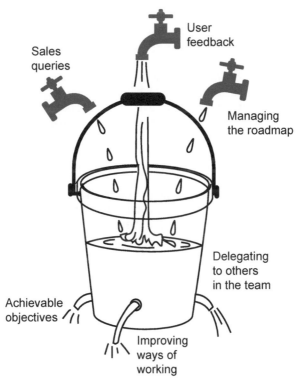

Sales queries

User feedback

Managing the roadmap

Delegating to others in the team

Achievable objectives

Improving ways of working

---

6   A. Brabban and D. Turkington (2002) 'The search for meaning: detecting congruence between life events, underlying schema and psychotic symptoms'. In A.P. Morrison (ed.) *A Casebook of Cognitive Therapy for Psychosis*. New York: Brunner-Routledge. 59–75.

7   Chris Smith provides an example of this model for tech leads. C. Smith (2022) *The Taps Model: A tool to explore cognitive overload*. Available from https://medium.com/ingeniouslysimple/the-taps-model-a-tool-to-explore-cognitive-overload-f2ad72c2f208

Different things work for different people, so the inputs and outputs will be different for everyone. As with pretty much anything in product management, experimentation is key to finding out what helps to maintain a comfortable level of cognitive load. Some product managers only check email at certain times of the day, rigorously ringfence break times or insist on 'no-meeting Fridays' to catch up on thinking time and documentation. Most connectivity apps such as Slack, Teams and so on, allow you to set times of the day when notifications can be silenced. This can be particularly helpful if you are working with a geographically disparate team, where people are likely to be working at different times of the day and night.

When there is a lot going on, it can feel counterintuitive to say no to meetings or ringfence time for quiet work. Even if you regularly set aside time, it takes mental discipline to actually use it and not schedule meetings during these periods. As so much of product management requires nuanced decision making and the balancing of different, conflicting perspectives, it can be impossible to do this well if your stress bucket reaches overflow point. Helping yourself to avoid overload helps the team – and, in the long run, the product.

Accidental team parent syndrome

As product managers are by nature problem solvers, your team's natural admiration of your ability to fix absolutely anything can sometimes add to the pressures on your time. If some of the problems you are starting to solve are less product problems and more general administrative or organisational issues – or you've also become the team agony aunt, counsellor or shoulder to cry on – then you may have become an 'accidental team parent'. Of course it's great to be a supportive colleague, but if you're the person in the team everyone has a coffee with when they need some calm and balanced advice, it can start to feel like a second full-time job.

Some practical tips if you find yourself in this situation:

- Make a list of practical places people can get help (the IT service desk number, for example, or the phone number for the building reception) and pin it somewhere easy to access like the team Slack channel or the team's whiteboard.
- Buddy people up: particularly with new starters, nominate someone in the team to help with any queries, so they don't get used to asking you by default.
- Just don't do it: gently explain that you don't have time for a coffee right now but perhaps someone else will.

Managing remote teams

Managing through influence in remote teams can be even more challenging than in person. It takes time to build trust with those around you – usually even more time if you are collaborating over video conferencing software. Spending a lot of time on video calls is also exhausting, as it takes more concentration to communicate and listen to one another when online. Studies have shown that delays in the call transmission can affect relationships negatively, as people can perceive the slowness in response as being caused by unfriendliness or lack of focus.[8] While it is tempting to have a lot of calls as you try to mimic the experience of being in the office, this can actually reduce team effectiveness. But working remotely also makes it easy for misunderstandings to spread, or for the team to start working in silos. This is particularly risky in product teams where, as we have seen, without seamless communication and facilitation it is easy for the different areas of specialism to pull in different directions.

Where it is difficult for everyone to participate at the same time, using asynchronous communication can help to build consensus without the whole team continually staring at one another over cyberspace. This is the opposite of synchronous communication, such as a conversation or a web chat. Essentially, this means setting up collaboration spaces or processes that allow people to contribute ideas over a set period of time, where they might not be able to respond immediately. Examples of this include:

- setting up a shared document for people to contribute to, as and when they want;
- uploading a video of an explanation of how to do something;
- using a virtual whiteboard to build up design ideas/collect feedback;
- using public channels on Teams or Slack rather than small group chats, so others can add to or learn from the messages.

These types of ways of working encourage transparency and allow the members of your team to dip in and out of conversations relevant to them. It's almost like overhearing colleagues talking in the office. However, it's important to discuss openly as a team what needs to be done synchronously and what not. The grid shown in Figure 8.3 can help to facilitate these conversations so you don't spend all your time in meetings – or end up never speaking to your team.

Getting in or out of the building

From time to time, changing the environment you are working in can really help the team to work together more effectively. If you're used to working in the same office, this may mean getting out of the building. For remote teams, this could quite easily be the opposite – all being in the building at the same time can have a very similar effect.

During design or ideation phases or for team retrospectives, it can be especially valuable to spend some time brainstorming in a new or different location. Looking at a different backdrop can give people permission to challenge the status quo, and bring a sense of energy that helps with idea generation or problem solving. You don't have to wait for an expensive corporate away day to achieve this. Even simply going for a walk around the office can lead to new ideas, as it gives some space to mull over different concepts and put them together in different ways.

---

8   K. Shoenberg, A. Raake and J. Koeppe (2014) 'Why are you so slow? – Misattribution of transmission delay to attributes of the conversation partner at the far-end.' *International Journal of Human-Computer Studies*, 72 (5). Available from www.sciencedirect.com/science/article/abs/pii/S1071581914000287

Figure 8.3 The time and place grid[9]

Same time and place	Different time but same place
• In-person meeting • In-person whiteboard session	• Physical whiteboard
Same time but different place	**Different time and place**

• Video call
• Phone call
• Instant messaging
• Online whiteboard
  (used in a video call)
	• Email
	• Recorded video
	• Shared document
	• Virtual whiteboard
	  (without an accompanying
	  video call!)

Team get-togethers are often used as a celebration when things have gone well – for example after a launch, or the release of a new feature. But getting outside the building can also be essential if things have gone particularly badly. When the senior management has just ripped up the roadmap, pulled the funding for the next release or you've had some devastating but accurate user feedback about a key feature, it can actually be more productive to down tools than carry on. If the rest of the day is likely to be spent in increasing doom-spirals of discussions that end up with team members blaming one another, it may be better to take the whole product team for coffee/a drink/ out to lunch or for a walk in the park. This forces a stop. It also introduces some wider perspective, because it forces you all to look at things outside your immediate product problems, so when you return it can make it easier to focus on what does actually need to be done next. Even if you are working entirely remotely, you could:

- go on a walk together – but in different locations, connected by a video call or just by sending pictures of favourite/nearby locations;

- play an online game together – online versions of popular games like Pictionary and Battleships exist in free multiplayer versions, for example.

9   Johansen Inst.eecs.berkeley.edu (1988) 'Johansen's time/space grid'. Available from https://inst.eecs.berkeley.edu/~eecsba1/sp97/reports/eecsba1d/collab-2/sld009.htm and P. Pullen (2016) *Virtual Leadership: Practical Strategies for Success with Remote or Hybrid Work and Teams.* London: Kogan Page, p. 96.

FINDING AND STARTING PRODUCT COMMUNITIES

Sometimes, standing in the middle ground and making those around you compromise can feel like a lonely place to be. This is especially true if you work in a small organisation and you are the only (or one of the only) product managers there. If this is the case, it's helpful to look for groups outside your organisation where you will be able to meet, learn from and discuss product problems with other people with the same specialism as you.

Good places to start looking outside your company include:

- Agile and product meetup groups – these are often advertised on networking sites or on Meetup.com or Eventbrite or similar.
- Product conferences.
- People you have worked with in the past. Because people come into product management from a number of different backgrounds, there's a good chance that some of the people you already know are now product managers – maybe they would like to grab a coffee and compare experiences.
- If you are a nervous or reluctant networker, interest and inclusion groups can be a friendly and informal place to begin, because they exist to broaden participation.

Starting a community of practice

You can also look for different groups within your own organisation and try to form your own community of practice. Even if there are no product managers or only very few, there may be people in other related roles such as business analysis and UX design, or who are generally interested in learning more about product management techniques.

These communities of practice can help you and your organisation in a number of ways. In organisations that have a number of different business areas, they can be a great way of breaking down silos and finding out what other parts of the business are up to. You might even gather information that informs your own roadmap. Similarly, they are a good place to bring and share problems – other people may have experienced something similar before, know someone who can help or have some insight that helps you unblock things. Finally, they can be a great place to invite stakeholders along to. If you're working with people who struggle with concepts like prioritisation, giving them the chance to see inside your world can help them to understand more about why you work the way you do, as well as reassuring them that these new ideas are working well in other teams and organisations.

Getting up and running

So that may all sound very helpful, but how do you get a community of practice off the ground? And once it's lifted off, how do you keep it flying? Most successful groups start a bit like this:

1. Check what already exists: just in case someone has simultaneously had the same idea. Check places like intranets, wiki pages and chat channels for clues – this can also help with step number 2.

2. Find like-minded people: start the conversation in the smallest way you can – this could just be a post in a chat channel, a poster on a noticeboard, an all staff email and so on.

3. Do not wait for someone else to start it: they are probably waiting for you to start it!

4. Meet informally at first and agree some simple guidelines for the community.

Initial guidelines for an example community of practice might look a bit like Figure 8.4.[10]

Figure 8.4 Community guidelines

Community name Something easy to understand for others	Community rhythm How often, when and where will you meet? When will your first meeting be?
Community members Who should join the community? What are their job role(s), concerns, passions or interests?	Community leaders/core community members Who are the people taking a role in running the community and keeping members motivated and coordinated? What will they each be doing?
Community purpose Why does the community exist? What problems does it solve, and for whom?	Community goals What does success look like for the community, what would you like to look back and celebrate in a year, what will you do first to get there?

5. Keep going! This is by far the hardest part of all. Lots of communities start out with an initial burst of enthusiasm, but then the novelty wears off, everyone gets busy and you will find attendance will inevitably drop off after a few months. This is a great time for a social event to reinvigorate things, or a brainstorming session on what members would find more useful for future sessions. Even if your community has a hiatus, people and organisations do change over time, so it is worth trying again even if it wasn't successful the first time around.

10 Community of practice kick-off canvas © Emily Webber. Available from hellotacit.com/community-of-practice-kick-off-canvas

KEY TAKEAWAYS

- Find the root cause of any conflicts by understanding people's motivation – and help your team move beyond their individual disciplines to collectively find the right direction for the product.

- Be there for your team by making sure you have time to remain calm yourself.

- Diverse and inclusive teams tend to be more successful (and more fun to work in).

- Investing time in finding and building product communities is rewarding – they can provide a great source of inspiration and support.

RECOMMENDED READING

Cadle, J., Paul, D., Hunsley, J., Reed, A., Beckham, D. and Turner, P. (2021) *Business Analysis Techniques: 123 Essential Tools for Success*. Swindon: BCS Publishing.

Christensen, C. M., Hall, T., Dillon, K. and Duncan, D. S. (2016) *Competing Against Luck: The Story of Innovation and Customer Choice*. First edition. New York: HarperBusiness, an imprint of HarperCollins Publishers.

Fraser, H. M. A. (2019) *Design Works: A Guide to Creating and Sustaining Value through Business Design*. Revised and Expanded edition. Toronto: University of Toronto Press.

Gray, D., Brown, S. and Macanufo, J. (2010) *Gamestorming: A Playbook for Innovators, Rulebreakers, and Changemakers*. Cambridge: O'Reilly Media, Inc.

Haines, S. (2021) *The Product Manager's Desk Reference*. Third edition. New York: McGraw Hill.

Hamel, G. and Prahalad, C. K. (1986) *Competing for the Future*. Boston: Harvard Business Review Press.

Hammond, J. S., Keeney, R. L. and Raiffa, H. (2015) *Smart Choices: A Practical Guide to Making Better Decisions*. Boston: Harvard Business Review Press.

Kalbach, J. (2021) *Mapping Experiences: A Complete Guide to Creating Value through Journeys, Blueprints, and Diagrams*. Second Edition. Sebastopol: O'Reilly Media.

Kim, G., Behr, K. and Spafford, G. (2018) *The Phoenix Project: A Novel About It, Devops, and Helping Your Business Win*. Portland, OR: IT Revolution.

Kim, W. C. and Mauborgne, R. (2015) *Blue Ocean Strategy: How to Create Uncontested Market Space and Make the Competition Irrelevant*. Expanded edition. Boston: Harvard Business Review Press.

Knapp, J., Zeratsky, J. and Kowitz, B. (2016) *Sprint: How to Solve Big Problems and Test New Ideas in Just Five Days*. New York: Simon & Schuster.

Lafley, A. G. and Martin, R. L. (2013) *Playing to Win: How Strategy Really Works*. Boston: Harvard Business Press.

Lombardo, C. T., McCarthy, B., Ryan, E. and Connors, M. (2018) *Product Roadmaps Relaunched*. Sebastopol: O'Reilly Media.

Magretta, J. (2012) *Understanding Michael Porter: The Essential Guide to Competition and Strategy*. Boston: Harvard Business Review Press.

Olsen, D. (2015) *The Lean Product Playbook: How to Innovate with Minimum Viable Products and Rapid Customer Feedback*. New York: Wiley.

Osterwalder, A., Pigneur, Y. and Clark, T. (2010) *Business Model Generation: A Handbook for Visionaries, Game Changers, and Challengers*. Hoboken: Wiley.

Osterwalder, A., Pigneur, Y., Gregory B. and Smith, A. (2014) *Value Proposition Design: How to Create Products and Services Customers Want*. Hoboken: Wiley.

Perri, M. (2019) *Escaping the Build Trap: How Effective Product Management Creates Real Value*. First edition. Sebastopol: O'Reilly Media.

Pink, D. H. (2011) *Drive: The Surprising Truth About What Motivates Us*. New York: Riverhead Books.

Reinertsen, D. G. (ed.) (2009) *The Principles of Product Development Flow: Second Generation Lean Product Development*. Redondo Beach: Celeritas.

Ries, E. (2011) *The Lean Startup: How Today's Entrepreneurs Use Continuous Innovation to Create Radically Successful Businesses*. New York: Crown Business.

Rumelt, R. (2011) *Good Strategy, Bad Strategy: The Difference and Why It Matters*. New York: Currency.

Stickdorn, M. and Schneider, J. (2012) *This is Service Design Thinking: Basics, Tools, Cases*. Amsterdam: BIS Publishing.

Stickdorn, M., Hormess, M. E., Lawrence, A. and Schneider, J. (2018) *This Is Service Design Methods: A Companion to This Is Service Design Doing*. Sebastopol: O'Reilly Media.

Sutton, R. I. (2012) *Good Boss, Bad Boss: How to be the Best – and Learn from the Worst*. New York: Business Plus.

Wodtke, C. (2021) *Radical Focus: Achieving Your Most Important Goals with Objectives and Key Results*. Palo Alto: Cucina Media, LLC.

GLOSSARY

Acceptance criteria: A testable set of requirements that must be met for a piece of software development work to be considered completed.

Backlog: A repository of all product work that needs to be done in the future.

Basic attribute: In Kano analysis, a product attribute that must be present for a product to be considered acceptable, but which doesn't increase the product's desirability once it meets an acceptable level. Also called 'must-have' attributes.

Beneficiary: A person outside your enterprise who receives value from your products or services, but who does not use them.

Business capability: A capability common to all enterprises with a similar business model, typically mapped to processes and technology as part of a business architecture. Also known as an operational capability.

Business model: A definition of how an enterprise creates and captures value.

Business-to-business (B2B): A product intended to be sold to other businesses.

Business-to-consumer (B2C): A product intended to be sold in the general marketplace.

Business value: A measure of progress towards an enterprise's strategic objectives.

Buyer: A person outside your enterprise who purchases your products or services but who does not use them.

Capability: A set of differentiated skills, assets, processes and knowledge that enable the delivery of a particular business outcome.

Customer: A person outside your enterprise who purchases or uses your products. Client or citizen may be preferred in non-profit or government contexts.

Customer experience: The overall experience of a customer with your enterprise, based on every interaction they have before, during and after the acquisition and use of a product or service.

Customer journey map: A visual representation of the experiences that a customer has with your company, ordered into a timeline.

Customer segment: A subset of customers with similar tastes, demographics or other attributes that allow them to be marketed to as a group.

Delighter attribute: In Kano analysis, a product attribute that gives the customer unexpected pleasure when using your product.

Design: A usable representation of a solution.

Developer: In Scrum, any member of the product development team other than the Scrum master and product owner. More generally, a person who is involved in the creation or maintenance of software code.

Driver: A force outside the scope of your product, service or enterprise that creates or changes behaviour.

Epic: A user story too large to be completed in a single iteration, and which will need to be decomposed into greater detail before development begins.

Feature: A set of related product functionality that enables a customer to realise value.

Goal: A desired outcome or result.

Job-to-be-done: The customer problem that they are using your product to solve.

Lean startup: A methodology for product development that focuses on early exposure to the market and use by customers to determine if a product and its business model are viable.

Measure: The value of a metric at a specific point in time.

Metric: A quantifiable indicator of a product's or enterprise's performance.

Minimum marketable product (MMP): The minimum set of product features that must be delivered for a product to be competitive in the market.

Minimum viable product (MVP): The minimum functionality that must be delivered to allow customers to assess the usefulness of a product idea and provide feedback.

Objective: A desired outcome or result with a specified timeframe and measurable results.

Outcome: A change in the world or in a person's behaviour, brought about by a series of actions.

Output: A deliverable, product or feature.

Performance attribute: In Kano analysis, a feature or attribute that increases customer satisfaction in a linear fashion as it improves.

Product: An object, system or service created in response to customer demand and made available for use by them.

Product manager: The person responsible for delivering a product to market and ensuring its success through understanding of the customer's needs, developing a strategy to meet those needs through one or more products and services, and working with the product team to realise that strategy and deliver that product or service.

Product owner: In Scrum (and generally in Agile), the person responsible for prioritising the value of the efforts of the development team, typically through managing the product backlog and prioritising the work of developers.

Product vision: A concise description of a product, its value to customers and key features or attributes.

Requirement: A usable description of a need.

Risk: An event that, if it should occur, will negatively affect the ability to deliver a set of goals and objectives.

Roadmap: A high-level visual overview of a product's vision and direction over time.

Service: Work performed in response to customer demand intended to deliver a desired customer result.

Stakeholder: Any person affected by the process of developing or use of your product or service.

Story: A short description of functionality, capability or characteristics of a product, service or result.

Story point: A relative estimation of the work required to deliver a story.

Substitute product: A dissimilar product in the market that serves a similar set of customer needs. Customers who buy substitute products will reduce their use of your product.

Theme (of a roadmap): A grouping of related problems or features on a product roadmap.

Touchpoint: Moment in a process or service that involves direct interaction with a customer.

User: A person who uses a product or service, particularly one who will not purchase it.

User experience (UX): The overall experience of a customer or user interacting with your product.

User story: A story (q.v.) written from the perspective of a customer or user.

Value: A person's subjective assessment of the worth or importance of a product in a particular context.

Value proposition: A concise statement of the value a customer segment (q.v.) gains through the use of their product, and which provides a compelling reason to select it over alternatives.

INDEX

Page numbers in italics refer to figures or tables.